KV-422-192

POLLUTION

& PERSONAL INJURY

TOXIC TORTS

II

POLLUTION
& PERSONAL INJURY
TOXIC TORTS
II

by

Charles Pugh & Martyn Day

CAMERON MAY
LONDON

Copyright © Pugh & Day 1995

Research: Daniel Oudkerk, a practising barrister

Published 1994 by Cameron May Ltd.

All rights reserved. Except for the quotation of short passages for the purpose of criticism and review, no part of this publication may be reproduced, stored in a retrieval system or transmitted, in any form or by any means, electronic, mechanical, photocopying, recording or otherwise, without prior permission of the publisher.

This book is sold subject to the condition that it shall not by way of trade or otherwise, be lent, re-sold, hired out, or otherwise circulated without the publishers prior consent in any form of binding or cover other than that which it is published and without a similar condition including this condition being imposed on the subsequent purchaser.

ISBN 1 874698 16 3

Printed by Watkiss Studios Ltd

The authors assert their moral right to be identified as the authors of this work.

CONTENTS

11. THE SELLAFIELD LEUKAEMIA ACTION

PART II: THE LAW

12. NEGLIGENCE

13. PRIVATE NUISANCE

14. PUBLIC NUISANCE

15. RYLANDS -V- FLETCHER

16. BREACH OF STATUTORY DUTY

22. CONTAMINATED LAND

23. GRAHAM v. RECHEM

FOREWORD TO THE SECOND EDITION

In the three years that have elapsed since the first edition of this book in 1992 there have been many developments in the field which we have sought to incorporate into this edition.

Part I, The Practice, has been amended to include lessons learned from 2 major toxic tort trials which have taken place: the Sellafield leukaemia claims, tried between October 1992 and July 1993; and the Bonnybridge cattle poisoning claims, tried between October 1993 and December 1994. We have added new chapters to deal with these cases. The Bonnybridge Judgment was handed down on 16th June 1995 and Chapter 23 has been added as we go to press, and is therefore not indexed.

As to Part II, The Law, the Cambridge Water decision by the House of Lords in December 1993 casts a broad shadow, touching claims in negligence, nuisance and Rylands v Fletcher and leaving its mark on land contamination claims, particularly for "historical" pollution. This important decision has been woven into this text together with numerous other decisions of lesser courts, such as the decision of the Court of Appeal in the Camelford water cases which has effectively put an end to exemplary damages as a recoverable head of damage in toxic tort claims.

Finally, in response to comments of colleagues and reviewers, we have added chapters on the four main fields for practitioners, namely noise, water, air and land contamination. Our aim is in part, to de-mystify technical concepts where these are apt to cause difficulty, such as "quantitative standards", particularly in the field of noise nuisance. In part we try to draw attention to aspects of the law which a practitioner tackling a case in that field will need to have in mind. We believe that Part III, which contains these new chapters, adds an important new dimension to the book.

At the same time we have pruned the book. The chapter on European Community Law has been removed, firstly because an introductory guide is no longer thought necessary, and secondly because, sadly, we can find no reported decision as yet in which a toxic tort claim has been effectively advanced by direct application of Community law, although no doubt that day will come.

We would like to express our gratitude to the many people who have given their time to help us with this edition, most notably the members of our own Environmental Law groups. In particular we say "thank you" to Sally Moore and to Daniel Oudkerk for their painstaking research and general assistance. We also thank the Environmental Law Foundation for allowing us to access their database for background material for Part III.

The law is as stated at 30th June 1995.

Charles Pugh

Martyn Day

PART I: THE PRACTICE

CHAPTER ONE

INTRODUCTION

Toxic Tort Claims

Toxic tort cases are difficult. Without doubt they are amongst the most difficult of all tort actions.

A number of people have suggested, having read these words in the first edition of this book, that the intention is to put off the reader from venturing into this field. This could not be further from the truth. This is an area of the law where the more solicitors and barristers there are who are interested and keen the more that it will be developed to the benefit of individual victims, the environment, and those who already work in the field. The key, however, is for the lawyer to be clear as to what the work entails.

To come to terms with most toxic tort claims, the lawyer is likely to have to understand a whole series of complex issues including industrial processes; the reason why a particular process creates waste; the composition of the waste; how the waste is disposed of into the environment; how the waste then disperses in the environment; what routes there are from the environment into the human body; what are the likely concentrations of the waste in air, water and food; how specific components of the waste then reacts with the body; what illnesses can develop from that reaction; the possibility of interaction with other substances in the body; what are the other possible causes for the same illnesses and the likely latency period for the illnesses as brought on by the waste rather than any other cause.

This list is only an outline of the main problems. It does not take account of other "legal nightmares" such as having to deal with a multi-party action; locating the proper defendants; finding and persuading often reluctant experts to assist and working within the context of an area of law that, as yet, is only just beginning to be defined.

Finally, there is the central problem that defendants do not like losing toxic tort claims. Many of the defendants will be multi-national corporations with a major reputation to protect. To say the least, the corporation will not be enthusiastic at the prospect of a court finding that its industrial waste is killing or seriously injuring local people, particularly where that involves children. At its worst, claims can seriously undermine the financial and moral credibility of the whole company in the way that Distillers were damaged by the Thalidomide claims.

As a result, these are the types of cases where the defendants are likely to put all the resources at their disposal into defending the action. This can mean literally millions of pounds being spent on the defence. One of the main issues for plaintiffs' lawyers is being able to determine whether it is possible to fund such a case when facing this sort of opposition.In short this is a challenging field, not just for the lawyers representing plaintiffs and defendants, but also for expert witnesses and for the court which has to manage the litigation.

What is a Toxic Tort?

The term "toxic tort" is a shorthand phrase used throughout the book for any case where an individual claims to have suffered damage to person, property or to the quiet enjoyment of his/her property as a result of environmental pollution. The term therefore covers damage resulting from the disposal of industrial waste, whether chemical or radioactive into the air, land, sea and rivers. It also covers claims for damage from the widespread use of pesticides and chemicals in the environment and nuisance resulting from noise, dust, smells, vibration and even, most recently, interference with television reception.

The basic starting point for a toxic tort claim is that the person who has suffered the damage is an innocent victim whose only link with the cause of the pollution is likely to be that of living within the vicinity of a toxic source (or having a parent who was exposed to a toxic substance). Not included are claims by workers in the industry causing the pollution and damage. The reason for the separation of environmental and occupational claims is twofold. The first is that although the injuries sustained by workers are often the same or similar, the problems of identifying how the exposure was sustained are not so great. Secondly, it is often the case that the levels of exposure in an occupational setting will be more severe so that the problem of establishing causation may, relatively speaking, be easier.

Recent toxic tort claims have included the childhood leukaemia victims around the Sellafield and Dounreay nuclear reprocessing plants; the residents of Camelford whose contaminated water supply is alleged to have caused chronic illness in the local population; the Docklands residents who allege that their quality of life has been massively reduced as a result of the dust, general disturbance and interference with television reception caused by their living next to Europe's largest building site; people who allege that they have suffered a variety of illness resulting from their own or their parents' exposure to pesticides used in or around their properties; the farmers and property owners of Bonnybridge, Pontypool and Derbyshire who allege that their properties (including livestock) have been damaged by dioxins emanating from waste incinerators and other industrial processes; victims of damage resulting from homes being built on landfill sites; and alleged and potential victims of electromagnetic fields. Some of these cases have now been resolved either through the courts or through settlement. Others are still continuing. Their implications on the future conduct of this type of litigation will be discussed in this book. The implications of living on contaminated land and old land fill sites are the cause of great concern to home owners who find themselves unable to sell their properties and where mortgage lenders' security is worthless. Not only are the financial consequences severe, the implications to health of living on contaminated land are of growing concern.

Why Now?

Only a few years ago there would have been little if anything to say about environmental litigation. Most of the significant cases brought in Britain are recent. The claims described above all started since 1989 and it is only in the last 2 years that decisions have been made by the courts. What is it that has sparked off a willingness to go to law to seek remedies for environmental wrongs?

There are a number of reasons. First and foremost is the enormous increase in public concern regarding environmental pollution. The political changes seen at a macro level, personified by the large numbers of votes received by the Green Parties throughout Europe in the late 1980's, and the public concern over major environmental issues such as global warming have clearly translated into a much greater and wider public awareness of the individual's personal environment. People seem no longer prepared to accept intrusions into their local environment simply because of the claimed "needs of progress".

Of almost equal importance has been the development of scientific research. One of the major problems with environmental cases is that pollution tends to cause illnesses of the most complex aetiology, eg radiation and other toxic substances are known to cause, amongst other things, a whole variety of cancers, congenital abnormalities and hereditary illnesses. Apart from diseases such as mesothelioma and hepatic angiosarcoma it is rare for the illnesses to be solely attributable to a particular pollution. What has greatly assisted the environmental lawyer in these toxic tort cases has been the major developments in understanding the stages of complex illness. That said, there is still an enormous distance for the scientists to cover before we understand completely the cause and effect relationship of exposure to pollutants and disease. Recent developments have made the lawyer's job easier, although it remains far from simple.

Alongside these developments has been a great expansion in epidemiological work. Epidemiology is the study of the causes of illness through the use of medical statistics. Increasing amounts of public funding have been put into epidemiological studies over the last ten years resulting in a great increase in the understanding of the patterns of cancers like leukaemia. The studies around the Sellafield and other nuclear plants have been a prime example of how the epidemiologists have a key role to play in this field. Another relatively recent innovation has been the Small Area Health Statistics Unit at the London School of Hygiene and Tropical Medicine. This unit was set up in 1987 to develop methods for investigating reported clusters of disease around nuclear and industrial installations, such as solvent incinerators, benzene and vinyl chloride works, coke ovens, smokeless fuel plants and municipal incinerators. The work has proved more difficult than expected and only a few studies have so far been concluded.

Whilst the advances in scientific understanding and research techniques are of major importance where illness is obviously caused by an environmental pollutant, the lawyers should not necessarily await the development of science. Courts apply common sense to the issue of causation and the fact that the exact causal mechanisms are not known to science should not be an insuperable hurdle where primary evidence allows a commonsense inference to be drawn. This important proposition, often overlooked, is dealt with in Chapter 6 at pages [59 to 61].

As to the increasing interest in studies of clusters of illness,

Sellafield is a case in point. Since the excess childhood leukaemias were located around the plant in 1983, the number of experts who have been given grants to carry out studies of one sort or another in the area is quite extraordinary. This is despite the fact that on the wider scale of things the actual number of affected children is quite small. Despite the fact that the Court rejected the plaintiffs' case that paternal exposure to radiation had caused leukaemia in the children, new studies here continue to take place and many of the concerns raised by this litigation remain unsatisfied. There can be no doubt that it is the widespread public concern about this issue which has led to this development.

There is quite clearly a direct link between public concern, the politicians' awareness of these concerns, and the direction of scientific research. The increased public concern for the environment has brought about increased funding into scientific research work directly related to this area.

CHAPTER TWO

COMMENCING AN ACTION

The Lawyer's Role

There are two ways that a toxic tort claim is likely to be commenced. The first is through the initiative of the affected individuals and the second is by the actions of interested lawyers.

a) Claimant Initiated Cases

Some toxic tort claims are clear and obvious to the affected individuals. The prime example would be the one-off incident such as occurred at Camelford in 1988. About 20 tonnes of aluminium sulphate were accidentally put in the wrong tank with the result that the drinking water supply received a massive injection of this compound. Immediately afterwards people in the area started to develop symptoms of nausea. It was, therefore, very clear that there was the potential of a claim to the affected individuals. They subsequently approached a local solicitor, Mr Christopher Key, who handled a number of the cases until their settlement in 1994. He had to start from scratch in terms of understanding, and dealing with, this type of case.

The Camelford example is a good one in that the initial view was that the claims were only likely to be small as the resulting effect on the local population had appeared at first to be minor. However, as time passed there was an increasing concern that the polluted water affected the local population in a more far reaching way than was first thought. The claims included an element for mental impairment for a number of people. All but a couple of the cases settled out of court for sums that by no means fully compensated them for any mental impairment they may have suffered.

Christopher Key is, therefore, a good example of a lawyer with little, if any, knowledge of toxic tort actions who was thrown in at the deep end when a specific incident occurred in the neighbourhood.

It is probable that these one-off incidents will continue to occur around the country. The lawyer approached by the affected people will have to decide whether there is the expertise and capacity in the firm or law centre to undertake such a case. In a speech to the Law Society Annual Conference in 1989 Mr Key described how his was the type of small local practice where he was able to pop off at lunchtime for a sunbathe and a dip on his local beach at Camelford. He had to give all that up as the cases slowly devoured more and more of his time and energy.

It is highly likely that, in all but the least significant incidents, properly conducted toxic tort claims will take up at least one lawyer's time completely and also require major input from others in the firm or law centre. A decision needs, therefore, to be taken at the outset as to whether there are the resources available to undertake the claims. The lawyer needs to be realistic about the commitment and back-up within the firm from the start.

b) Lawyer Initiated Cases

Toxic tort claims are sometimes started as a result of the initiative of the lawyers. As previously mentioned, toxic tort claims can be enormously complex and the injuries are often not obviously linked to a particular pollutant, as a result of which neither the affected individuals nor the treating doctors will realise that illness has been caused by environmental pollution. It is in this type of case that the environmental lawyer can have a major role.

The increasing relaxation by the Law Society of the rules on advertising since 1984 has greatly enhanced the environmental lawyer's ability to reach individuals affected by environmental pollution. Where a lawyer is confident that there may be a claim it is now possible specifically to advertise for cases. That said, this method should not be used lightly.

In any claim initiated by a lawyer there is a heavy burden placed on his/her shoulders to be clear that the claim has a genuine chance of success and is not simply a flight of fancy. In most claims involving toxic torts it is likely that the victims will have undergone great suffering or at the least great inconvenience. There can be little doubt that this type of case imposes a great deal of stress on the plaintiff as it is pursued through the courts. Lawyers should not add to the victim's stress by the pursuit of a claim unless the background work has been done to enable the lawyer to be clear that the case has a solid foundation. For this reason alone the lawyer must undertake a good deal of research in the particular field before any direct approach to clients is made.

There are likely to be two types of lawyers who become involved in this field. There are those like Christopher Key who were simply in the right place at the right time. Once such a lawyer has developed an interest in this area through one case the depth of research involved is likely to mean that they will have become very knowledgeable about the wider issues relating to toxic torts. That knowledge is likely to be transferable to other types of claim within this field. It is, therefore, to be hoped that, in the same way a number of tort lawyers have become experts in the field of medical negligence, the same will slowly become true in this field.

The second type of lawyer is the one who works in a region where there is a high level of industrial activity, resulting in high levels of pollution. Although the British manufacturing base has reduced in size over recent decades there are still areas with very major industrial complexes, such as Cleveland, Humberside, Merseyside, West Yorkshire, Greater Manchester, Tayside and Derby to mention a few. Revelations of abnormal clusters of cancers, respiratory problems, etc. in these areas, are likely to unfold as we move in to the 21st Century.

It is to be hoped that there will be lawyers in these regions, whether in local law firms or law centres, who will take an interest in their own area and will pay particular attention to any report suggesting the possibility of personal injury being caused by local industries. Local knowledge is vital in these types of case.

In most instances the media, whether on a local or national scale, are fascinated by environmental damage issues and therefore health problems that may be associated with certain industrial processes and pollution are well reported. The interested lawyer would therefore do well to keep an eye on the national and local media.

Any lawyer keen to become involved in this field should become a regular subscriber to the main scientific journals such as the British Medical Journal, Lancet, Nature, and the New Scientist. There are also increasing scientific "on line" services, such as "Medline" which operate in the same way as "Lexis".

By going through these journals regularly, the lawyer will become more aware of the state of scientific thinking on the central issues in any possible claim. This will ensure that when a new study is published which increases the possibility of initiating a claim in a particular field the lawyer will be aware of the issues involved and will ensure that the decision is supportable scientifically. Further, the lawyer will have a better idea of the scientists, epidemiologists and experts involved in the particular field.

Once the lawyer has determined upon an area where there may be a real possibility of a claim succeeding research becomes fundamental. Experts and possibly other lawyers should be consulted to see whether or not it is supportable. Scientific literature reviews may also assist. It is often the case that specialist journalists in the field may have information that is helpful in determining the prospects of the claim at this initial stage and certainly checks should be made to see if there are any local groups campaigning on the issue.

From all this a decision can be made as to whether the claim is worth pursuing.

The question may be raised as to how on earth the lawyer can take on all this before the claim is even begun. The work will certainly not be paid for even if the claims go ahead and succeed. The point goes back to what has already been stated. This is an area where it is highly appropriate for the lawyer to take an interventionist rather than passive role in the initiation of actions. In doing so, however, the lawyer takes on a much greater responsibility to ensure that the claim is viable before contacting potential clients. Not to do so is not only morally reprehensible, but if the claim quickly turns out to be non-viable, the lawyer's credibility in this field will be affected. The lawyer who is interested in toxic tort cases should therefore accept that in many cases there will be sizeable expenditure on developmental research which will not, largely, be recoverable.

Advertising for Clients

There are a number of ways that a lawyer can now attempt to contact potential clients in toxic tort claims.

a) Groups

Relevant groups may be in a position to circulate information. There are various types of group that may help. Sometimes there are victims' groups where people have got together without being aware that there may be a legal cause of action.

Going back to the Sellafield example, around the nuclear installation there were two leukaemia local groups where parents with children affected by the cancer regularly met together to discuss ways of collecting funds for leukaemia research and generally to help affected children in the area. Once the advert appeared in the paper they contacted the lawyers and immediately set up a meeting between the lawyers and their members so that they were clear as to what was being suggested. It meant that those victims who had a potential claim could readily and speedily seek specific advice. It had the further benefit of ensuring that those interested in pursuing a claim did not feel isolated.

Another value in working with and through groups is that they can provide a forum for developing issues that arise in the conduct of the action. Pursuit of a claim often brings up issues that have wider implications. The lawyer's role must always focus centrally around the claim itself but the existence of a group allows the legal action an outlet for such issues to be aired and if necessary pursued and given a public airing.

Groups are almost invariably pleased to be contacted in this way. This is partly because it gives them a focus and also because it gives them further legitimacy. That is not to say that there may not be an element of suspicion, often quite rightly, that the lawyer is making the contact more out of self interest rather than in the interests of the victims. It is the lawyer's task to allay those fears.

It will sometimes be the case that no victims' group exists in which case consideration should be given to approaching the wider based environmental groups such as Greenpeace and Friends of the Earth (their contact numbers appear in the appendix). They are generally very helpful and understand the significance of the pursuit of individual claims in this field. They may be able to assist in providing contacts or even suggestions on advertising as they have a very good knowledge of the media and its impact at different levels.

Finally it is often the case that where the pollution has been recognised as being a real problem by the local community a group will have been set up in opposition with the intention of monitoring the industrial plant and lobbying for the clean up of the pollution. They, again, are often a useful point of contact with potential clients.

b) Using the Media

Publicising the case through the media can often be a very good way of contacting clients in an easy and largely non-controversial manner. In the breast implant litigation two appearances by the lead lawyer in the case on ITN News produced some 1500 calls.

For the media to be interested it usually requires that the issue is a new one, that it is of general interest and that the lawyer has at least one client who is prepared to be interviewed for the piece. Without a client the media will usually regard the inquiry as ambulance chasing by the lawyer.

It is important that the lawyer does not at anytime use the client for the firm's benefit, i.e. simply to obtain other clients, when this may not be in the client's best interests. It may often be the case that the client's interests will benefit by other claimants coming forward, for example to share the costs, but this issue must always be considered on a client by client basis. Indeed, in many cases the client will only be too happy to be given the opportunity to bring their problems, which often raise issues of wide public importance, to the attention of the media.

Where publicity is not in the clients' interests or the clients are not keen to have their problems publicised the lawyer must use other routes to bring in more clients where it is deemed necessary for the success of the case. For example, writing articles on specific topics or teaming up with interested journalists to write about a particular issue or incident can be effective ways of publicising a specific issue and the lawyer's specialism in that area.

c) Advertising

Another possibility is to carry a straightforward advertisement in a newspaper. The style of the advertisement and the particular newspaper would depend on the people the lawyer is attempting to reach. If, therefore, the affected victims live across the country, for example in some pesticide claims, there is little point in doing anything other than advertising nationally. This can however be expensive and an advertisement in one national paper is unlikely to be picked up by many of the victims.

Where, on the other hand, the victims are all likely to be living in a certain region advertising in the local media is the obvious choice. Different elements of the local media, i.e. radio, regional television, and the local newspapers are all likely to take an interest which gives the issue a much greater focus than would normally be the case with one advert. Equally, simply placing an advert is likely to create discussion in the local area which increases the chances that the local victims will hear of it. Where the issue is of sufficient interest to the national media a small advert placed strategically can overcome the problems of the advert not being seen by a sufficiently wide group of people as it is picked up in other news stories.

The point for the lawyer to focus on is where the victims are likely to live and also what they are most likely to read. There is therefore little point in advertising in "The Times" if all the victims are people who would never dream of reading that particular paper.

Reference is made here to advertising in the newspapers. It is also possible to advertise in other ways. Advertising on the television or on the radio should also be considered. The cost of the former and the ephemeral nature of the latter (i.e. an advert read by the friends of a victim can be shown to the victim, but the same is not true of a radio advert) means that it is unlikely that this would be particularly appropriate but there may be particular circumstances where they become so.

The ability of lawyers to advertise has been extended enormously by the Law Society and what is particularly important is that lawyers can be very specific in what they are advertising. In the Sellafield case, it can be seen that the advert was not describing the firm's general work but very specifically describing the position on the particular cases envisaged. Having made this point there are still some restrictions imposed by the Law Society and it may therefore be sensible to check the draft advert with the Law Society's Professional Standards and Development Directorate, Ipsley Court, Redditch, Worcestershire, B98 OTD (Tel: 0527-517141).

Lawyers should be aware, however, that notwithstanding the freedom to advertise, advertising for clients will often lead to criticism from Legal Aid Board, the defendants and in some circumstances the court. A lawyer should not be put off by such criticism but should be prepared to deal with it. Defendants, particularly at the outset of the case, mention at every possible opportunity the fact that the action is "lawyer led" rather than plaintiff led. Allegations of "ambulance chasing"; attempting to profit from the victims' misfortune; that the claim is more about the pursuit of the lawyer's rather than the victims' interests, are all arrows that can be shot at the lawyer who takes this route. What is clear is that when the potential defendants resort to these allegations the resolve of the lawyer should harden since it is probably a sign that a raw nerve has been hit.

The approach of the court to lawyer led litigation is rather mixed. In the recent drugs multi-party cases the courts have criticised plaintiffs for "jumping on the bandwagon" and for lawyers advertisements which have encouraged this. The courts and defendants have indicated that the amount and type of advertising has lead to a large number of weak speculative claims which were eventually dropped. It does not appear that any detailed research has been undertaken by the defendants before resorting to the criticism and it may well be that the defendants' claims are without foundation.

Where advertisements are tightly drawn to attract specific groups it is not so easy for the defendants to level this complaint. Furthermore, the courts are becoming more accustomed to handling multi-party actions and accept, particularly where cut-off dates are imposed, that advertising is a useful tool their disposal. It is therefore to be hoped that as lawyers become more adept at advertising, the courts become more familiar with it and that there will be less mileage for the defendants to gain in their criticism.

There are, therefore, a number of routes through which the lawyer interested in initiating a claim can make contact with the victims to see whether they want to pursue a claim. The most appropriate route will depend on the circumstances of each particular case. The lawyer should consider the various possibilities and then pursue the route chosen.

CHAPTER THREE

FUNDING

1. Civil Legal Aid: the legal merits test

Under the Legal Aid Act 1988 s15(3) a person shall not be granted civil legal aid for the purpose of any proceedings unless he satisfies the Area Office that he has reasonable grounds for taking, defending or being a party to the proceedings.

This is the legal merits test. Except in relation to certain Children Act matters both this test and the reasonableness test must be satisfied before legal aid can be granted. The use of the word "reasonable" in both tests may at first sight be confusing but for this test it means reasonable grounds for taking proceedings or reasonable grounds for being a party to proceedings rather than an overall concept of "reasonableness" which is the criterion of the second test.

The Area Office must be satisfied that, on the facts put forward and the law which relates to them, there is a case or defence which should be put before a court for a decision. Notice will be taken of the availability of evidence to prove the alleged facts. The Area Office must assume for this purpose that the facts are as stated. They see only one side of the case, and are in no position to adjudicate on issues. The likelihood of success is also a factor which the Area Office must bear in mind but it is of the essence of litigation that there are two opposing points of view on which the court is required to adjudicate. Litigation is also notoriously uncertain so that any attempt to restrict legal aid to certainties or near certainties or even those cases with a probability of success would not only be doomed to failure but would also be a denial to many applicants of an opportunity to obtain justice.

The aim therefore must be not to be over-cautious but not to grant legal aid for cases where there is little or no hope of success. If legal aid is granted in hopeless cases it raises the expectations of assisted persons too high, forces opponents to defend their rights and wastes public money, perhaps doubly if costs are awarded against the fund.

Therefore there are reasonable grounds to proceed if:

(a) there is an issue of fact or law which should be submitted to the court for a decision;

(b) the solicitor would advise the applicant to take or defend proceedings privately, i.e. if he had means which were adequate to meet the likely costs of the case or would make payment of the likely costs possible although something of a sacrifice; and

(c) the applicant shows that, as a matter of law, he has reasonable grounds for taking or defending proceedings, i.e. that there is a case or defence which has reasonable prospects of success, assuming the facts are proved.

An application must, however, not only satisfy this criterion on the legal merits but also the reasonableness test.

2. Civil legal aid: the reasonableness test.

Under the Legal Aid Act 1988 s15(3) the rule is that a person may be refused legal aid if in the particular circumstances of the case it appears to the Board (i.e. the Area Director/Area Committee) unreasonable that it should be granted. This rule is in addition to and not an alternative to the legal merits test. The discretion is wide on the face of it but there are well recognised circumstances in which the decision has to be made, and the most common cases in which legal aid is likely to be refused as unreasonable include proceedings which are not likely to be cost effective, i.e. the benefit to be achieved does not justify the costs.

Without legal aid very few cases would or indeed could ever be commenced and so the legal merits test and the reasonableness test will need careful appraisal at the outset.

There is little prospect that even a person of substantial wealth could afford to take on the major corporate interests in these circumstances never mind the averagely resourced citizen.

The plaintiffs' lawyers should from the start, therefore, be looking to obtain the support of the Legal Aid Board for the claim.

3. Multi-party actions and legal aid

Most toxic tort claims are likely to affect a number of people and therefore will be multi-party actions. The concept of group litigation is something which has become increasingly significant in the British legal system over the last ten years due to the number of mass disaster, drug and now toxic tort claims. The courts do not recognise the concept of "class actions" that exist in the United States. They have, however, come to realise that multi-party actions need to be dealt with differently to most cases and a series of procedures have been developed, some of which relate to legal aid.

On 1st June 1992 the Legal Aid Board's special procedure for dealing with multi-party personal injury actions came into effect. Their definition of this type of action is that there must be at least ten common individual claims, i.e. ten legal aid certificates, and that the claims must have a personal injury element.

The special procedure is summarised in the "Multi-Party Actions Manual" produced by the Legal Aid Board dated May 1992 and available from the Policy and Secretariat Department, Head Office, Sixth Floor, 29/37 Red Lion Street, London WC1R 4PP.

Where a firm becomes involved in a multi-party action which is likely to involve more than ten legal aid certificates the lawyer handling the claims should contact the Area Office and inform them. Under the procedure the Area Office has to appoint a liaison officer and arrange for all other legal aid applications relating to the same action to be referred to the same Area Office.

Once ten certificates have been issued, the Director of the Area Office will prepare a report for the specially convened Multi-Party Action Committee of the Board. (The Committee will consider the position regarding all types of legally aided multi-party actions i.e. not only toxic tort actions). The Committee decides whether the action meets the Board's criteria and whether the cases are sufficiently complex to be dealt with under the terms of the scheme. If it accepts that an action does fit the criteria the firm and any other firm involved (i.e. those acting for clients who have been granted legal aid certificates) will be invited to submit reports dealing with the conduct and co-ordination of the action. This report, known as the "tender report", will have to include a large amount of information relating to the proposed conduct of the action, details of the firm(s), the relevant staff, the expertise, the firm's technology, proposals for the co-ordination of the other firms involved in the claim as well as the clients and, if the case has advanced far enough, details of potential costs and damages.

4. Entering into Contracts with the Legal Aid Board

The liaison officer from the Area Office then forwards the details back to the Committee who will decide whether or not to make a "contract" with the firm. They can decide to ask more questions and, if they deem it necessary, even invite the lawyer to attend a meeting of the Committee. They can also make the decision not to enter a contract with the firm and can turn to another firm or groups of firms to take over the lead work.

There are detailed arrangements when there is a large group of firms involved which is more likely to relate to disaster and drugs cases than it is to toxic tort claims. Where a toxic tort claim does involve a large number of firms the lawyer should pay great attention to the powers of the Committee to determine who should be awarded the generic work contract.

Once agreement has been reached on the contract it will be signed by the Chairman of the Committee and the lawyer(s) from the firm(s) to which the contract has been granted.

Contracting firms have onerous responsibilities. It is the responsibility of the firm to report back to the Committee every six months giving details as to the past and future conduct of the action, the strengths and weaknesses of the case, the current and future costs, likely quantum, numbers of existing and likely future legally aided and private clients, as well as copies of reports made to the claimants and other firms and details of any unresolved complaints. The firm has to keep other firms and claimants fully informed of the progress of the claim by means of regular reports.

The Committee has, therefore, the right to allocate a specific firm of lawyers to handle the generic aspects of the work. What is meant by this is that where there are several firms with a handful of cases each, all relating to the same incident, or at least the same type of toxic tort, rather than having each firm duplicating the work necessary to determine liability, the Committee will choose a group of one, two or more firms to do that work. The other firms are then left simply to do the work on quantum for each of the cases in which they have instructions.

The reasoning behind this is to avoid duplication of work by a number of firms involved. The initial contracts have, without exception, gone to the firms doing the central work, i.e. leading in the area, where they have a significant number of cases. That may not always be the case and the lawyer moving into this field should be aware of the issue. There could be few things more upsetting than undergoing a lot of the research work into a potential toxic tort claim, even appointing additional staff to do the work, only to find that the legal aid certificates are all marked "not to include any generic work".

It should therefore be the toxic tort lawyer's goal not only to locate the victims but also then to ensure that the firm is awarded the contract or part of a contract for that particular group of cases.

This whole issue has become all the more acute in the light of the Benzodiazepine litigation. Hundreds of law firms dealt with some 17,000 individual cases and the cost to the Board is said to have been some £35 million in an action that did not even reach trial. Following this, in the tobacco claims contract the Board awarded the successful tenderers not only the generic work, but also the individual work, in an attempt to ensure that they can keep control of costs.

5. Making the applications

Some toxic tort claims will have only perhaps a handful of victims and on the odd occasion perhaps only one. Often there will be tens if not hundreds of victims. In those instances careful thought needs to be put into the completion of the legal aid forms.

For a lawyer to take a statement from an individual, and then assist in the completion of a Green Form, the Statement of Means, Legal Aid Application form, and employer form often takes an hour or so. If there are 500 clients, all applying for legal aid, a system needs to be worked out to deal with them all in what may be a short period of time. The lawyer should be quite clear that, at this initial stage, there are no short cuts. Since there are no class actions as that expression is understood in the USA, it is not possible simply to take a handful of claims to trial and leave the rest to see what happens. The time it is likely to take before the cases reach trial may well mean that the other claims will become statute barred. Further, the longer the gap in time between the events and their investigation leaves more time for memories to fade and documents to go missing.

It may be possible to agree with the defendants to waive the statute bar to ensure that they do not face too many cases at the same time.

It is, however, more often the case that the defendants will want and in some cases insist on knowing the details of all the individual cases against them so that usually the lawyer will have to either take full instructions from all the victims who want to pursue the claim or alternatively persuade the courts to take a "generic issue first" approach, perhaps looking at 20 or so individual representative cases, with the rest of the individual actions left until after judgement is obtained on the generic issues.

Insistence that individual cases be dealt with before certain cut-off dates was substantially to blame for the costs in the Benzodiazepine action and the indication is that the courts are keen to avoid this re-occurring.

Where there are a large group of victims living in the same area it may be best to set up a meeting where the victims are all invited and where the lawyer can set out the basis of the case to one and all. The lawyer should ensure at any such meeting that each individual is given the opportunity of having any statement taken down in private. Further, the meeting should be treated as a meeting between clients and solicitors and therefore the media and other interested parties should be kept out.

Sufficient forms and staff should be taken along to process the applications. In the Docklands case some 300 people turned up to such a meeting and the twenty legal staff present were just about able to deal with the applications within the four hours available. There were however many days of work to be done back at the office tidying up all the loose ends arising from the meeting. Despite the problems associated with undertaking the task in this way it did ensure that the lawyers were made fully aware from the outset of the extent of the disruption to the lives of the local people.

Where a large number of applications are to be made at the same time the Board should be forewarned. A hundred or more applications will take up a lot of their staff's time and by giving them advance warning they will be able to make efforts to divert resources to ensure the applications can be processed without undue delay. Taking this step should again encourage the Board's Multi-Party Action Committee to place the contract with lawyers who are perceived as being well organised.

The applications should be accompanied by as much information as the plaintiffs' lawyers can muster. It is crucial that, the Board can see the claim is well founded and feasible. The cost of this type of case is usually high and the Board's resources so stretched that unless the claim is strong, even at the start, there is a serious risk that it will be refused. Whilst a "flier" in a straightforward personal injury case may succeed there is no chance of it doing so here.

6. The Board's decision

In the Docklands and Sellafield cases legal aid was originally refused by the Board's officers. It is worth considering what happened in these cases since there may be lessons for future applications.

In the Sellafield group of cases, some 30 or so applications were made in August 1988. Research papers, statements, experts' comments and counsel's opinion accompanied the applications. In October of that year the Board officer dealing with the applications wrote saying that legal aid was likely to be granted and that the Board were simply waiting for the financial details before making a final decision. In December, British Nuclear Fuels' lawyers wrote to the Board saying that the claims had absolutely no foundation whatsoever and would be an enormous waste of public funds. A few weeks later legal aid was refused.

When some 500 applications were made for legal aid in the Docklands case in September 1991 the only debate with the Board officials was in relation to how the claims would operate once legal aid had been granted. It was never suggested that legal aid might be refused.

The applications included large amounts of supporting evidence and the expectation on the plaintiffs' side was that legal aid would be granted. It was therefore a great shock when it was announced that legal aid had in fact been refused.

In both instances appeals were lodged against the decisions. In the Sellafield case the plaintiffs were represented by leading and junior counsel together with one of the experts. In the Docklands case the plaintiffs were represented by junior counsel and accompanied by a number of clients. Following the representations, on both occasions the Area Committee reversed the earlier decision.

It is of course, difficult if not impossible, to be clear as to exactly how the decisions to refuse were arrived at within the Board. It would however appear from experience in the Sellafield and Docklands claims that in multi-party toxic tort cases the applications are scrutinised in minute detail. The Board also seems to have a much greater expectation as to how much exploratory work should be carried out prior to the applications being made than would be normal in any other type of personal injury case. It would also indicate that the initial decisions on the granting of legal aid are taken at the higher levels of the Board. Taking into account the enormous costs involved in funding these cases this is perhaps not surprising. The fact, however, that in two of the largest cases of this kind legal aid was refused at the first instance does not bode well for future decisions.

In the tobacco related claims, legal aid was eventually granted in 1995, after a fight lasting almost three years. This suggests that the gaining of a certificate is going to become more, rather than less, difficult in the future.

The great majority of toxic tort legal aid applications of which the authors have experience has been refused at first instance. Furthermore, it has often been the case that legal aid has been granted by the Area Committee without further detailed representations. It is, however, clear that this is one of the ways the Board monitors these types of actions closely. It is not unusual these days for an Area Committee to require the solicitor to report to them regularly on the progress of the toxic tort action.

It could be thought that to have taken leading counsel into the Area Committee appeal on the Sellafield action was a case of overkill. However this seems to have been crucial in persuading the Area Committee that the case was strong enough to be supported. The same was true in the tobacco related claims, although this is by no means always the case and for lesser actions there is a lot to be said for the solicitors to present the appeal, as they are the people who know the case best.

Two reasons for refusal, over and above the direct merits of the case, which need careful consideration are:-

a) that there are other individuals with the same interest as the applicant who could benefit from the action; and

b) that the applications are premature in that there are other bodies who can take action to prevent the nuisance/damage.

a) Other individuals with the same interest.

Regulation 32 of the Civil Legal Aid (General) Regulations 1989 gives the Board a discretion to take into account others with the same interest in the action as those applying for legal aid.

The exercise of the Board's discretion under this Regulation has not as yet been the subject of a challenge to the Divisional Court and therefore the court has yet to rule on what is meant by 'same interest' but it is difficult to see how the provision could be applied in the context of a nuisance or personal injury claim because every plaintiff's claim is different.

The examples cited in the Legal Aid Handbook relate first, to an application by tenants of a block of flats to repair common parts where other tenants are cited as, in certain circumstances, having the same interest. The second example relates to six home owners benefiting from proceedings involving a liability to maintain a road where all six are considered, in certain circumstances, to have the same interest. Both examples cited are linked by a statutory or contractual nexus, are easily and clearly identifiable and all have an identifiable financial interest in the proceedings. In cases of nuisance, personal injury or where an individual wishes to exercise a public law right, it is arguable that in exercising the discretion under Regulation 32 the Board should determine that there are no persons with the same interest or that it is not reasonable to seek a contribution from any others on the grounds of uncertainty in determining who those others are and that it would be manifestly unjust to allocate a contribution between an arbitrarily determined number of people.

A more difficult point is whether a person can be said to have the same interest where he/she refuses to take any legal action.

b) Other bodies who can take action

This is a popular ground of refusal where the legal aid application relates to injunction proceedings in nuisance actions. Since the clients' primary objective in these cases is to stop the nuisance, this is a serious obstacle.

The main body contemplated as being able to take action (see Regulation 30(i)a)) is the local authority. For example, local authorities have a duty to investigate nuisance under the Environmental Protection Act 1990. The difficulty is, that in reality, enforcement action is not always taken by local authorities, and even when enforcement action is taken the injured party rarely benefits in terms of compensation as distinct from abatement or injunction,(see Chapter). If it is possible that legal aid may be refused on these grounds, attempts should be made to determine exactly what, if anything, the local authority are doing about the problem.

7. Defendants' representations

The position of the defendants submitting representations to the Legal Aid Board at the outset of cases and, more recently, throughout their duration is controversial. In multi-party actions and toxic torts in particular these have become routine. The Legal Aid Regulations are largely silent on the subject, although they do provide that Legal Aid can be withdrawn on the representation of a third party. In a recent paper on multi-party actions, published by the Legal Aid Board in May 1994, which is of general relevance to toxic tort litigation, the Board states that although it does not encourage representations it takes the view that when they are served they must be fully considered.

The defendants in these types of cases may well be multi-nationals with unlimited resources of both experts and lawyers to counter the submissions made in the applications for legal aid. A firm acting for an applicant in these circumstances may find itself faced with pages of detailed representations which will need to be answered if legal aid is to be granted. The Board has resisted requests that limited legal aid should be provided to answer these representations. Where applicable the lawyer may be able to obtain Green Form extensions.

The Board's paper also suggests that special area committees might be formed to consider particularly complicated cases where funding for the plaintiffs' representation would be made available. However they also suggest that the committee should have the power to invite representations from the defendants where they think they would be beneficial to the decision making process.

It is clear that in the last 2/3 years lawyers acting for the defendants have become much more aggressive in attacking the grant and continuance of legal aid. Clearly, lawyers for applicants must be prepared to counter such moves, with or without the funding to do so.

8. Challenging decisions on legal aid

It should be remembered that there have been many significant challenges to the final refusal of legal aid in recent years. In order to be successfully challenged the decision must be flawed by reason of illegality, irrationality or procedural impropriety, (see per Lord Diplock in *Council of Civil Service Unions v Minister for the Civil Service* [1985] AC 374). In *R v Legal Aid Committee No.10 (East Midlands) ex parte McKenna*, The Times 20 December 1989, Mrs McKenna successfully challenged the refusal of legal aid by the Area Committee to permit her to continue proceedings against Eli Lilly, the manufacturers of Opren. It was held that the decision was flawed in that it was based on a demonstrably mistaken view of the facts. It was also held that the cost of the litigation (the reason for the withdrawal of legal aid) should not be the sole or even the decisive factor in legal aid decisions since otherwise "it would place multinational corporations in a position of advantage vis-à-vis individual claimants which, in my opinion, such commercial concerns ought not to enjoy."

In *R v Legal Aid Area No 8 (Northern) Appeal Committee* ex p Parkinson, The Times 13 March 1990, (a medical product liability claim involving vaccination) it was held that relief could be granted requiring an Area Committee to provide proper reasons for its decision.

Legal aid is available to challenge the decisions of the Area Committee. Lawyers in these cases will need to consider carefully whether or not they have grounds to proceed by way of judicial review in important toxic tort cases. If successful the decision is likely to be remitted to the same Area Committee unless they have shown bias. There are therefore no guarantees that a successful judicial review will lead to the grant of legal aid but the Divisional Court may give indications to the parties about how the decision should be redetermined. In the judicial review of the Newcastle Area Committee's decision to refuse legal aid to take proceedings against the tobacco industry for personal injuries, Popplewell J made very significant findings on the question of whether the litigation raised generic issues which had been in issue at the original hearing before the Area Committee.

The defendants in the Docklands case took the highly unusual step of issuing judicial review proceedings against the Board's decision to extend legal aid to allow proceedings to be issued. The case is still outstanding. However it is indicative of the tough stance which the defendants are now taking to attack the litigant's legal aid. In these proceedings the Docklands plaintiffs are not parties to the action but are persons "directly affected" under the terms of Order 53. They can make representations in the action if they have anything additional to add to the respondents, the Legal Aid Board. It is important therefore for the plaintiffs to ensure that the Legal Aid Board are fighting their corner adequately should the defendants take this step. It is to be hoped that the generally negative view which the court has taken of these particular proceedings will, in future, dissuade defendants from taking such action.

Furthermore, in a judicial review application against the Board in the tobacco related claims, the manufacturers, having already made detailed representations about why legal aid should not be granted, fought tooth and nail to join the proceedings as persons directly affected but failed. The plaintiffs argued that until legal aid was granted the tobacco industry were not persons directly affected and that the judicial review application was a matter between the applicants and the Board. The Court agreed. This is yet another illustration of the effort which defendants will make to prevent legal aid being issued to their potential opponents.

9. Limitations on legal aid certificates

In the Sellafield case the limitations imposed on the certificates were relatively standard and indeed once legal aid was granted the Board officers were extremely helpful. When the certificates were granted in the Docklands cases the limitations imposed on the certificates ran to two pages. The implications of this are that the Board, in the larger toxic tort cases, are likely to keep a very watchful eye over what is done under the certificates.

Essentially, the Board is concerned to ensure at the outset at the very least that individual work on these types of cases is limited to avoid escalation of costs when there may not be a viable claim.

What is a matter of concern is the extent to which the Board or indeed the Multi-Party Action Committee intend to attempt to oversee the detailed running of these actions. They are able to do this through lengthy limitations which prescribe in great detail what can and cannot be done and by costs limitation which is a further check on the actions of the plaintiffs' lawyers. It will be a matter of great concern if it becomes the case that the Board starts to determine the course of the action rather than the lawyers. Only time will tell whether or not this concern is justified, but we do not know of any specific instance since the first edition of this book which would reinforce concern.

Having made this point it should also be accepted that the Board have the right to ensure that public funds are being well spent. It is only to be hoped that the Area Committee attain a reasonable balance between the two perspectives.

10. Claims for Costs

One great value of being granted the generic certificates in a multi-party action claim is that special funding arrangements will have been made by the Board. These new regulations bypass a lot of the difficulties with ordinary legal aid interim payments.

In the case of ordinary certificates a claim for payment can first be made to the Legal Aid Board accounts department after the certificate is eighteen months old and then after 30 months and finally 42 months. The claim is paid by the Board in 1992/3 at 75% of the costs. (Regulation 100 of the Civil Legal Aid (General) Regulations 1989). Work done under a legal aid franchise allows claims to be made every 9 months at 75% of the costs and would be applicable to a toxic tort claim if the firm concerned had a franchise in the appropriate field, which is most likely to be personal injury.

There is also provision for special hardship claims to be made. However, for a claim to be made under a certificate the court proceedings are supposed to be twelve months old and judgement more than twelve months away. Further, the firm making the application has to show it is in financial difficulties which usually means providing bank statements showing a large overdraft. (Regulation 101). Within these parameters the claim can be at any time and for whatever proportion of the costs that seems appropriate. A word of warning is, however, necessary. In these cases the costs will often be large and as a lot of the work is breaking new ground, the attitude of the Supreme Court Taxing Office on the taxation of costs is not at all clear. The lawyer should therefore be wary of over claiming and should leave a good margin for error.

Counsel claim for their own payments on account and the solicitor is obliged to send on to their clerk a copy of the legal aid certificate (Civil Legal Aid (General) Regulations 1989).

In a multi-party action it is often necessary for a firm to take on additional staff to deal with the group of cases. For the firm to bear the costs of this, the additional computer facilities, and the administrative back-up can, for all but the largest firms, be crippling. The new regulations take account of this and for those multi-party actions where there are more than ten claims with a personal injury element and where a contract is granted the firm can apply for regular payments at 75% of the costs whenever the firm considers an application to be appropriate. There are no restrictions and therefore it would appear that a firm can apply as often as every month or so. There are also no time limits in relation to how soon after the certificate has been granted or how near a claim is to the judgement. This represents an important and beneficial change in the scheme.

Under the "contract" scheme in multi-party actions it is important that the lawyer is fully aware of the position of privately funded clients. In particular, any private client who joins the action late will still be expected to bear an equal proportion of the costs with those who joined earlier. The Multi-Party Action Committee can also reduce the amount of costs paid on account if there are private clients. It is up to the lawyer to obtain money on account from the private client.

11. Legal Insurance

More people are taking out legal insurance, sometimes as direct cover and sometimes as a part of their household insurance. If an individual is covered by legal insurance, it is possible to contemplate taking on their case privately. The legal cover is often in the region of up to £25,000 on costs (the fine print of the policy should be checked) but that is just for the plaintiff's costs. The insurers do not cover the defendant's costs if the claim is lost and an order for payment is made. This greatly reduces the potential for the use of legal insurance in these actions.

12. Conditional Fees

In June 1995 a new system of funding came into operation for bringing personal injury actions, insolvency claims and claims to the

European Court of Human Rights. This conditional fees scheme is a hybrid of the contingency fee system in existence in the United States and British distaste for allowing lawyers to take a percentage of the damages.

The system allows the lawyer to take cases on a "no-win no-fee" basis. The client and lawyer can decide whether or not the disbursements such as experts fees are funded by the client as the case progresses or are also part of the no-win no-fee agreement. Counsel's fees can be treated as a disbursement which are funded by the client throughout, alternatively, the barrister concerned to take the case can also take the case on a no-win no- fee basis or the solicitor can fund counsel's fees themselves. Is generally thought that this latter option will only be acceptable in rare cases.

The incentive for lawyers to take on the risk is that they can charge their clients a "success fee" in the event that the client wins their case which is not a percentage of damages as in the USA but is an enhancement of the solicitor's and, where appropriate, the barrister's costs. This is allowed to be between anything up to twice the normal fees that would be charged. The percentage success fee should reflect the degree of risk which the lawyer is taking on and the fact that the lawyer only gets paid, if at all, at the end of the case.

The success fee will ultimately come out of the plaintiff's damages. The Law Society's model agreement includes a cap on the success fee where it is suggested that the total success fee should be limited to no more than 25% of the damages recovered. It is to be hoped that solicitors will abide by the Law Society's suggested cap and that only in the most complex cases will the lawyer insist on a high percentage success fee.

The great advantage of the scheme to the client, especially where they are outside the legal aid eligibility limits, is that for a premium of less than £100 they can buy an insurance policy which will cover them for up to £100,000 of the other side's costs payable if he or she loses. This insurance policy will enable clients to sue where otherwise they may have been put off by the rule that costs follow the event. The insurance scheme called "Accident Line Protect" will only apply to personal injury cases other than those involving medical negligence. To offer the insurance policy firms must be a member of the Law Society's Accident Line scheme which means that they must have at least one solicitor on the Law Society's Personal Injury Panel.

All clients entering a conditional fee agreement with the lawyer must also take out the insurance policy. The insurance companies offering protection will have no discretion to refuse particular individuals insurance. Presumably the nominated insurers think that lawyers will not agree to do cases on a no-win no-fee basis unless they consider there is a strong probability of success.

It is not clear yet how great an impact conditional fees will have on personal injury work and less so as to whether there will be any significant impact on more complicated cases such as arise from exposure to toxins and pollution. Clearly, the reduction in legal aid eligibility levels indicates that there are large sectors of society who are too well off to be eligible for legal aid but who are unable to take on the risks of funding litigation privately. Conditional fee agreements for personal injury work will clearly satisfy a gap in the market for this particular group.

However, other than in the most straight forward toxic torts cases, for example, injuries suffered as a result of a one-off leak or escape it is thought that conditional fees will have little impact on the conduct of toxic tort litigation. It is thought that at the outset of the scheme few lawyers will be prepared to take these cases on a no-win no-fee basis because the lawyer and barrister will not be prepared to take the risks association with this type of litigation.

It is early days yet and until the scheme is up and running it is difficult to predict how it will work. It may be that if the scheme is a successful funding alternative in ordinary personal injury cases lawyers will become more confident in their risk assessment abilities which may persuade some firms to take on more complex cases under the scheme.

It is useful to compare the American contingency fee system here particularly in relation to what may be perceived as the British lawyer's refusal to take risks with their own money whereas in the States there is no shortage of "speculative" or high risk litigation. It seems that the fundamental difference is that the levels of reward available to the lawyer in the American system are infinitely greater because the level of damages there is significantly higher. It follows that the money available as a cushion against losing cases is that much greater and, accordingly, greater risks can be afforded.

13. The White Knight

In rare circumstances, it may be possible to find a "white knight" to come up with the financial backing for these types of claim. In the Opren litigation, the plaintiffs' lawyers were able to obtain the support of a millionaire to back the claims. The chances of this happening are slim, but always worth considering.

14. Professional Indemnity Insurance

An issue recently identified as important is the special precautions which have to be considered in respect of professional cover for negligence in the context of group actions.

The Solicitors' Indemnity Fund (SIF) forces all solicitors in practice to insure themselves against negligence claims up to a certain level, depending on the size and turnover of the practice. The solicitor then can decide whether or not to top up that minimum amount. The same principles apply to counsel.

The problem for lawyers involved in doing generic work in this field is that where a negligent act arises out of one particular decision made on the generic work that leads to claims from many if not all of the clients, the SIF says that under Clause 17.2 of the 94 Indemnity Rules (they are revised annually) they will treat all the claims as being one claim. The significance of this is that if there are say 1,000 claimants, whose claims are worth £10,000 each, who then pursue the lawyers for negligence, their joint claim will be worth £10 million, but it may well be the solicitors will be insured for a sum far less than this.

This is an issue about which lawyers in the field need to be very aware. The way round the issue is either to enhance the lawyers' overall insurance or to look for a one off cover for the particular case. The best route will depend on the scale of the exposure, as against the existing cover, and the increased costs of the premiums of the two alternatives.

The Legal Aid Board are becoming increasingly concerned about this issue and are likely to insist on such cover being taken out in major cases, and particularly where contracts have been awarded.

CHAPTER FOUR

CONDUCTING MULTI-PARTY ACTIONS

The Supreme Court Procedure Committee have produced a very useful guide book (May 1991) on the running of these actions. It is called "Guide for use in Group Actions". Any lawyer interested in this field will need a copy, which is available from the Lord Chancellor's Department.

1. Client Coordination

One of the major difficulties in a multi-party action is simply handling the large numbers of clients involved in the same action. Although many lawyers are used to representing large numbers of plaintiffs in separate actions there are a number of differences between this and the handling of large numbers of people involved in the same action.

One of the classic difficulties is that energy is often focused around the "lead cases" with the tendency to ignore the others. It is crucial for the morale of all the clients that the lawyer develops systems of contact which ensures that all clients are kept informed about how the case is progressing. In the days of word processors, databases and mail merge programmes this is relatively easy but time and thought still needs to be put into this vital area of work. This is also a fundamental part of being granted a contract by the Legal Aid Board's Multi-party Action Committee, as described in Chapter Three above.

Another role the lawyer can usefully play is that of ensuring the clients have access to each other where there is no other coordinating group. In toxic tort actions the pressure on those taking court action can be enormous. Clients will be in a position to give each other support and ensure that no one feels isolated.

One of the alleged Sellafield leukaemia victims was Gemma D'Arcy, a five year old, whose father worked at the nuclear plant. Her case against British Nuclear Fuels was being pursued through the courts when she died in 1990. At the funeral service the church was packed with other families taking part in the same action. This was a source of great comfort to Gemma's parents, and encouraged Gemma's mother, Susan, to remain a leading spokesperson for the families.

It is often the case that one of the families will take over a coordinating role for keeping the clients in regular contact with each other. This takes some of the burden off the lawyer who should give them every assistance.

To ignore the needs of individual clients can result in some families pulling out of the claims, leading to a general demoralisation amongst them all. Once this starts the lawyer may see the claims slowly dissipate.

2. Lawyer Coordination

In disaster and drug multi-party actions the tendency is for the firms instructed to set up a lawyers co-ordinating committee, with the appointment of Executive Committees, Chairs, Secretaries, Press Officers, etc. This is clearly necessary where there are many firms involved in the same basic action. This allows the co-ordination of the legal action, the gaining of evidence, and also allows joint approaches to be made to the defendants, and joint statements to the media.

There will be occasions when this approach is necessary in toxic tort actions but it is unlikely to be as usual as in disaster or drugs related cases. In the latter instances the victims are likely to be spread far and wide and will therefore tend to go to many different lawyers. In the toxic tort claims so far there have been one or two firms centrally involved in each group of claims with perhaps one or two instructed in the odd case. This is mainly because most of the claims have concentrated in a particular locality. That is not to say that there may not be circumstances where a large number of lawyers do become involved and a coordinating committee would then be most appropriate.

Where a lawyer has been approached to act or is taking the initiative in developing a multi-party claim, the Law Society should be informed. This ensures that they are aware of the claim and therefore if victims contact them they know to whom the caller should be referred. The Law Society's current coordinator of multi-party actions is Ms Edwina Dunne.

Where it becomes clear that there are other lawyers who have been instructed by claimants in a multi-party action contact should be made with them. The point made above regarding the Multi-Party Action Arrangements operated by the Board should however be borne in mind. Indeed the lawyer should be aware that there will be an element of competition between the firms until the issue of who is to be granted the "generic certificates" is determined.

Where there are just a handful of lawyers involved the setting up of a formal committee may not be needed. It is likely that the firm granted the generic certificates will be the main source of information to be passed onto the other lawyers involved. This role should be taken seriously with regular reports concerning the progress of the action.

3. Proceedings

There is no mechanism in the courts for a "group class action" which means that the claims have to be pursued by traditional methods.

The main way of pursuing claims through the courts are set out below.

a) Test Cases

A handful of the best and/or most representative cases can be pursued through to trial, with the agreement of the defendants either that the other claims are not statute barred or that the proceedings are issued and are stayed until the other claims are completed.

If the test cases are successful it is likely that the defendants will agree to settle the outstanding claims without the need for a further trial unless there are clear distinguishing features between the successful claims and those outstanding.

Equally, if the claims are unsuccessful, unless there is good reason to distinguish the other claims the Legal Aid Board will almost definitely refuse the extension of legal aid to take the outstanding cases through to trial.

The benefit of pursuing claims in this way is that it allows the lawyers to concentrate their minds on just a handful of cases, without having to deal with all the bureaucracy of keeping many claims going, with all their different histories, injuries and losses. One of the problems with taking this route is that the very fact that there are such a large number of claims may be one of the strengths of the case. Equally, even if the first group of cases is successful it does not necessarily mean the defendants will agree to compensate the rest which can mean another long wait while the follow-on group of cases go to trial. Perhaps most important, however, are the difficulties the applicants will face in meeting the Board's cost/benefit test, i.e. showing that the value of the claims outweigh the costs of the actions. Finally there is the problem that it will be difficult to avoid the plaintiffs, in these circumstances, ending up with a very stiff reduction of their damages through the operation of the statutory charge.

The test case procedure should not be confused with Representative Actions under RSC ord 15 r 12 of the Rules of the Supreme Court. Plaintiffs suing in a representative capacity under this rule may be granted non-monetary reliefs such as injunctions and declarations. Where, by contrast, a personal injury damages claim was brought under the rule, it was struck out on the basis that one plaintiff's interest in personal injury damages is not "the same" as others, see *Jones v Cory Bros* (1921) 152 LTJo 70. The Court of Appeal has recently indicated, however, that "same interest" may be interpreted more broadly, see *Irish Shipping Ltd v Commercial Union Assurance Co plc* [1990] 2 WLR 117. Nevertheless, whilst *Jones v Cory Bros* remains good law Order 15 r 12 would seem to have no general application in toxic tort litigation.

b) One Claim

The second possibility is to take all the cases together in one action where each claimant is named in a schedule to one writ. Thereafter directions are sought from a judge appointed to run the case. The litigation proceeds by a "Master" Statement of Claim and Defence which set out the fundamentals of all the claim and the defendant's response to that. Appended to the claim would be a series of "individual statements of claim" setting out the basic facts of each individual's case including their injuries, losses, and any additional allegations not covered in the Master Statement of Claim.

The benefit of taking this route is that it ensures that all the cases are dealt with together. It also circumvents the problem of having to issue a separate set of court documents for each case, with all the additional costs and administration that this would involve.

The lawyer will need to keep on top of all the cases as they move on toward trial. The classic case where this would be appropriate is where all the claims result from the same incident so that there is only one joint issue on liability. The lawyer will, therefore, only have to assess each individual quantum claim which should not be too difficult.

More recently the move to trial by lead actions is favoured in multi-party cases. This would be appropriate where a single Writ had been issued for all plaintiffs and where the issues of liability and causation are similar for all those claiming. Trial by lead cases would involve the court or the parties selecting a representative sample of cases by which the "generic" issues of the case would be tried. Despite the costs savings of such an exercise defendants object to this process, although the prevailing opinion today is that this will be the way forward for multi-party actions in the future.

c) Separate Claims

The final possibility is that the lawyer pursues all the cases under their own action numbers through to trial, having them consolidated as they are set down for trial.

This may be most appropriate where the claims have started in a spasmodic and uncoordinated manner. It is difficult to imagine circumstances when this would be a suitable way to commence an action where the lawyer has control over all the cases from the start as it involves all the work of pursuing each of the cases through to trial and has none of the benefits of the trial by lead action.

d) Making the choice

The most appropriate route for any action will depend upon the circumstances of each case. In the Sellafield claims the route chosen was that of the "test cases" mainly because each case is so different in terms of the circumstances and therefore liability that it was felt it would be unnecessarily complicated to have them all proceeding to trial at the same time.

The Camelford claims were pursued by the "Master Statement of Claim" method. There, the cases were sufficiently similar in terms of liability that was no great problem in pursuing them all through to trial at the same time.

Similarly, in the Docklands case the plaintiffs are applying to the court for trial by lead actions having issued one writ for all the plaintiffs and exchanged master pleadings. The suggestion is that lead actions can be jointly chosen by the parties in order to decide generic issues and liability on causation. The defendants do not favour this approach. They are arguing that each case should be individually pleaded before any generic issues of liability can be decided.

Recent pesticide and electromagnetic field claims have been pursued separately, mainly because the claims are spread throughout the country and relate to entirely distinct incidents; the specific pesticides to which the individuals in the former instances were exposed differ and the defendants in both instances are usually not the same. There is sufficient difference between each case that to group them together would produce no overall net gain in terms of costs, although there is work that can be shared to cut down the net unit cost per case.

It is important for plaintiff lawyers to reach a view as to the preferred method of progressing a particular multi-party action before applying for legal aid. This will assist the Board in determining whether to grant full certificates to every plaintiff or generic certificates to representative plaintiffs and limited certificates to the rest.

4. The Court Procedures

Unfortunately if the cases are issued separately and they are worth less than £50,000 proceedings have to be commenced in the County Court regardless of the number or complexity of the cases. This does not apply to cases where all the claims have been issued together, providing the joint value of the claims is worth more than £50,000.

Where a group of individual claims have to be commenced in the County Court immediate application should be made for transfer to the High Court. Such an application is likely to be treated sympathetically by the County Court.

Once proceedings have been commenced in the High Court or transferred from the County Court an early procedural application to determine the special problems and issues arising from the multi-party action should be made. The first decision is whether to apply for a single judge to be designated to deal with all procedural matters. In most cases this is a sensible step since it will ensure that interlocutory summonses are dealt with by the judge making procedural appeals less likely. Further, it ensures a degree of consistency in the decision making on procedural matters. This application is usually made to the Senior Master in the Queens Bench Division in London, elsewhere to a District Judge. The White Book recommends that environmental claims where there is no personal injury, for example nuisance cases, are Official Referee's Business. Under the standard procedure for OR Business a judge will automatically be appointed to run the action and a Summons for Directions should be taken out once the defendants have indicated their intention to defend the action. It is preferable for the directions application to be made in conjunction with the defendants.

Unfortunately, as a result of the number of judges already assigned to long trials and to multi-party actions together with the shortage of judges, applications in the QB for the assignment of a judge, even when agreed by both sides, are not always successful. The Senior Master, in conjunction with the Lord Chief Justice keeps a list of applicants and depending on which judges are available and what prior claims on the judges' time have already been made will determine the decision. The complexity of the issues and the importance of having a judge appointed will also be significant factors in the decision.

Issues to do with the Statute of Limitations can also be considered by the courts. It has been increasingly the case that in multi-party actions the appointed judge will decide a cut-off date after which no further claims can be brought. At times this has been overcome but the lawyer should try and ensure that all potential claimants are aware of this date and are told of the problems of not claiming within that period.

Other procedural matters such as consolidation and discovery will also have to be carefully considered early on in the proceedings.

To date the only multi-party actions that have reached the courts have been the test case type of action. Accordingly no multi-party toxic tort claim has yet been tried, as a result of which it is difficult to know exactly how the courts will handle them. It may well be that each judge will act differently but it will be interesting to see how the courts react to dealing with many hundreds if not thousands of claims issued as one claim.

One thing is clear. This kind of litigation is unmanageable without a degree of co-operation between the plaintiffs' and defendants' lawyers and a willingness on the part of both to assist the judge to "manage" the action. This requirement is sometimes at odds with the wish on the part of some lawyers to display aggressive litigation tactics. Unless the judge is given this assistance and co-operation he may be forced to be more vigorously intrusive in the preparatory phases than he would wish. That said we are unlikely to reach the level of judicial intrusiveness seen in some US class actions. In the Agent Orange litigation for example the judge having, according to the lawyers involved, worked very hard to persuade all parties to the class to agree a £200 million settlement then proceeded to strike out the claims by all those plaintiffs who had refused to join the class on the basis that they disclosed no reasonable cause of action!

The Practice Direction of 8th February 1995 (1995 1 AER 385) by the Lord Chief Justice encouraging judges in longer actions to take a more interventionist stance in curtailing the scale of large actions and particularly of trials, is an indication that the courts will in future be keen to become more involved in the running of these actions.

The drugs litigation may provide toxic tort lawyers with a glimpse of how the courts and defendants will, in future, deal with multi-party toxic tort claims. The Benzodiazepine litigation has been brought to its knees by the defendants' insistence and the court's agreement that all individual cases should be pleaded as opposed to lead cases being taken on generic questions of liability and causation. The amount of public money spent on the thousands of individual cases, where only a limited amount of individual work has been carried out, was enormous. The defendants now argue that cases are crippled with these costs and therefore do not satisfy the statutory test for the continuance of legal aid. Thus, by insisting on individual pleadings the defendants have now put themselves in the position to argue that the cases are no longer financially viable.

Tactics such as these need to be carefully considered and pre-empted wherever possible. The problems associated with the Benzodiazepine litigation have been highlighted in the Legal Aid Board's report on multi-party actions. It is now recognised by all but the most hard bitten defendants' lawyers that practice rules must be devised to allow multi-party actions a realistic chance of progression through the courts without becoming overwhelmed with individual work and costs due to the defendants' insistence that individual cases should be pleaded before the generic issues are resolved.

A Law Society Special Committee was convened in 1994 to consider all issues arising in multi-party actions. Its members comprise senior officers at the Legal Aid Board and both plaintiff and defendant lawyers with experience in this field. In the wake of the Benzodiazepine litigation the committee is investigating whether a practice rule on the conduct of multi-party actions can be drafted to avoid problems that have occurred in the Benzodiazepine cases repeating themselves in the future.

CHAPTER FIVE

THE DEFENDANTS

The authors' litigation experience in this particular field is plaintiff based. It is however instructive to consider what is going through the minds of the defendants and their lawyers in a mainstream multi-party action toxic tort claim. It must be stressed however that what is set out below is the perception of what is happening from the "other side of the fence". It is accepted that the reality may be entirely different.

1. The defendants' initial approach

The typical response of defendants when a claim for toxic torts is intimated is vigorous denial that there is any substance to the allegations whatsoever. It can only be presumed that defendants take this line on the basis that to give any credence to the allegations would only give support to those thinking of claiming and also to the lawyers representing the claimants.

The problem for defendants in taking this approach is that if it can be shown that there is any support whatsoever for the allegations being made they can be forced to retreat very early on. It is then difficult for them to stop retreating.

A good example is that of the childhood leukaemia excess around the Sellafield plant. When the claims were first intimated in the Summer of 1988 British Nuclear Fuels plc went out of their way to refute the allegations being made. It was the defendants line that there was not the slightest chance of the leukaemia families being able to prove their claims.

The publication of the Gardner report in 1990, suggesting that the excess childhood leukaemias around West Cumbria was linked to the fathers who worked at the Sellafield Plant, led to a clear change in attitude.

The same sort of line has been taken in the claims of the Docklands residents where both the London Docklands Development Corporation, the Docklands regulatory body, and Canary Wharf Limited, the builders of Canary Wharf, have taken the line that the claimants case is totally without foundation.

From the plaintiffs' side this "dead bat" approach by the defendants makes it all the more important that the claim is well researched before it is commenced. A case which the lawyer takes on, hoping that the defendants will settle at an early stage, has virtually no chance of success in toxic tort claims.

For almost all types of multi-party toxic tort claims the prospect of defeat for the defendants is likely to be very damaging. A large corporate body may well have no difficulty in principle with settling the rather doubtful claim of the worker who has fallen off a ladder and broken his leg; on the basis that it is cheaper to settle the particular case than to fight it. However, when it comes to settling the claims of a group of inhabitants, allegedly suffering from illnesses caused by toxic emissions emanating from the company's plant, the corporate body will do all in its power to resist. The ramifications of either settlement or defeat are extremely serious both in relation to that particular concern and those carried out in other locations. For most large companies their public image, locally, nationally, and internationally, is of the utmost significance. Companies spend millions of pounds promoting their image including the sponsoring of local groups, charities, the arts, as well as, of course, enormous sums spent on advertising. A successful claim by local inhabitants, particularly where injury is proved, is likely to lay waste to most, if not all, of that carefully planned and expensive image. Spending hundreds of thousands, if not millions, defending a claim in these circumstances can be seen by the company to be an efficient use of their resources.

For the plaintiffs and their lawyers the crucial point to recognise is that in a legally aided case worth, say £250,000, where the costs are likely to run into hundreds of thousands of pounds, the defendants are still very unlikely to settle the claim simply because of the economics of the litigation. They are more likely to look at the claim in a much wider context. An example of how seriously defendants take environmental claim can be seen in the case of Mr and Mrs Graham against Rechem International Limited, the details of which are referred to in detail below. In the trial, which lasted over a year, Mr Graham was in the witness box for some 30 days, of which the great majority consisted of his being cross examined. This may well be the longest period in English civil legal history. Commentators argued that this type of treatment was, in all the circumstances, oppressive. However, the judge took the view early on in the case that he wanted to hear all the evidence the parties wished to submit. Irrespective of these arguments the case is illustrative of the point that the defendants will go to great expense to discredit claims that they are causing environmental damage.

Having said all this, it is also the case that whilst settling such a claim may cause the defendant company a lot of public relations difficulties, losing the case at trial would be a disaster for them. Pressure can still be brought to bear, for the defendants to settle, particularly in the early stages of the case. An example was the Camelford litigation which settled at the door of the Court on significantly improved terms to those previously offered, although part of the incentive was probably to avoid having the case opened at trial with considerable media attention.

2. Defendants and Legal Aid

As stated in Chapter 3 defendants are entitled to make representations to the Legal Aid Board regarding the granting and continuation of legal aid to the plaintiffs and this practice is becoming routine in toxic tort and multi-party litigation.

The difficulty for the plaintiffs is that during the early stages of the case the defendants will always have two major advantages. They will have greater knowledge of the problem that has occurred and also the resources to carry out early investigations. They are therefore always likely to be in a position to put forward a strong case to the Board. The Board should, unless the claim clearly does not have foundation, grant legal aid to enable preliminary investigations to be undergone. The fundamental decision as to whether the claim should be funded through to trial ought to be left until those investigations are concluded. Instead what appears to happen is that the Board expects the plaintiff's lawyer to be able to answer the defendant's representations at this initial stage.

Under the current system once legal aid has been granted it is less likely that intervention from the defendants will have the impact of the letter sent before the decision is made. It is, however, still common for defendants to continue to write to the Board with their comments regarding the continued funding of the case. In the electromagnetic field actions, having made one such set of representations that failed to persuade the Board to discharge the certificates, they simply tried again. On the second occasion the different officer considering the position took a more pessimistic view of the action than the first and discharged the certificate.

3. Defendants and their lawyers

Most of the major companies involved in toxic tort litigation will instruct one of the big city firms. It will usually be the same firm that represents the company in its commercial affairs. Often the experience of those firms is exclusively that of dealing with other large firms. Until recently, most had little knowledge of personal injury work and limited experience of how the legal aid system operated. Their state of knowledge in relation to legal aid has changed dramatically as they have learnt that often the key to stopping a toxic tort action is either to prevent legal aid being granted at the outset or continually to challenge the viability of the claims.

A firm which does not normally deal with personal injury cases is unlikely to have the "settlement" mentality which most personal injury specialists acquire with experience. City firms are also likely to be far more used to the large scale litigation involved in toxic tort actions.

The key point to understand is that in this type of litigation the lawyers and their clients will spare no expense if they consider the objective worthwhile. Useful examples of this can be seen in the Merlins family's claim for damage caused by the presence of radioactivity from Sellafield in their home. At the trial the defendants' lawyers and clients took over a floor of the Waldorf Hotel, had an office in the Royal Courts of Justice, and a host of secretaries brought down from Cumbria. They even went to the lengths of trying to follow one of the plaintiffs' experts to Germany to listen to one of his lectures simply to assist in their cross examination.

This is not the nature of ordinary personal injury litigation!

4. The Defendants' weaknesses

The main problem for the defendants is that they have a much larger agenda than simply the financial issues related to winning or losing any one case. They have their own public image, including their relations with the media, they have their relationship with the company's workforce and unions, as well as the local people and local press. As a result of this they may take the tactical decision that to pursue a particular avenue, albeit potentially fruitful in the litigation, may be harmful to one of their wider interests and therefore not take the point. Establishing links with local groups, unions, press etc. is likely to assist the plaintiffs' lawyer in gaining a clearer picture as to what the defendants might do in particular circumstances.

There are indeed times where close links with bodies such as the trades unions and local pressure groups may be appropriate where the goal of the lawyer, the unions and/or the groups coincide. There are, of course, limits as to how appropriate such links are and the crucial point should always remain in the lawyers mind that the case is being run for the purpose and benefit of the clients and not any third party. That does not however rule out assistance between the various interests where they coincide.

5. Multi-Defendants

The crucial point is to focus in on the central defendants. Who were the two/three or so most to blame? By commencing an action against them it then leaves the decision in their hands as to whether other parties are added. In most instances the defendants are jointly and severally liable for damages and as long as each of them has a part of the responsibility they will be obliged to pay the full damages if the claims are successful. It is then up to the named defendants to add third parties to the action. A decision can be made once this has been done whether to join the third party as a defendant.

If an attempt is made to involve in the action all the defendants where there are clearly a large number, it is likely that defendants may be involved who in fact share no part of the blame. The problem with this is that when the position becomes clear and the claim against them is withdrawn their costs may have to be paid by the plaintiff. It is therefore generally a better policy to proceed against the few apparently most culpable and then wait and see if these defendants add in any other party. They are likely to know who else was involved at an early stage and they can decide whether to add other parties into the action. The plaintiff can then respond by adding the party with much greater confidence that their costs are unlikely to be a major problem.

Where the action relates to a particular toxic substance but details about the manufacturer are not known it would usually be appropriate to sue the supplier and let the supplier add in the manufacturer. They will know much more about the position than the plaintiffs' lawyers. There is a danger, however, that the supplier may decide not to join the manufacturer either because they think they can defend successfully on their own or for other commercial reasons.

Clearly if the proposed defendants respond immediately to the letter before action saying that they are the wrong defendants for any reason or indeed that other companies are equally or even more to blame then they should be written to and, if necessary, incorporated into the claim when proceedings are commenced. The originally proposed defendants can then be left out of the proceedings without any risk on costs.

CHAPTER SIX

CAUSATION

Probably the greatest hurdle to be overcome in most toxic tort claims is that of causation, i.e. proving that the pollution emanating from a particular source caused the specific illness, injury or condition. The legal principles applied or likely to be applied to the issue of causation in this type of case are considered first. The evidential issues in particular types of toxic tort claims are then put under the microscope albeit that it is not intended that the comments are intended to be anything other than illustrative, based on the authors' experience. This section is not intended to be prescriptive, since circumstances will vary greatly.

1 The Law

The first question to be determined is what exactly does the plaintiff in a toxic tort claim have to prove? There have been three key judgements that need to be considered.

The first case is that of *McGhee v National Coal Board* [1973] 1 WLR 1. The plaintiff in that action worked in a brick kiln, where he was continually covered in brick dust. Having worked at the kiln for some time he began to suffer from dermatitis, one of the causes of which was known to be brick dust. He claimed against his employers on the basis that they had not provided a shower which would have enabled him to wash off the dust.

The central issue in the case was whether the plaintiff would have suffered from the illness regardless of a shower not having been provided. The experts were unable to say whether or not this would have been the case but what they were able to say was that the provision of a shower would have materially reduced his risk of contracting the dermatitis. On this basis the House of Lords decided for the plaintiff although it was not possible to determine the extent to which the failure to provide showers had contributed to the occurrence.

In 1987 the House of Lords case of *Hotson v East Berkshire Area Health Authority* [1987] AC 750 it was held that, despite *McGhee* the burden still lay upon the plaintiff to prove that the negligence more probably than not caused the injury. It was accepted, however, that causation would be sufficiently proved if it was shown that the negligent act "was at least a material contributory cause" of the injury.

Finally, the case of *Wilsher v Essex Area Health Authority* [1988] AC 1074 came before the Lords the following year. Lord Bridge approved *McGhee* but in a rather restricted way. In that case the infant plaintiff suffered from a condition known as RLF. There were four possible causes of this syndrome, one of which was excess oxygen, which was the basis of the negligence action. The problem for the plaintiff's lawyers was that they were unable to show that the cause complained of was any more likely to have caused the RLF than any of the competing causes. (In fact the plaintiff failed to prove that excess oxygen was a cause of RLF in any event).

Lord Bridge held that the plaintiff had to show the act complained of had either caused or materially contributed to the onset of the injury.

In short, the burden is and remains upon the plaintiff to show that the act or omission complained of was probably a material cause although not necessarily the only one. The plaintiff cannot discharge this burden where he can only establish that it was possibly a material cause.

In any specific case it is this test that will have to be passed for the claim to succeed. In coming to a decision the judge will consider all the evidence including expert evidence. However the court must approach the question broadly and on a common sense basis, see *Stapley v Gypsum Mines Ltd* [1953] AC 663 at 681 per Lord Reid.

The fact that experts cannot identify the precise mechanism of causation does not preclude the court from making the inference, on all the facts, that the defendant's negligence materially contributed to the plaintiff's injury. This important principle was restated by Lord Bridge in *Wilsher* in the following terms [1988] AC 1074 at 1088:

" But where (as in *McGhee*) the layman is told by the doctors that the longer the brick dust remains on the body the greater the risk of dermatitis, although the doctors cannot identify the process of causation scientifically there seems to be nothing irrational in drawing the inference, as a matter of common sense, that the consecutive periods when brick dust remained on the body probably contributed cumulatively to the causation of dermatitis."

The Supreme Court of Canada has recently applied the dictum of Lord Bridge and interpreted it as promoting "a robust and pragmatic approach to the facts to enable an inference of negligence to be drawn even though medical or scientific expertise cannot arrive at a definitive conclusion"; see *Snell v Farrell* [1990] 72 DLR (4th) 289 at 297.

McGhee was an occupational disease case. Snell was a medical negligence case. The issue of causation has not yet been directly addressed by the UK appellate courts in a toxic tort case although it was addressed in the High Court, in the Sellafield childhood leukaemia trial, which is considered later in the book. The Dublin Supreme Court, in *Hanrahan v Merck Sharp & Dhome (Ireland) Limited* (1988)ILRM 629, held that in this class of case that the primary evidence was very important and that where, on the direct evidence in that case of the plaintiff farmer and his witnesses, it was a legitimate inference that the defendant's factory emissions damaged the plaintiff's livestock the plaintiff had made out his claim. To hold otherwise, said the Court, would be "to allow scientific theorising to dethrone fact".

There may well be a parallel approach by the court in this class of case to that taken in the medical product liability claims which have given rise to problems when dealing with the issue of causation. If so, the court may follow the guidance of Lord Justice Stuart-Smith in *Loveday v Renton* (1988, unreported), the whooping cough vaccine litigation, where the judge considered 5 evidential sub-headings as follows:

(a)evidence that the substance concerned can cause the condition complained of; (b)evidence of "temporal association", i.e. relation in time between exposure and onset consistent with the way in which the condition is known to develop; (c) evidence that the plaintiff was not exposed to another substance as or more likely to have caused the condition; (d) evidence that the plaintiff was not subject to the disease naturally; (e) epidemiological evidence.

Having considered the approach of the court to the issue of causation it is now necessary to look at some of the categories of evidence which are likely to be adduced as relevant to the issue in toxic tort cases.

2. Biological Evidence

Biological evidence in these types of cases is likely to fall into the following categories:

(a) Data from experiments using whole animals; (b) in vitro ("test tube") experiments with animal and human cells; (c) biological testing of clients' specimens, (including blood, skin and sperm).

Biological evidence may be used to establish causation on its own or in conjunction with epidemiological evidence. In cases involving alleged chemical exposure, it may be possible, by genetic testing of clients' cells, to determine whether or not DNA damage attributable to the chemical has occurred. This is due to the specificity of chemical interactions with DNA. On-going scientific research should make this possible in a substantial number of cases in the not too distant future.

Of course, even if chemical damage can be shown, it is then necessary to establish that damage of the type occasioned to the cells which have been tested gave rise to the injury. This is dependent on some understanding of the underlying cellular mechanisms which cause injury. This is not to say that the plaintiff is required to explain the precise mechanism which gave rise to the injury. However, if the defendant adduces evidence to the effect that the exposure could not have caused the injury, then the plaintiff will certainly need to demonstrate a plausible mechanism by which it could have caused the injury. Evidence as to the plausibility of the mechanism might be obtained from animal experiments in which comparable injuries have been induced in animals by chemical exposures.

Where epidemiological evidence, showing a statistical association between the exposure and increased risk of the injury in question, is available this will usually need to be supported by biological evidence (unless the defendant is unable to cite any contradictory biological evidence). The plaintiff may need to refer to biological evidence first, to demonstrate a plausible mechanism and secondly, to prove that the level of the exposure (i.e. dose) is more likely than not to have caused the injury. For example, in the Sellafield cases, there were major arguments regarding the plausibility of the genetic mechanism (i.e.

whether radiation induced damage to a man's sperm can cause leukaemia in his children), and whether the pre-conception doses were sufficient to have generated a leukaemia excess to the extent observed in Sellafield. Included in the arguments was animal data considering whether they showed a similar increase in the level of leukaemia in the offspring of animals and evidence considering the quality of the radiation exposures in Sellafield (for example, the length of time over which the exposures occurred, the distinction between the biological effects of internal and external radiation and biological differences between effects of different types of radiation).

It should by now be apparent that the rate of progress of science means that the plaintiff's lawyer, in this type of case can no longer hope to avoid coming to terms with the scientific detail in environmental personal injury cases by adopting the "res ipsa loquitur" approach i.e. "I was well before I came into contact with the chemical and thereafter I felt ill. Therefore the exposure caused the illness". The scope of that kind of approach is diminishing rapidly. Nevertheless, scientific advances should ensure greater certainty of outcome in legal cases.

3. Epidemiological evidence

As has been discussed above this is an area where there are large numbers of epidemiological studies. Where this is not the case the decision has to be made by the lawyer as to whether one is necessary. This is considered in detail below. Where there is epidemiological evidence the question arises as to how the courts will deal with it in terms of assisting them in coming to a decision on causation. The Sellafield trial illustrates that the courts here are prepared to consider epidemiological evidence on the question of causation and will take such studies into account when deciding whether the plaintiff has proved the case on the balance of probabilities.

Epidemiology tries to determine by statistical analyses whether or not there is evidence of an association between suspected causes and increased risk of injury. Such an analysis can be used to test which is the most likely of competing causes to have brought about the particular group of illnesses. If, for example, there is a reported cluster of cancers around a particular chemical plant the epidemiologists attempt to see whether the excess is real, as opposed to it being a chance phenomenon, and whether there is any consistent pattern emerging in terms of the links between the individuals and the plant, including perhaps how long those with the cancers had lived in the area before the onset of the cancer.

They then compare the pattern in the incidence of the cancer under investigation with what is known about the plant in terms of emissions and potential carcinogens.

An example would be the cluster of leukaemias around the Dounreay nuclear reprocessing plant in Scotland. A study published in 1991 attempted to look at the various possible causes. What the authors concluded was that there was an excess of childhood leukaemia but that there did not appear to be a link between the radiation exposure of the fathers working at the plant prior to the conception of the children, as there had been in the Gardner study at Sellafield. What was "statistically significant" was that a number of the children played on the beach close to the plant and the closer the child lived to the plant the higher the risk of the child contracting leukaemia.

In that example, despite the statistics, the epidemiologists stated that in their view the link between the radiation emitted from the plant into the air and sea and the leukaemias was not sufficiently clear cut to be proven by this study.

It can be seen from this that although epidemiology can be of great assistance it cannot directly prove any hypothesis, it can only show a correlation. One of the reasons for this is that the epidemiologists, as with most scientists, by convention, require a relationship to be statistically significant before they will say that such a relationship or correlation is real. What is meant by this is that the epidemiologist needs to show, statistically, that there is a less than 5% probability that the correlation is due to chance.

The problem for the lawyer is in making the expert, and in particular the epidemiologist, understand that the test for the court is 51% certainty rather than this 95% figure. For an expert who has always adopted the 95% certainty figure this is a difficult concept to grasp. The lawyer should not be put off by an expert who states at the outset that the particular hypothesis forwarded by the plaintiff cannot be proved. They will usually be talking about it not being provable to a 95% degree of certainty.

One epidemiological approach is to look at the "probability of causation". What is meant by this is the determination as to what is the probability that in a particular case the illness has been caused by the particular toxic incident. This can be worked out by the use of complex formulae, particularly in radiation cases. This has become popular in the USA and has even gained Government approval over there in terms of its use in certain compensation schemes.

Whether it would ever be of great significance to the courts here remains open to question. The courts here retain their determination to weigh everything in the balance without needing to take any specific account of this statistical reasoning.

Although the statistical evidence does not constitute biological proof of causation, in the absence of contradictory biological evidence, statistical evidence may constitute proof of legal causation. It was so held by the Scottish Court of Sessions in the case of *Alexander - v- McPherson*.

There can be no doubt that where it is available and in the plaintiff's interests epidemiologists should be brought in to give evidence on the question of causation. The lawyer should simply be wary of laying the whole case at the epidemiolgists' feet.

Considered below is the evidence in relation to various environmental pollutants to provide a better understanding of the difficulties involved in proving the causative link.

4. Evidence in a radiation claim

There is a rather mysterious and even slightly sinister atmosphere surrounding the issue of radiation and nuclear power. In fact radiation is probably the most closely monitored of all environmental pollutants. The amount of public resources that have gone into monitoring people who are exposed to radiation are phenomenal when compared to the paltry sums spent in many other fields.

The crucial issues that need to be determined in radiation based toxic tort claims are: the dose received by the victim; the radiogenicity of the type of cancer (i.e. the tendency of radiation to cause the particular cancer); and the spontaneous frequency of the cancer in people of the plaintiff's age.

a) The dose

Radiation workers for many decades have been monitored for their exposure to external radiation by the use of dose badges. The badges operate in a complex way, which is outside of the remit of this book to explain, but the basic purpose is to determine the radiation dose of workers when they work in any area where it is likely that they will be exposed to radiation. Although the sensitivity of the badges have greatly improved over the years, for most workers in the nuclear industry it is possible to gain an immediate impression of the level of radiation exposure from their dose records. The industry are obliged to keep those records for at least thirty years and indeed, because of the interest in the impact of radiation, it is likely that the records will be kept for a much longer period.

Internal radiation dose, i.e. radiation that has been inhaled or ingested, is rather more difficult to ascertain as the measurement of urine and faeces, which is the main way of making any sort of assessment whilst the worker is alive, only started on a systematic basis in about 1970. Even then the determination of dose from those records is far from simple.

For people living in the vicinity of a nuclear plant the only way to assess dose is to try and determine the amount and make up of radiation emanating from the plant; how that radiation could have affected the local people and what dose this could have subsequently given to the local inhabitants. This assessment is far from easy. It is the case, however, that there are enormous amounts of monitoring data on radiation levels in food, milk, in the air, on the land and in the seas and rivers in the vicinity of our nuclear plants. This is carried out by a whole variety of Government bodies and the nuclear industry itself. It is, therefore, possible to have some idea as to the levels of radiation that were in the environment during the relevant period.

In the Sellafield cases one of the problems of determining dose to the local inhabitants was that the main cases related to what was happening in the 1950's and 1960's. At that time the monitoring data was far more crude than it is today and therefore attempts to determine what each monitoring document from this period means involves the lawyer in endless consideration of all the surrounding documents.

For the lawyer to determine the radiation dose received by any individual means understanding the operation of a nuclear plant; the reasons for radiation emanating from the plant; the different types of radiation and their different characteristics; the particle size distribution whether in the air or water; the interaction of the particles with the air, land, vegetation, sea, etc.; how it can either be inhaled or ingested through the food chain; then understanding the pathways the radiation takes in the body, depending on its route of entry, and then finally what dose that gives to the relevant organ (e.g. in the leukaemia cases the crucial question to be determined is what is the dose to the bone marrow).

b) Epidemiology and radiation

Once the dose is determined, the next question is, given the dose, for a person at a certain age and with a certain cancer, what is the possibility that the cancer has been brought about by the exposure to radiation as against it being caused by some competing cause, such as chemical exposure or indeed by chance?

The dropping of the Atomic Bombs in Hiroshima and Nagasaki led to a follow up study of the survivors which is without doubt the largest and most detailed epidemiological study ever carried out in the world. The follow up of the cancers sustained by the survivors and the comparison with cancer rates in other parts of Japan has enabled the experts to determine the so called "risk estimates", i.e. the chance of contracting any particular cancer having been exposed to a certain dose of radiation.

c) Sellafield and the genetic debate

The Gardner report, published in February 1990, indicated that the cause of the excess childhood leukaemias surrounding the Sellafield plant seemed linked to the fact that it was the fathers who had been subjected to high radiation doses who had a much higher than expected level of leukaemia amongst their children. The implication of the report was therefore that the radiation was creating some sort of mutation in the sperm of the father which carried through to the embryo and eventually became leukaemia in the infant.

The claims, which were heard over a nine month period between October 1992 and June 1993, were based on the principle that in contravention of the strict liability imposed by Section 7 of the Nuclear Installations Act 1965 (and the preceding similar statutory provisions) radiation had caused or materially contributed to the onset of the excess leukaemias. In respect of the mechanism it was the plaintiffs' case that the most likely route was that of the genetic damage to the father's sperm.

The Gardner report came as a great shock to the scientific community. The Atomic Bomb studies, described above, had not found any excess cancers amongst the children of the survivors and as a result, prior to the publication of the Sellafield study, the overriding view amongst epidemiologists and geneticists was that genetically induced leukaemia could only be caused by very high doses of radiation and certainly much higher than those described by Gardner.

Animal experimentation had previously suggested that radiation could induce cancers genetically at a relatively high frequency. However the A Bomb studies cast such a large shadow that most experts thought the animal data were not applicable to radiation induced human cancers. The publication of the Gardner report sent geneticists scurrying to their laboratories to repeat the animal data and has brought about a major review of the whole question of genetic damage.

One of the central features of the Sellafield claims was the debate between the epidemiologists and medical statisticians regarding the strength of the Gardner report and other studies determining there to be excesses around a number of nuclear plants. They also considered the question of what else could be causing the excess other than radiation; certainly viruses have been held up by some experts as being a plausible alternative. Another one of the debates was between the dosimetrists who argued that they knew what doses the mothers, fathers and children received. Finally, the geneticists considered the question of the feasibility of the genetic mechanism, per se and as an explanation of the Sellafield leukaemia excess.

It would be hard to imagine a more complex set of issues to put before a judge. However, on balance the judicial system worked well in providing a forum where these complex issues could be fully explored.

5. Evidence in a pesticides claim

a) Direct Effects

Pesticides are in common and widespread use throughout the country. As their name suggests they are chemicals used to kill pests. In the broadest sense pests are, animals, micro-organisms, plants and insects. Examples of pesticides are crop sprays used in agriculture and wood preservatives, primarily in terms of their use in the home.

Increasing concern is expressed as to whether the manufacturers and commercial users of pesticides have taken enough care to ensure that what can be extremely toxic substances are not used in the vicinity of individuals. Health effects can be acute or chronic. There have recently been a number of cases against companies including Rentokil on behalf of both workers, home owners and children where it was claimed that the use of/and exposure to particular pesticides in their vicinity has brought about illnesses.

Nearly all of these cases are "one-offs" rather than being group actions, although in 1995 a group action appears to be developing in relation to the alleged use by the Government laboratories at Porton Down of military personnel as human guinea pigs in the testing of various chemicals. Further in nearly every case the action has either been settled or withdrawn before trial.

The only exception to this is the case of *Gaskill v Rentokil* (unreported), which was heard by Mr Justice Otton, as he then was, in 1994. In that case it was alleged that the infant plaintiff had sustained a soft tissue sarcoma as a result of his sleeping in a bedroom that had been recently sprayed with "Lindane", a wood preservative. The court determined that there was not sufficient evidence to meet the level of proof necessary to link the illness with the exposure (the epidemiology was virtually non-existent because of the cancer being so rare). Further, the judge stated that the case did not meet the foreseeability test in that although it was foreseeable at that time that some injuries might result from exposure, this particular type of illness was not foreseeable at that time.

The important issues in any such claim are the stage at which the exposure occurred; the extent of the likely exposure; the question of whether the illness was the type likely to be caused by the particular pesticide; whether the exposure was sufficient to cause the particular illness when taking everything else into account; and whether adequate precautions had been taken to keep any exposure to a minimum.

One of the problems in this field is the bewildering number of different chemical formulae for the numerous different pesticides. Trying to get to grips with those formulae and their links to other similar pesticides and their effects is again far from easy.

There is, however, a distinct advantage in these actions being based on individual illnesses in that it allows the actions to settle with far less impact on the defendants, i.e. they are far more likely to take a commercial view of the case than they do in group actions where the principle of the action is of much greater importance.

b) Genetic effects

As with radiation there is an increasing concern that exposure to certain pesticides and toxic substances may lead to an increased risk of certain cancers and other malformations in the offspring of the exposed. A classic example of this is a syndrome known as CHARGE. Each of the letters describes a different malformation in the child which adds up to the child being born badly deformed and in some cases mentally handicapped. There seems an increasing suggestion that a proportion of the parents of the children born with such a defect have been exposed to pesticides immediately pre or post conception. More recently, investigations have been undertaken in relation to the number of babies born without eyes and others born without arms and the possible link with maternal exposure to pesticides whilst pregnant.

Cancers involve gene mutations/chromosome aberrations. Radiation is known to cause cancer in people who have been directly exposed. It is also known that radiation can induce gene mutations which can be genetically transmitted, in that the radiation induces cell transformation and chromosome aberrations. Certain chemicals can also cause DNA damage and/or chromosome aberrations and can induce cancers in animals exposed experimentally. As regards CHARGE the question is whether the observed chromosome aberrations (in some instances) are the cause of the syndrome and whether the substances to which the parents of the affected children were exposed are likely to have caused those aberrations.

Further scientific research is being undertaken in relation to the CHARGE children and their families and the syndromes of babies born without eyes and arms. If the scientific evidence supports a link with parental exposure to pesticides these cases may become a very significant category of litigation in this class.

6. Evidence in a dioxin poisoning claim

One of the greatest concerns in this field is the increasing level of dioxins permeating the environment emanating from incinerators and other industrial processes. A dioxin is usually formed by the incineration of toxic substances at temperatures which are not sufficient to enable the substance completely to vaporise. It is therefore a sub-class of the "product of incomplete incineration" class which attracted such attention following the Seveso disaster in Italy which occurred in 1977. Dioxins can also occur as a by-product of certain pesticides, of certain other processes such as paper manufacture, and even from vehicle exhausts. The points to note are firstly that dioxins are man-made not naturally occurring and secondly that by reason of the number of different processes that can generate dioxins they are now ubiquitous in the environment at background levels.

There is a body of research to show that dioxins are capable of causing great harm when taken into the body. There is evidence that dioxins are tetragenic (i.e. cause birth deformity); fetotoxic (i.e. cause abortions); immuno-suppressive (i.e. disruption of bodily mechanisms so as to impair healing ability) and that dioxins may cause certain types of cancer. Another typical feature is an impact on the skin which in humans is a particularly unpleasant form of skin condition called chloracne. However the feature of dioxin poisoning of most interest for present purposes is a disruption of biological mechanisms such that the ability to recover from normal ailments is severely impaired. Thus a dioxin poisoning case may initially be masked since death within the group may seem to be from many different causes. In the report on dioxins by the American Environmental Protection Agency in 1994 all the scientific literature on the hazards of exposure to dioxins was reviewed. The 2000 page report was conducted by some of America's most well respected scientists, and it has concluded that there is no known safe level of dioxins to which the population may be exposed. The report has led to a review of those industries known to produce dioxins as part of their process, and a commitment to phase out those processes in the future. In Britain, where incineration of waste is an activity promoted by government policy as one of recycling waste to energy, many people living close to both industrial and medical incinerators are increasingly concerned about the health implications of this policy.

In an incineration case involving an allegation of damage to livestock from dioxin poisoning the following classes of expert evidence will need to be available:

(a) Incineration technology; evidence will be needed both as to the design and the operation of the incinerator which bears on the propensity to emit products of incomplete incineration; (b) meteorological evidence which locates the pasture in question as a likely point of deposition; (c) toxicological evidence which brings together the sampling data, the emissions data, and the pattern of symptoms in the livestock into a coherent picture which is characteristic of a dioxin poisoning episode; (d) veterinary evidence as to the likely pathways of ingestion and pattern of symptoms in the livestock and by reference to Lord Justice Stuart-Smith's categories above, i.e. eliminating other possible causes of the pattern of symptoms.

These categories of evidence are taken from *Graham v ReChem* which was tried in 1993/4 and is dealt with in more detail below.

The Coalite plant in Derbyshire allegedly discharged dioxins into the local environment, not only causing concern to the local farmers and property owners, but also to the workers and the National Rivers Authority who found high levels of dioxins in the local river. The farmers commenced proceedings against the company and settled their actions for substantial sums. The central evidence was analytical data. Dioxin levels in soil herbage milk and tissue (of the grazed cows) were found to be elevated above background. The inquiry was triggered by routine MAFF milk sampling which identified the high milk levels.

7. Evidence in industrial air pollution cases

It is known that there are a number of noxious substances which, if inhaled in large enough doses, will cause respiratory disease. The diseases can be of varying severity and can be seriously disabling such as narrowing of airways and its more episodic relation asthma. Where an unusual cluster of respiratory disease is found adjacent to certain kinds of large scale industrial process with significant emissions of noxious substances going back over years it may be possible to establish a causative relationship.

An example is Monkton Cokeworks at Hebburn near Newcastle on Tyne. The plant is now closed but the local authority commissioned an epidemiological study by Newcastle on Tyne University and in February 1992. The study concluded that there did indeed appear to be a link between the plant and respiratory illness in the area.

There are many examples of housing estates abutting large scale industrial processes where there is now concern that there may be a link between illness and emissions and, indeed, the government has set in train epidemiological surveys in a number of such cases. At first blush this appears to be fertile ground for claims but there are serious evidential hurdles to surmount. A practical approach to garnering evidence is developed in Chapter 21 on Air Pollution.

There is a difficulty in assessing this type of claim because little epidemiological work has been carried out and it is necessary for the lawyer to decide whether an excess of respiratory disease actually exists or is in fact simply anecdotal.

If the excess proves to be real the next question is whether the pollution emanating from the plant is the cause of the respiratory problems. The cause may be something else such as poor housing conditions, traffic, smoking or some other unrelated cause. The only way of finding this out is to ascertain the type and levels of plant emissions. Unfortunately although companies in the USA are obliged to produce such information voluntarily the Environmental Protection Act 1990 only requires companies to make certain information on emissions available which is not as extensive and certainly not as accessible as it is in the United States.

If the defendant is uncooperative the only option for the plaintiff is to force the production of the information by making an application for pre-action discovery. This is a crucial application and therefore, in this as with other similar cases a lot of groundwork needs to be carried out before the application is made. A refusal by the court to make such an order may put an end to the cases before they have even begun. There has to be enough evidence to convince the court that there is at least a *prima facie* case against the alleged polluters.

Allied to the quest for obtaining information regarding the releases is a similar need to obtain monitoring data.

One of the ways of determining whether there is a link between the aerial releases from a particular plant and the onset of respiratory problems is to look at when the emissions occur and whether there is a correlation with the timing of the asthma attacks. The point being that if there is a clear temporal link between when the aerial emissions are at their worst and when the respiratory problems are at their worst this is strong evidence of a link.

It is clear that there will be many areas where atmospheric pollution can cause respiratory problems. There is a good deal of evidence to show that substances that are regularly emitted from our manufacturing industry such as nitrogen dioxide and sulphur dioxide can cause respiratory illness. In an attempt to show that on the balance of probabilities it is the industrial plant's emissions that have caused or materially contributed to the onset of the illness it will be necessary to eliminate other variables so far as possible. This can be done by epidemiological studies. However some of the more obvious significant factors, such as smoking or parental smoking in children, occupational dust exposure, and pollution from cars should be elicited in the first proofs taken, so that the chest physician will have an early appreciation of such factors.

8. Evidence in construction/demolition cases

a) Nuisance

Dust may be a considerable nuisance to a community. For example, the soiling of homes, gardens and vehicles resulting from the rapid collection of dust and dirt may well mean that constant cleaning is required. This can seriously impair the quality of life particularly where pavements, playgrounds and other communal areas also become very dusty.

There are various methods used to assess whether the dust levels in an area can amount to a nuisance in law. One method involves determining the rate of soiling caused by dust by placing glass slides throughout an area. Detailed evidence from those affected is also essential in proving that a nuisance has occurred. The plaintiffs must be able to give evidence of the effects on every day life and restrictions the nuisance has imposed, for example their inability to open windows or use the garden because of noise and dust. The monitoring evidence will back up the primary evidence but is no substitute for it. Once it has been established that a nuisance exists, it is then possible to trace, by scientific analysis, this back to its source. In most cases this will be obvious. In some, however, where there are other dust producing sources, this analysis will be a crucial part of establishing liability. Practical advice on dust analysis is given in Chapter 21 on Air Pollution.

To base a claim in nuisance in respect of noise, it is generally necessary to establish a pattern of serious noise problems over a period of time.   To assess whether noise constitutes a nuisance in law, noise levels should be measured and account taken of when that noise occurs. Noise during anti-social hours i.e. at night or weekends, is less tolerable than at other times. The duration of exposure to the noise complained of, whether it is short or long term, will also be taken into account when making the assessment of whether the noise amounts to a nuisance. Practical advice on noise level measurement is given in Chapter 19 on Noise Pollution.

The balance to be struck in terms of the value of the defendants' work in causing the nuisance, the cost of it being reduced and the damage to the plaintiff's quality of life is set out below. The point to note in looking at evidence is that establishing a nuisance is not sufficient.   In claims arising out of construction works for the nuisance to be actionable the court must be satisfied that the developer has failed to use all reasonable means to abate the nuisance caused by the construction work. This will involve expert evidence by construction engineers as to the practicability, efficacy and cost of abatement techniques which the developer could have but did not employ.

9. Evidence in other chemical poisoning claims

In addition to the categories described above there are numerous other examples of chemicals and toxic substances which can cause serious harm if the individual is exposed at certain levels. The principles in relation to proving causation are the same as for the examples quoted above.

Ideally in discharging the burden of proof which lies upon him the plaintiff will be able to do the following:

a) identify the chemical or chemicals;

b) identify the disease or condition complained of;

c) identify the precise dose to which each the person was exposed of each chemical;

d) establish by reference to scientific literature a plausible mechanism linking the condition to the exposure to the specified chemical, and the dose level at which the condition is likely to be caused by the exposure;

e) thereby establish a causal connection between exposure to the chemical and the disease in the person concerned;

f) identify other plausible causes for the disease complained of which are not associated with the chemical, and exclude them in the case of the person concerned.

The key word is "ideally". There are approximately 80,000 chemicals used in industry of which we have comprehensive toxicity data on some 300 and modest data (e.g. studies in other species such as rats) on about 5000. New chemicals are thought to be being generated at the rate of about 5000 per year. In other words the chances of a plaintiff being able to deal with the dose issue satisfactorily are remote. The question as to whether an epidemiological study of one sort or another can plug a gap in the plaintiff's ability to fulfil the above requirements in any particular case is a matter of judgement.

Where the plaintiff cannot deal satisfactorily with each step and cannot make good the evidential deficiencies with an epidemiological study the case will not necessarily fail. This is because the court is required to apply a common sense approach to the evidence overall. An example of this is the Irish case of *Hanrahan v Merck Sharp & Dhome (Ireland) Ltd* referred to previously in this chapter. There, an industrial complex was built next to a farming family. The family had no health problems until the industrial emissions started. After a few years a whole series of problems developed, not just amongst the family themselves but also amongst the livestock. The court at first instance held that plaintiff's claim failed for want of sufficiently conclusive analytical data. The Supreme Court in Dublin reversed the trial judge saying in effect that he must have left his common sense at home. The Appeal Court was not disposed to allow "scientific theorising to de-throne fact". .

If the courts are not willing to apply common sense robustly they will leave the citizen at the mercy of incomplete science or 'junk' science or inept theory or worse, as happened in criminal cases, where great reliance was placed on "scientific" tests undertaken by some forensic scientists. As the Prime Minister said at the Rio Conference on June 12 1992 "What every child knows today few scientists knew the day before yesterday." The courts have to deal with the situation 'the day before yesterday'.

That said, in an attempt to establish the link between exposure and illness the device most usually employed is the epidemiological study. The main difficulty with epidemiological studies is that they are very expensive. Carried out properly they often costs hundreds of thousands of pounds and can take many years to complete.

In some cases there will be publicly funded research. Where this is not so, it is necessary to decide whether one is crucial. If so, can it be done on a shoestring, within the normal legal aid parameters? The only way to achieve a result that would be at all acceptable to experts giving evidence in the case is if it had been carried out or at least ratified, by a respected expert.

If the study needs to be carried out on a more formal basis the question for the lawyer to determine is whether to ask the Legal Aid Board to pay for the study or whether to ask one of the country's existing epidemiology units to carry out the study within their own budget. There are obviously problems of timing on the second of the possibilities. Even if enough public concern brings along an epidemiologist willing to do such a study, the time it usually takes to have a study funded, the work to be carried out and then written up and published is often three to four years. The problems arising from the statute bar may mean that this is not an appropriate route in many cases. An example of this is in the area of electromagnetic fields where the United Kingdom Childhood Cancer Coordinating Study on this issue commenced in 1992 and is likely to be published in 1997/8.

The option of the Board agreeing to fund the study is obviously a last resort. It is not, however as impossible as it might at first seem but the lawyers would have to show they had exhausted every other avenue first and would certainly need to have some indication that a positive result is likely.

CHAPTER SEVEN

DISCOVERY

In a toxic tort claim the discovery process is vital. There are three areas of discovery to consider, ie non-party, pre action, and post action. There are also various decisions that the lawyers need to take in relation to the discovery process, the major one being who is best equipped to consider the documents "discovered". These issues are all considered below.

Non-Party

1. Access to Environmental Information

The first discovery question for the lawyer pursuing a pollution related case is what information is readily available through the regulations on access to environmental information.

The Environmental Information Regulations 1992 (SI 1992 No 3240) apply to information relating to the environment (as defined in reg 2(2) where there is no other statutory obligation of disclosure. They provide that Minsters of the Crown, Government departments, local authorities and all other persons carrying out functions of public administration who hold relevant information shall make that information available to every person who requests it. They must respond to every request as soon as is possible and in any event within 2 months. Where the request is refused the reasons must be given in writing. There are exceptions to protect information which is held for the purposes of judicial or legislative functions or which is capable of being treated as confidential.

By way of researching any toxic tort litigation it is vital to make use of this resource since the data is acquired on a non-partisan basis and the court will naturally have regard to this.

There follows a brief summary of the main statutory bodies, the statutory and regulatory provisions to which reference should be made, and the locations of offices where inspection can take place. However, since this system is still in its early days it is very important to "keep asking" until the seeker is sure that the correct department and the correct data have been found. It really is a question of persistence.

(a) HMIP (tel. 0171-276 8061) Her Majesty's Inspectorate of Pollution (HMIP.), is responsible for the largest and most complex plants. Part I Environmental Protection Act 1990, see particularly s20-22.

The HMIP offices are in Leeds, Sheffield, Cleveland, Lancaster, Warrington, Bristol, Bedford, Lincoln, Fleet, E. Grinstead, Sutton Coalfield, and Cardiff.

(b) Local Authorities

The starting point is the Environmental Health Department.

(i) Environmental Protection Act 1990 Pt I Air-born pollution from all non HMIP. industrial operations.

(ii) Control of Pollution Act 1974 s64.

(iii) Noise data. Control of Noise (Measurement and Registers) Regulations 1976 (SI 1976 No 37).

(iv) Air emissions. Control of Industrial Air Pollution Regulations (Registration of Works) 1989 (SI 1989 No 318).

(v) Land use, notifications. Town & Country Planning Act 1990 s69 cf. Planning and Compensation Act 1991 s16 (publicity).

Local Government Act 1972 s100 (Council Committee reports). Background material on proposed developments.

(c) National Rivers Authority (NRA)   Responsible for water quality data and records of discharge and abstraction consents. Information is obtained and made available pursuant to Part VIII of the Water Resources Act 1991. See also:-

(i) Water pollution s190 and the Control of Pollution (Registers) Regulations 1989 (SI 1989 No 1160).

(ii) Water quality s189 and the Water Supply (Water Quality) Regulations 1989 (SI 1989 No 1147) as amended by the Water Supply (Water Quality) Regulations 1989 (SI 1989 No 1384).

(iii)   Maps of (i) fresh water limits; (s192 WRA 1991) (ii) main rivers; (s193 WRA 1991) (iii) waterworks; (s195 WRA 1991)

The NRA offices are listed as Appendix 2.

(d) Waste Regulation Authorities

(i) EPA 1990 ss64-66 registers

(ii)EPA 1990 s67 Annual reports

(iii) COPA 1974 NB: Contaminated land use registers (see s143 EPA) will not be brought in; s143 has been withdrawn.

(e) Other Government or "Official" bodies.

It should always be carefully considered whether records are likely to be kept by such a body which may afford invaluable "independent" data. For example, in a farming case one would approach the Ministry of Agriculture, Fisheries and Food (MAFF), a government body, and also, say, the Meat and Livestock Commission as an "official body" who may have reported on the claimant's livestock.

2. Who to pursue?

Even with these improved access to information regulations, toxic tort claims are likely to involve applications for discovery against organisations who are not parties to the action. Environmental pollution is of sufficient public concern that there are a whole series of organisations at national and local government level who are involved in the control and monitoring of the release of toxic substances.

In the workplace itself the Health and Safety Executive retain prime responsibility for the safety of the workforce. There are however other organisations that retain an interest in terms of the operation of any particular industrial plant, such as the Nuclear Installations Inspectorate in the nuclear industry.

The manufacture of toxic substances, such as pesticides, is controlled by various government departments including the Department of Health and Ministry of Agriculture Farming and Fisheries. They are also involved in the monitoring of the environment. Other examples of watch-dog bodies who may have relevant documents are the Department of the Environment, Agricultural Research Council, environmental health departments in local councils, National Rivers Authority and Her Majesty's Inspectorate of Pollution.

Attempting to determine which particular body has been responsible for the authorisation of a product, checking on plant operations, and monitoring of the environment is never easy and it often takes painstaking research particularly when the period complained of is some years ago.

Often the local authority will be the most helpful, particularly when the authority supports the action being taken. Sometimes, however, professional pride can become an obstacle where the health problem was not previously spotted by the environmental health department.

The most important preliminary to non-party discovery is to remember that it can only occur in personal injury claims. Accordingly, if the claim is in nuisance or for chattel damage such as injury to livestock, non-party discovery is not available and the only way to compel disclosure of relevant material in these circumstances is by sub-poena duces tecum, which stage will not be reached until the action is tried. What follows relates to non-party discovery in personal injury claims.

3. The application

The type of application will depend on whether or not the action has already commenced. If proceedings have already commenced an application should be taken out for discovery of certain documents under Section 34 of the Supreme Court Act 1981. The application should be supported by an affidavit setting out the reasons why discovery of the documents should be given and why it is thought that the respondents to the application possess the documents.

If the application is made before the proceedings commence it should be made as an originating application under Section 33 of the Supreme Court Act 1981. It should be stated in the accompanying affidavit whether there is any intention of adding the respondent as a defendant to the action.

The hearing of the application should normally be before the Master in a private room appointment.

4. The costs

There is often an issue in these types of applications as to who bears the costs of the respondents. In the great majority of occasions they will be entitled to their costs but when the party is legally aided what does this mean?

Under the terms of the various legal aid provisions, the normal route is for the respondents' costs to be treated as a disbursement and be dealt with like any disbursement, ie the plaintiff lawyers obtain the funds from the Board during the action and then includes them in the bill submitted to the defendants if the claim is successful. A question arises because of Section 18 of the Legal Aid Act 1988, as to whether it entitles another party to claim their legal costs, per se, against the Board. That section suggests the costs can only be paid where it can be shown that severe financial hardship accrues. This is, of course, next to impossible for the relevant bodies here.

In the Sellafield cases, where the non-party discovery costs ran into six figure sums, the issue was controversial and the answer which has emerged in the context of that litigation is that where the respondents are not a party to the action all their costs are payable, including the copying and postage charges and the costs of lawyers, whether in-house lawyers or an independent firm of solicitors are used. These costs are all accepted as being disbursements.

It is possible to seek prior approval from the Board for the costs of the exercise under the term "disbursement" and that should be done whenever possible. However, often this will not be feasible in the time available, as a specific figure will have to be obtained from the respondent, and then referred on to the Board. In that case the lawyer should seek guidance from the local Area Office to ensure money is not paid out on fees that are not later recoverable.

In any order obtaining discovery from a non-party to the action, the most appropriate term to deal with the plaintiff's costs of the application is "as between the plaintiffs and the defendants, the plaintiff's costs be reserved". This means that unless the defendants (who should be sent a copy of the order) make a point regarding these costs at the trial or other procedural hearing, the costs will be deemed to be "in the cause".

5. The documents

The type of documents the plaintiff will be seeking to ensure have been disclosed, will depend on each case, but the more usual classes would be as follows: (These can be in the possession of either the defendants or non-parties)

i)   all documents relating to the government approval of the toxic substance including experts' reports made available to the deciding body;

ii)   all documents relating to the production process including receipts and invoices for the purchase of the key elements in the process;

iii)   those documents that describe the monitoring of the procedure itself;

iv)   the monitoring data for the emission of toxic waste from the plant;

v)   the monitoring carried on outside the plant showing pollution levels in controlled waters, in the air and on the ground;

vi)   any analyses carried out to determine the harm of the toxic substances to either the public or livestock;

vii)   any public or private enquiry documents relating to investigations carried out on the plant's activities and any suggested health problems. Here it should be remembered that the plaintiff is entitled to any such inquiry document provided the inquiry was not carried out for the   specific purposes of the litigation.

Pre-action discovery

In some cases pre-action discovery will not be necessary. The evidence regarding the case may be sufficiently clear without having to gain access to the documentation at this early stage. That, in many ways, is desirable as it is usually preferable for the discovery process to take place once the pleadings have closed. The reasons for this are that it ensures the process is carried out on a timescale of the plaintiff lawyers' choosing; it takes place with the prospect of the trial looming and therefore ensures that there is a degree of urgency attached to the exercise; it ensures that the process is carried out with the appropriate degree of seriousness by the defendants; it also makes sure that the process is carried out in one go, thereby saving time and costs. Most significantly of all it does not give the defendants the chance to stop the case in its tracks at this early stage by their successfully defending the application.

Having said this, in a number of instances it will simply not be possible to obtain legal aid to commence the court action or settle the pleadings without clarifying the strength and weaknesses of the case through the discovery process.

In the Sellafield case the original legal aid certificates were limited to certain pre-action events including discovery. However, the publication of the Gardner report gave sufficient strength to the case to enable the lawyers to persuade the Legal Aid Board to withdraw the limitation which allowed the claims to be taken all the way through to trial. This meant that instead of applying for pre-action discovery the discovery process did not commence until after pleadings had closed.

Where an application for pre-action discovery is made there must be sufficient evidence set out in the supporting application for it to succeed. An unsuccessful application will totally undermine the Legal Aid Board's views of the prospects of success and although it may be possible to keep the case going in one way or another a defeat at this stage is likely to create an underlying feeling of weakness about the case which will be hard to overcome.

The lawyers should, of course, obtain approval from the Board for such an application. It would be usual for them to incorporate this into the first or second limitation on the certificates. Where the case is particularly complex the lawyer may want to apply to the Board for authority for Leading Counsel to conduct the application.

The lawyer should, in the affidavit supporting the application, be able to set out the grounds for suggesting that there is a link between the toxic substances and the plaintiff's illness and further the grounds for considering that the substances emanate, in one way or another, from the defendants' property. There is a balance to be struck in the affidavit between the lawyer giving too much away in terms of the plaintiff's longer term action and revealing sufficient information to ensure the application is successful. Generally the importance of the application together with the likelihood that the defendants will already be aware of the plaintiff's claim militates in favour of putting in more rather than less.

The defendants will see this application as being absolutely crucial. If they are able to defend successfully the request for pre-action discovery they will have stopped the action in its tracks. Equally, if they are defeated the claim will begin to develop a real credibility. They are therefore likely to devote considerable resources into opposing the application.

Taking this into account, thought should be given by the lawyers to obtaining experts' reports even at this early stage. A short report or letter from a known expert expressing the view that there is the genuine possibility of a link between the illnesses and substances emanating from the defendants' plant will give the application a credibility that the defendants would find hard to resist. Again there may be a concern that if this is done, the defendants will know early on the experts to which the plaintiffs have turned but this is only a minor tactical problem when weighed against ensuring the cases are able to move off base.

It should be remembered that the plaintiffs only need to show a prima facie case against the defendants and there is, therefore, a balance to be struck between making sure the application is strong without spending enormous amounts of time and effort in making the case water tight. This will only delay the eventual trial and it is always crucial that the lawyers' sights be firmly placed on this longer term goal.

Discovery after close of pleadings

The discovery process under the automatic directions both in the High Court and County Court commences 14 days after the close of pleadings. The close of pleadings is the term describing the main exchange of pleadings being the Writ and Statement of Claim, (Particulars of Claim in the County Court) the Defence and finally the Reply, if any. Usually it is receipt of the Defence that completes the exchange of pleadings and thereby "closes the pleadings".

The automatic directions provide for the service by both sides of their list of documents within 14 days with inspection to take place 7 days thereafter. In the minor type of toxic tort claim this may suffice as a direction. In most cases it will, however, be totally unrealistic.

The plaintiff may well be able to comply with such a direction but the defendants almost certainly will not. The likely size of most discovery exercises will be a very major task for the defendants and their lawyers. Whilst it is the role of the plaintiff's lawyer to keep the pressure on the defendants, it would be both naive and counter productive to insist on the application of the terms of the automatic directions in relation to discovery, as the defendants are almost certain to obtain an order varying them, if not abandoning them altogether.

Although the Sellafield case was, in some ways, an extreme example it may assist in comprehending the point to set out the extent of the discovery process in that court action.

The exercise effectively commenced in April 1990 on the close of pleadings. The whole process took until May 1992, involved a large number of lawyers in the defendants' team, and by the end, the defendants had served on the plaintiffs sixteen lists from British Nuclear Fuels, eight from the Atomic Energy Authority, and then numerous lists from the Ministry of Agriculture, Farming and Fisheries, the Department of the Environment, Department of Employment, the Health and Safety Executive, Agricultural Research Council, Medical Research Council and the Department of Energy. Although the documents were never individually counted they amounted to hundreds of thousands of pages of the most complex scientific documentation.

In anyone's terms this was a serious discovery exercise and not one envisaged in the terms of the automatic directions.

The most sensible line is to agree that an application for directions be made immediately following close of pleadings. In considering the terms of any directions the plaintiff's lawyer should look very carefully at the defendants' views as to how long the discovery process is likely to take them. The plaintiff's lawyer should consider whether the proposals are reasonable. The basic point is that the defendants are the people most aware of the actual situation, and the court will be wary of pressing them harder than the timescale they suggest unless it is clear they are being very pessimistic, or it can be shown there is an urgency about the situation not appreciated in the defendants' proposals.

To ensure that the delay is as short as possible it should be feasible for the defendants to provide a rolling process of discovery, ie providing lists at reasonable intervals. This ensures that the plaintiff's lawyers can keep an eye on what is being produced to ensure there is not some fundamental objection. Perhaps most importantly it also gives the lawyers the chance to start getting to grips with the documents as soon as possible.

In the Sellafield example the first main list arrived some four to five months after the discovery process began with lists being produced every three months or so thereafter.

It is likely that despite the large nature of the discovery process it will be necessary to apply for an order for specific discovery. Indeed it may well be the case that in going through the documents, as they arrive, it will become apparent that there are others that have not been disclosed that relate to those that have. They should generally be requested immediately, rather than waiting until the end of the process.

One of the difficulties in this type of exercise is reading between the lines to try and understand the decisions that have been made by the defendants as to which categories of document not to disclose. The main point is to be both patient and persistent.

If it is necessary to make an application for specific discovery it is important that the plaintiff's experts support the requirement for further documents. After such a major exercise the court is unlikely to grant such an order unless the reasons for it are quite clear and usually only if supported by one of the experts. The application is made under Order 24 Rule 7A of the Rules of the Supreme Court.

Under the Practice Note of the Lord Chief Justice in February 1995, discovery is one of the areas where the judge overseeing the case is asked to take reasonable steps to ensure the level of discovery is kept within manageable proportions and is kept to the key issues in the case. The exact impact of this Note is still under observation, however, there can be little doubt that any attempts by the defendants to "snow" or "dump truck" the plaintiffs, with oceans of documents or, alternatively, any attempts by the plaintiffs to go on lengthy fishing trips into the defendants archives will be met with stiff resistance from the courts.

Who does the scrutinising?

One of the central issues in a toxic tort claim is the decision as to whether it is the lawyers or the experts who do all the scrutinising of the discovered documents. The answer will depend to some extent on the case but as a rule of thumb this is a task that should primarily be that of the lawyers.

The extent of discovery in most toxic tort claims is likely to be far, far greater than that in most personal injury claims. It is also highly likely that the fields of expertise relating to discovery will be numerous. In the Sellafield instance the discovery process raised issues to do with the operation of nuclear plants, occupational radiation doses, environmental doses, dose modelling, toxicology, epidemiology, genetics, and health physics.

There were in the region of thirty five experts involved in the case on the plaintiffs' side. It would have been quite impossible simply to send each of the experts hundreds of thousands of pages of documents, saying "you decide which documents are relevant to your field, and you comment on them and you then write your report." In any event such a procedure might leave the plaintiff's solicitor open to a charge on complaint of `contempt of court' since some experts might receive documents they should not have been shown.

It is essential that the lawyer keeps hold of the case in all but the minutest of detail. In that way the lawyer will be able to identify the legal issues in the case, will know the areas of expertise that the case covers and will be able to ensure that the experts are only covering, in their evidence, issues relating to their own expertise and receive documents accordingly.

It is, therefore, the lawyer's task to go through the discovery documents and then forward to the various experts any documents that need their attention or need further explanation.

Where this may not be the case is where it is quite clear that a case only covers one area of expertise. Where that occurs, it may be more appropriate to leave the expert to go through the documents as this may be more time and cost efficient. Further, with the lawyer going through complex documents there is always the fear that an important piece of information will pass the lawyer by simply because it is too complex to be understood by the lay person. The expert should always be asked to advise the lawyer if the case impinges on another area of expertise.

This latter point makes it all the more crucial that where the lawyer does take on the scrutinising role that the documents are not simply "skimmed" but are read thoroughly. This means the lawyer taking the time and effort to get understand the complexity of the issues involved in the case. This is not the type of work where the solicitor simply acts as a post box receiving documents, and then passing them from expert to expert and then to counsel without ever making any attempt to understand them.

Technology

Where there are a lot of documents to be assessed it is important to spend time before they come in and the assessment process begins to set up a system for the recording of important information from the documents. The most sensible and useful is a computer data base system which can record key words and then recall those document numbers when a cross check needs to be made later in the case. This is a time consuming process but is likely to reap rewards as the case nears to and then reaches trial. It is vitally important to set up a system which enables the lawyer to retrieve information easily particularly during preparation for and trial of the case.

There are now available scanning machines that will scan pages of the discovery documents and then store the information. By inputting issues or key words, the computer will then print out all the documents which deal with that point. Again, used properly this can be a very valuable litigation tool, although the simple scanning exercise can cost a lot of money and, therefore, the lawyer needs to be clear about the benefits and costs before this route is taken.

If computer facilities are not available it is still important that the documents are noted up in a systematic way that will be most easily considered at a later stage.

During the course of a major toxic tort claim the lawyers are likely to obtain a lot of scientific papers that have some import to the issues in the case. Again, if it is possible, it is best to have a computer system record each report with brief details and key words so that it is possible to recall all those reports that relate to a particular issue at the flick of a switch, rather than having to go through a list manually.

It is likely, if the firm specialises in the toxic tort field, that the accumulation of scientific reports will prove to be a significant resource, particularly when doing research into a new field of work. The lawyer should, however, always keep in mind the rule that documents obtained from the defendants for use in one case cannot be used in any other case, without the authority of the defendants or the courts. This is a strict rule and means that, if in a multi-party action, there is more than one set of court proceedings, the documents in one action cannot be used for the benefit of the others without specific authority.

What to look for

If the lawyers are taking on the role of scrutinising the documents themselves, the first point to ensure is that there are sufficient resources within the firm to do this properly. There is no point in only one lawyer being left with the task of going through hundreds of thousands of pages of documents as it will mean either that the trial is delayed for years, or the job will not be done properly.

In the same way it is important for the lawyers carrying out such a task to have their minds firmly fixed on what they are seeking. An unfocused trawl is unlikely to reap rewards.

As a starting point it is highly likely that the industry will have given the impression of knowing exactly what emissions have come out of the plant, where they have gone to, and why they will not have even caused minimal damage to the local people, livestock, crops or land. In most instances the industry plays a major role in its own policing. The regulatory authorities rely heavily on the assistance of the plant operators in assessing emissions and their impact on the local environment.

The problem here is that companies are keen to ensure that they come within existing government limits for the emission of pollution. Providing that they achieve this they rarely seem to look much further. For instance, if the advancement of scientific understanding means that previous maximum levels of emission are in fact unsafe, there may be no reassessment to determine whether what had been emitted has in fact caused damage.

Whether, through lack of resources, because the personnel within the regulators come from a similar background to that of the regulated, because the regulators simply accept what the regulated give by way of data, or whatever, the fact is that they do not generally carry out as rigorous a set of checks as is often suggested.

The lawyer should therefore not accept anything at face value. This is particularly the case where the investigation is historic. Clearly it is likely that the pollution would have been worse in the 1960's and 1970's compared with the 1980's and 1990's because the public concern regarding the environmental impact was a lot less than it is now. A lot of the industry do not, however, like to admit that any mistakes have been made and will defend practices that would quite clearly, today, be thought inadequate.

Equally, reports that have been brought out more recently may be more up to date in terms of knowledge but may in fact be based on ideas and data from many years ago which are totally wrong. The fact that a report is brought out in the 1990's tends to give the original data credibility. The lawyer should be prepared, if it is an issue in the case, to go back to the earlier reports and data, extracting the key features to compare them against what is now known and what is being stated in current reports.

Scientists, although in some ways quite scrupulous when it comes to drafting a report, can also be quite naive when it comes to accepting other people's work. The training of the lawyer to have an enquiring mind and not to accept things at their face value is a real asset when carrying out this task.

CHAPTER EIGHT

EXPERTS

1. Which experts?

Understanding the areas of expertise covered in any particular toxic tort claim is one of the most difficult tasks for the plaintiff's lawyer. Whilst in most personal injury cases the type of expert needed is well defined, toxic tort claims are so new that this is far from being true in this field.

One of the main difficulties in making this decision is that hardly any of the experts involved in this type of work will have any court experience. It is not, therefore, generally an area where a request can be made to a particular expert to provide a full critique of which others should be brought in to support that person's view, which often happens in more conventional personal injury claims. That first expert is often unlikely to have any concept of the nature of giving evidence, of what happens in cross examination, and of the importance of only covering their field of expertise. The lawyer's task is therefore all the greater here than in other work.

At the start of the case it is likely that the lawyer will turn to an expert who is favourably inclined toward the case. Whether it is because the Legal Aid Board has asked for an expert's opinion or simply because the lawyer needs to obtain a clearer picture of the science in the case, it may be necessary to go to an expert rather earlier than in other areas of personal injury work.

Where the Board has not asked for a specific opinion from an expert it can be more useful simply to arrange meetings with various experts, without specifically requesting a report. In this way the lawyer not only gets to grips with the science of the case but is also able to sound out potential experts without committing the plaintiff to a fee, which may not be recoverable on taxation, if the experts' work is not used.

It should certainly be borne in mind that the people to whom the lawyer turns in the first instance may well not be the experts who appear for the plaintiff at the trial. The reasons for this are that the expert who gives the initial advice may be rather more generalist than the needs of the case determine and further may be notably too pro-plaintiff.

The lawyer should not worry about the fact that there will be an enormous learning curve in operation as the case develops. The generalist expert who seems to the lawyer to know everything at the start and, therefore, may well be an enormous asset in bringing the case to life, may become a liability in the witness box when pitted against a number of different experts each covering separate areas of expertise. If such a disaster occurs, the fault lies with the lawyer and not with the expert. It is very much the lawyer's role to determine the course of the case and an important part of that is knowing which areas need to be covered by which experts. This in turn means that the lawyer has to have a clear understanding of the scientific issues.

The best sort of expert is the one who responds to a letter asking for a written opinion on subjects A, B and C by saying that A and C are areas that can be dealt with, but that B is an area outside the expert's knowledge. The worst sort is the one who says that not only A, B & C can be dealt with, but also, in the report, mentions a number of other areas that are quite clearly not within his/her experience.

There will be cases where an opinion from an expert is needed immediately and in others it may not be needed until after the discovery process is complete. The main difference will relate to the lawyer's own knowledge. If it is a new field it is likely that an expert's opinion will help sooner rather than later. If, however, it is an area familiar to the lawyer, it may well be possible to wait until after discovery.

The question of exactly which expert to approach is a tricky one because there has been so little court experience in this field. The scientists with the most litigation experience usually work for the eminent firms of Consulting Engineers, but these firms will often have past or present consultancy contracts with the defendant or an associated company which may lead them to decline instructions.

At first blush the most fertile source of independent high calibre scientific expertise would seem to be the universities. There does, however, seem to be some reluctance on their part to assist. It may be that scientists in academia do not wish to be distracted from their research. It may be that they do not relish the prospect of the witness box in a tightly contested action with a powerful team ranged against them, (who could blame them?). It may be a simple failure of communication since there is no central information exchange. Some experts have indicated that the failure of the academic establishment to recognise proofs of evidence and expert reports as being set to gain academic credit is a great disincentive to involvement in legal proceedings.

It is possible to look to the few lawyers with work in this field to ask for the names of experts to approach, or to contact the Environmental Law Foundation, which was set up to help with this very kind of problem, or to contact one of the main groups whether it be Greenpeace, Friends of the Earth or Campaign for the Protection of Rural England or one of the more specific groups such as the Pesticides Trust, or Cumbrians Opposed to a Radioactive Environment.

A full list of those environmental groups that the authors consider may be able to assist, together with a note of their areas of interest is listed at the back of this book. Lawyers involved in this field should also consider joining the Association of Personal Injury Lawyers, which has a special interest group on the environment.

Another very useful way of locating experts is to go through the main scientific journals. The most useful are those such as Nature, the British Medical Journal, Lancet, and the New Scientist. These are all rather generalist but they contain most of the key ground breaking reports or certainly reviews of the main reports. There are many other journals of the most obscure sort which maybe useful where it is very clear as to which scientific issues are crucial to the case.

A perusal of the journals may well reveal experts' names in the appropriate field. A telephone call to those experts should be an appropriate starting point in the search. Most experts seem not to mind a discussion on the telephone. It is the thought of actually drafting a report and appearing in the witness box that seems to alarm so many of them.

Most lawyers know of "Lexis" the system for calling up, by computer, all the relevant legal issues relating to a particular point of interest. The medical world has a number of similar systems, often advertised in the journals mentioned above, where a search of say a particular chemical should give details of all articles and reports written on the subject. Examples are, Data Star, Dialogue, Maxwell Online and the British Library who operate a service called Blaize Link. Obtaining those articles and going through them, at least as far as they are comprehensible, so that the lawyer has some understanding of the scientific issues, will ensure that the expert is not totally put off from the start. It is generally true that experts who feel that they will at least be understood by the lawyer are more likely to take the plunge and assist in the case, than those who are contacted by complete novices.

2. Numbers of experts

The fact that the defendants are likely to take a toxic tort claim so seriously means that they are almost certain to turn not only to the world's experts in their fields, but will also ensure that they only cover those areas in which they have genuine expertise. In claims involving complex cancers and other illnesses, the problem is that an expert is in fact only au fait with a very small area of the case. This can lead to a very large number of experts being involved in this type of case.

The question that should be uppermost in the lawyer's mind is whether each of the central scientific issues in the case has been covered by an expert who will be able to withstand potentially severe cross examination in the witness box. In the Merlins' claim against British Nuclear Fuels (*Merlin v British Nuclear Fuels plc* [1990] 3 WLR 383) one of the plaintiffs' experts was kept in the witness box for two weeks, the great majority of that time being under cross examination. That may be unusual but it should be borne in mind that these are not normal personal injury cases where having an expert kept in the box for a whole day would be seen as something very much out of the ordinary.

3. The type of expert

This is the type of work where there is little point in lining up a team of young experts in their thirties, with a lot of bright ideas but no proven academic standing. Obviously there may be the odd person of this sort but the great likelihood is that the defendants will calling experts who are eminent in their field.

Obtaining the assistance of experts able to oppose such an array is not easy. Often actions in this field are at the very frontier of scientific understanding and therefore it is unlikely to be the mainstream of expert opinion which supports the claims. Clearly in looking for experts those who are at the very top of the scientific community should be enlisted if they support the case. If not, other senior experts should be sought. It is worth reiterating here that the lack of enthusiasm by an expert may be due to a lack of appreciation of the legal standard of proof.

Whilst Britain has some areas of science where it still leads the world, and epidemiology certainly seems to be one, there are many others where we are well behind advances made abroad. Whilst prejudice against experts from overseas must remain an imponderable, it is hoped that the "Little Englander" approach is on the wane. It may well be the case, therefore, that the most appropriate experts in terms of experience, knowledge and prestige, are overseas, and the lawyer should have no hesitation in looking for an expert abroad.

Having said this there can be little doubt that if the expert is non-English speaking, unless his/her opinion is quite crucial to the case, it is still probably better to look elsewhere. Whilst it is, of course, possible to have an interpreter assisting it may well be that the complexities of the evidence combined with the problems of having an interpreter outweigh the benefits of that particular expert.

4. Legal aid and experts

The rule regarding legal aid and experts fees is that it is necessary to gain prior approval for an expert's fee to ensure that the Board meet it at the end of the case. To do this the lawyer must write to the Area Office setting out why a particular report is required, the area of expertise, the skills of the expert, and the likely fee. The lawyer will have to obtain a quote from the expert to be able to do this.

The problem then arises when the Board starts to query the cost, or the expert, or both. It can often take months before any agreement is reached.

The alternative is for the lawyer to take the limited risk that the expert's fee will be partly or wholly disallowed on taxation. Where the fees are clearly reasonable, ie below about £500 a day depending on experience and qualifications, and the report is crucial to the case there are unlikely to be problems on taxation and it maybe well worth taking the slight risk. Where, however, the fee is over say £1,000 a day and the report is peripheral to the main thrust of the case the lawyer should think more than twice about incurring the fee, unchecked by the Board.

Where the expert lives abroad it is again possible to ask for the Board's approval of the cost of travel to see the expert. The same kind of points arise in terms of the decision whether to go to the effort of obtaining prior approval or whether it is worth the risk of simply travelling and then waiting to justify the cost on taxation.

For the trial itself it is of course the case that the costs of the expert travelling to and from the hearing, including flights, hotels, etc., will be paid as a disbursement unless it is suggested that the bringing of the expert to the hearing is totally unreasonable.

The point should be made here that the plaintiff's lawyer should keep a very watchful eye on solicitor and own client costs. In cases of this potential size, the costs can be enormous and where a claim is only worth a few thousand pounds, it is not at all beyond the realms of possibility that the case can be won and the plaintiffs receive nothing because the costs have wiped out the damage award. The increased concern of the Board over the cost/benefit analysis in each case means that this position is now far less likely to occur than was previously the case, but it is still an issue to be borne in mind.

5. Experts' reports

The point has already been made that most of the scientists who are likely to be asked to give evidence in these cases will be new to the legal world. They are highly unlikely ever to have written a report before or to have appeared in the witness box. The writing of a report in the way preferred by the courts will be a mystery to most of them.

These are not the kinds of case, therefore, where a short letter will produce a standard medico-legal report. The expert will have to be nurtured through every stage.

The main hurdle to overcome is having them actually put pen to paper to write a report. Almost invariably the expert will be the head of a busy scientific department where the writing of a report is the least of his/her worries. Indeed the feeling often comes across that the expert considers the agreement to act for the plaintiff an enormous favour, and therefore any pressure applied to have them write the report can be seen as being a bit of a cheek.

The first impression that the expert will make both on the other side and on the judge is through the written report. Given the importance of first impressions it is vital that the report is full, well laid out, and avoids pitfalls for the unwary such as references to privileged documents which may then be subject to disclosure on the basis that privilege has been waived.

In order to make the best of this task the expert needs a thorough briefing note before reporting which covers the documents, the issues to be addressed, the list of headings which should be incorporated, the importance of a full CV and of an appendix setting out all published research and texts upon which reliance is placed, traps to be avoided, and so forth.

In the case of a novice such as an overseas expert giving evidence in the UK for the first time, it would be desirable to show her/him a well laid out report from another piece of litigation as an example of the format which most assists the court. It cannot be over-emphasised that the quality of the report will be affected by the thoroughness of the lawyer's input at this stage.

Once the draft report is finished alterations can be, and generally are, made with the expert's consent after consultation with the lawyers before the report is signed and becomes part of the material for pre-trial disclosure. However alterations at this stage may properly be cross-examined to and, other things being equal, the weight of the report will be undermined in proportion to the number and nature of the changes elicited.

Furthermore, whilst the Bar Rules permit counsel to help draft experts' reports, the courts have been quick to condemn the practice of amending the report even with the experts' consent to delete the "bad news" (such as criticism of the plaintiff that could found contributory negligence). Accordingly whilst nobody can object to lawyers inviting experts to make changes particularly in respect of matters of legal procedure, (such as reference to privileged documents), there is a risk, depending on the sort of alterations made, that the credibility of the report will be damaged.

There are two points to be made. Firstly the problem of alterations should in all possible cases be pre-empted by the pre report briefing note. Secondly it would be desirable for practitioners to have unified guidance upon what they may and may not do since at present the Bar's Code of Conduct sits rather uneasily with some judicial utterances, particularly the speeches of some of their lordships, in effect ordaining that experts' reports should be and remain all their own work in form and in content. Lord Woolf's Civil Justice Reort (June 1995) is likely to result in such guidance.

6. Exchanging Experts Reports

There have been changes to the rules regarding the exchange of medical evidence which means that reports can now be exchanged sequentially, with the plaintiff's first medical report accompanying the Statement/Particulars of Claim in personal injury cases. Despite this significant shift, when it comes to reports in relation to liability, the plaintiff's lawyer should, as a general rule, ensure that reports are exchanged mutually.

In the Sellafield claims, British Nuclear Fuels pressed for an order for sequential exchange based on the premise that until they had the plaintiffs' reports, they were not clear as to the key issues in their. This was despite there having been a number of very lengthy requests by the defendants for Further and Better Particulars.

It was the plaintiffs' argument that mutual exchange ensured that the case was fought on "a level playing field" and that as the issues relating to the claims had been discussed at conferences of scientists throughout the world, it could hardly be suggested that anything the plaintiffs' experts were likely to say in their reports, would take the defendants by surprise.

The court accepted the plaintiffs' arguments and ordered mutual exchange. It would give the defendants a very great advantage if an order for sequential exchange were made and any such application should be rigorously resisted.

CHAPTER NINE

THE ADJUDICATION OF THE CASE

1. Background

The point has been made, that toxic tort claims are difficult for the lawyer to comprehend and deal with properly. One of the further problems arising from the complexity of the issues involved in these claims is that the action will be determined by a judge who is likely to find the issues equally difficult to adjudicate. The Merlin family's case against British Nuclear Fuels (*Merlin v British Nuclear Fuels plc* [1990]) was described by the judge, Mr Justice Gatehouse, as being the most complex he had ever had to try.

2. Environmental Tribunals

The problems for the courts in trying environmental cases have been recognised by some members of the judiciary. Lord Justice Woolf in a speech to the United Kingdom Environmental Law Association in December 1991 suggested that the complexity of this class of litigation is such that the only way for it to be determined properly is by the setting up of a special Environmental Tribunal. His idea is that the Tribunal would have officers and experts attached to it. In May 1992 the Association held a seminar attended by distinguished observers including some from jurisdictions where Environmental Tribunals already operate to debate the proposal.

It is outside the scope of this book to look at this important proposal but it is pertinent to recognise the enormous difficulties the court has deciding these cases within the context of the adversarial process. More recently, both the Legal Aid Board and practitioners in the field have called for a revision to the court proceedings dealing with the multi-party cases to make the system for deciding cases which raise complex issues of liability and causation fairer and more cost effective. The Legal Aid Board proposed that tribunals may be more suited for this purpose. This suggestion has been rejected unanimously by plaintiffs' lawyers on the basis that legal aid is not available for tribunals and that the constitutional safeguards taken for granted in court procedures are not necessarily present in a tribunal set up.

3. Expert assistance for the court

The question of whether the Judge should have at his disposal expert assistance is a difficult one.

It is likely that the plaintiff will consider this more advantageous than the defendant. For the plaintiff the most significant difficulty is that the case will often be pushing back the boundaries of the law and science. It is a matter of human nature that a judge is unlikely to take such a bold step unless he feels very confident of his grasp of the scientific issues. In some cases such confidence may be hard to achieve unless the judges have their own experts to assist them in their decision making, as is usually afforded to courts of inquiry into major disasters.

That said, a court expert could have an enormous influence over the judge and the question of his impartiality would be of vital importance to both parties.

Although we are not aware of the court having had such assistance in any toxic tort litigation so far, there are in fact three possible ways that this can happen. The expert can be appointed as arbitrator, court expert, or court assessor. Each role entails the use of the expert in a rather different way.

The use of experts in this way is virtually unheard of in the Queen's Bench Division of the High Court but is common in other areas, such as the Commercial Courts.

a) Arbitration

Whilst there is no specific rule in the White Book and no precedent to provide for arbitration in the Queen's Bench Division, the Court has an inherent power to make an order for reference to arbitration of any part of the case. Under this power it is possible for the two sides to appoint an arbitrator to determine a particular issue in the case. Accordingly where there is an issue which both sides consider would be better determined by an outside expert rather than by the court an independent arbitrator can be appointed prior to trial.

The arbitrator would then consider both sides' position on the issue and would then come to a view. Both sides must agree to the appointment. It is a fundamental requirement of such an agreement that they would both be bound to accept the outcome. That outcome would then be presented to the judge at trial as an agreed position between the parties.

It is possible that in a complex toxic tort claim a particular area may be best determined by this approach. One major problem (4th ed, para 48 37 Halsbury's Laws of England) with this approach is the question of costs. It would appear that the plaintiffs would not be covered by the legal aid certificates under s14 of the Legal Aid Act 1988 for such a process and the costs of the arbitration could be considerable. Where arbitration appears to be beneficial to the plaintiff, the lawyer should be careful to ascertain the Board's position before taking the matter further.

b) Court Expert

By agreement or by court order an expert can be nominated by the court to consider a particular issue and report back (under RSC Order 40). It would appear, as with the arbitration, that the expert would have to agree to the appointment (Atkins Court Forms, Vol 33 page 281). There are very few examples where this particular Order has been put to use in recorded proceedings.

However it would appear that the court will be more likely to appoint an expert to report on an issue of fact than of opinion. For example, where the issue was between different epidemiologists, which will always incorporate a matter of opinion as well as fact, the judge would almost certainly decide that this is a matter for the court and which could not be dealt with by a nominated expert.

For a court expert to be appointed, the applicants would have to persuade the judge that there is good reason why the court's normal judicial function should be bypassed. Arguments regarding the amount of time that the issue would take if put before the court, the complexity of the issue and that it is an area of the case capable of having an absolute answer are all matters which favour the appointment.

A problem common to all "court expert" procedures lies in the selection of an expert who is perceived as being independent by both sides, who has sufficient "gravitas", and who has the qualifications in the particular field.

Once appointed, the role of the expert would be to determine the issue which he has been asked to consider. RSC Order 40 sets out the general procedure that would apply following the experts' appointment, although there is a good deal of flexibility within the basic rules. The likely format is that the expert would be appointed on the exchange of experts' reports, when it became clear that no agreement is likely to be reached between the parties. The expert would then consider both sides' arguments, by considering the reports and possibly by meeting with the experts either separately or together, depending on the particular circumstances. Rule 3 even allows the expert to carry out tests to assist in the determination of a particular issue.

Once the court expert has come to a view, that would be provided in the form of a report to the court and subsequently to the two parties. That would give both sides the opportunity to accept the court expert's view prior to trial. If that happens the court expert's view would be presented to the court as an agreed report. If not, both sides would on giving notice have the opportunity to put forward its own evidence in the area. Rule 6 limits this to one expert without leave of the court, which can only be given in exceptional circumstances. Rule 4 allows the court expert to be cross-examined by both parties. Although the court expert's view is then only one of the experts whose views the judge would have to consider, the likelihood is that the judge would pay particular attention to that view.

c) Court Assessor

The third possibility is that the court appoints an assessor to sit with the judge in open court, during the course of the case. (The power to do this is contained in Section 70 of the Supreme Court Act 1981 and RSC ord 33 r6.) The idea of this is that, as with planning inquiries, the judge has available its own expert to turn to for advice and ideas to assist in coming to a view. It is not the assessor's role to make any sort of determination.

Again, the parties can apply for an assessor by consent or individually. It would be up to the applicant to persuade the court that such a person was necessary. The agreement of the possible assessor would have to be obtained.

The assessor would not come to a formal view in the sense of the court expert who produces a report. Instead the person would have listened to the evidence and would have the ear of the Judge. It would appear that the assessor is not able to ask questions during the course of the trial, nor indeed to take any other active role and further, cannot be questioned by the two sides. (37 Halsbury's Laws, (4th edn) para 475).

d) Advantages and Disadvantages

It seems unlikely that the arbitration process will be often used as it is unlikely that the circumstances would arise where both sides felt that their own case would benefit from such a step. The cost of the arbitration may also be a major stumbling block. The main benefit of arbitration is that it would ensure that the particular issue was determined before trial.

The problem with the court assessor is that it would be unclear as to how the assessor had assisted the judge in the judgement. The benefit is that it may help the judge come to terms with complex and at times incomprehensible scientific matters. The largest problem here is likely to be finding someone to do the job who would not be seen to be prejudiced in any way.

It is the use of the Court expert that would seem more appropriate in these cases. Knowing what the expert has said and having the ability to put forward other evidence, at the hearing, ensures a fall back position if the expert's view is unfavourable. Above all, it would ensure that complex issues in the case could be properly considered by someone independent of either side, but knowledgeable about those particular areas. Subject to the problem of selection this is the route that promises to find most favour with the parties.

Lord Denning in Re-v-Saxton [1962] 1 WLR 968 at 973 said "I hope, however, that in future, careful consideration may be given to the appointment of a court expert". His words seem to have been ignored for some 30 years, but Lord Woolf has now revived the notion.

Lord Woolf's Civil Justice Review Report, published in June 1995, addresses the role of experts and in certain instances recommends restriction to a single court-appointed expert.

CHAPTER TEN

THE TRIAL

1. The Build Up

The period building up to the trial is the time when the plaintiff's legal team will be at their busiest. They will need to be checking the experts' reports, obtaining new reports, ensuring the discovery process is complete, ensuring witness statements are fully up-to-date, briefing counsel, and preparing all the bundles.

The particular points that the lawyers need to have in mind are as follows.

a) Experts

The exchange of reports is likely to have raised serious gaps in the plaintiffs' case, and the lawyers must, therefore, spend some time checking through the defendants reports to see where the plaintiffs' case is weak. It maybe that the court has ordered a specific secondary report exchange date, in which case all of the main experts will need to have prepared their reports in response to those of their opposite numbers in the defendants' team within this period.

The February 1995 Practice Note from the Lord Chief Justice made it clear that it is the role of the two legal teams to cut down extraneous issues in the case, and to keep experts down to a minimum. There is no question but that in the new regime the courts are likely to look very unfavourably upon experts giving evidence as "fillers". The plaintiffs' lawyers should always have an eye to ensuring that issues dealt with by the experts are still of relevance.

The exchanging of reports can continue even into trial. In the Sellafield action there were many, many reports exchanged after the trial commenced, and one expert served his sixth report before the case was concluded.

b) Documents

The plaintiffs' lawyers must ensure that the discovery process is complete and be clear that there are no significant loose strands to be tied up before the trial commences. Although the courts will be wary of late discovery applications, better that than having key points missed.

The bundling in these cases is important. There is no great magic formula to be adopted other than having the bundles in chronological order, properly paginated, and in handleable quantities, (i.e. ring-binders with about 250 pages). The most important job is to ensure that the bundles are the same, from one set to another. Where it is obvious that within a given category containing many ring-binders (say daily incinerator operation records) some will be referred to very often,(key dates) then a single ring-binder, a "core bundle", of selected documents will be useful.

c) Counsel

One of the greatest difficulties for the plaintiffs' solicitors is that this is the time counsel starts to take a greater role, and is the time that the handover needs to take place as smoothly as possible.

In the Sellafield action, the opening speech was drafted by counsel, but then reviewed by the solicitors and experts, to ensure accuracy and that counsel had fully understood what was the most complex of cases. This was a painful exercise, not least because neither side of the profession had ever done it before, but it was very worthwhile in ensuring that counsel understood the case, that there was agreement about the direction of the case and that the case was accurately stated as far as the experts were concerned.

d) Pre-Trial

The Practice Note referred to above calls for a pre-trial review in the immediate run up to the case in any action likely to last more than ten court days. At that hearing the judge will want to consider the orderly running of the action, including whether to take the action in the normal way or whether to try it in blocks, as happened in the Sellafield case.

The judge may also want to consider having short weeks to allow for the preparation to take place of the next witnesses, reading time etc. This was the case in the Sellafield action where the weeks were generally four days. This probably saved time in the long run because it allowed both sides to make decisions as to whether experts were definitely needed, whether final reports should be written, and whether peripheral issues should be accepted or dropped, all cutting down on the time before the judge.

The court will also want to consider some form of electronic transcript of evidence such as "Livenote". In such a system not only do the questions and answers come up on screens as they are given but pieces of transcript can be "filed" as they emerge and passages of transcript can be recalled by word search. In the Graham case which lasted 198 days of which 166 were evidence the use of such a system resulted in a great saving of time. Indeed in a case where factual evidence given on Day 10 was being put to another witness on Day 80 or to an expert on Day 139 the thought of Counsel having find it in their notebooks, notebooks disagreeing, wait while shorthand writer finds the passage, would not only have greatly extended the trial, but would seriously have disrupted it.

2. The Opening

The opening in the Sellafield case was some 350 pages long. It was agreed with the judge that it need not be fully read out, and under the new regime of keeping trials shorter and tighter this is likely to be the position in future. Counsel did, however, read out the key parts to ensure the media and public present were fully aware of the background to the case.

The defendants' opening is likely to be far shorter as they keep their cards, largely, up their sleeves at this stage.

In the Graham case by contrast the parties' opening statements were on the basis of full skeleton arguments and oral submission, taking some 5 days per side. This process enabled the court to indicate where matters needed further elaboration.

Witnesses: It is likely that following counsel's opening, that the plaintiffs' themselves will have to give evidence. The courts will increasingly be taking the statements as their evidence in chief, and therefore it is important that if there is anything for the witness to add that it is put in a supplementary statement before the witness gives evidence.

In the case of *Graham v Rechem* the defence counsel was allowed to cross examine the plaintiff for nearly 30 days. It is questionable whether the courts will allow the time of the court to be taken up in this manner in the future, but is perhaps a sign of the keenness of the defendants in these cases to break the plaintiffs down, and it bore fruit in the Graham Case.

Normally in this type of case, the evidence of the lay witnesses will be taken relatively shortly when compared to the time taken by the experts. In the Sellafield all the lay evidence was agreed so that the time in court was taken up almost exclusively by the experts.

3. Experts

One of the key problems for the plaintiffs' lawyers is to determine the order of experts. This will partly depend on the decision by the judge as to whether to take the case in blocks and partly on defence counsel as to the length of time cross examining experts. There is little doubt that the time to be taken by each expert on the stand will reduce as the case moves along, as the judge becomes more familiar with the issues and terms.

It is important to have a working relationship with the defendants' solicitors at this stage, to ensure the best running of the action. The judge will not look too kindly upon delays in the action because of experts not being available, at the right time, or upon issues being raised that are entirely peripheral to the action, so it is important that the process of honing down the case continues right through the trial.

When the defendants' experts are giving evidence it is extremely helpful to have the plaintiffs' expert from the same area present in court, passing notes to counsel regarding questions and answers. The reality is, however, that this is often unrealistic because of the amount of pressure on the experts' time and, therefore, the lawyer from the solicitor's team who specialises in the area of the case being dealt with should be in court to give counsel that assistance.

In the Graham case the factual evidence was all taken first (plaintiff side then defendant). Thereafter the expert evidence was taken in blocks: incineration; meteorology; veterinary; toxicology and so forth, in each block the plaintiff experts followed by the defendant experts.

4. Submissions

In the Sellafield action the judge requested that submissions be passed to him, in writing, shortly after each expert had left the stand, from both sides saying what each team felt to be the key points arising from that expert's testimony. This was an extremely time consuming exercise. However there was little doubt that it was a task worth doing because it ensured that both sides kept on top of the case, having to reconsider its own case each time an expert had been examined. Further it ensured that the task of noting up the transcript was not left until there were literally tens of thousands of pages of transcript before the noting up exercise took place.

In actions where the judge does not make such a request, it may well be worth the plaintiffs' team taking the same course, but simply not revealing the submissions until the end of the case.

The final submissions usually take some time to prepare after a long action, and the judge will usually allow a reasonable period for this work to take place. However, the writing of submissions can be taken to extremes and the judge certainly called a halt in the Sellafield action where both sides produced submissions on the other sides' submissions, and then submissions on those submissions.

In the Graham case 15 days were allowed for preparation of final submissions, to be delivered orally but with full skeletons. Each party was then limited to 7 days for the oral submissions. Then each party was permitted 2 days for "tidying up".

5. Judgment

The judge will almost certainly take quite some while to produce a judgment in anything other than the most straight forward of cases. It is usual for the judgment to be in writing, and in the Sellafield action it ran to some five ringbinders, albeit that a large amount of this was appendices of the judge's view of each of the expert's evidence.

The judge will usually allow the two legal teams sight of the judgement a day or two in advance of it being read out in court, to allow them time to prepare for any points that need to be raised, not least being on the issue of costs.

It is specifically stated that the lawyers must not give sight to anyone or tell anyone of the contents of the judgment, prior to it being read out in court. Although there might be a great temptation to tell the clients before the judgment is given this must, of course, be resisted.

At the judgment there may well be a large number of journalists and it is important that the client is well briefed beforehand on what is likely to occur win or lose, with the media. The client's wishes as to their preparedness to give interviews must be heeded, but the clients should be told that it is often easier to deal with the media in one block, outside the court, rather than having them constantly harassing the clients at home or on their way home.

The interest of the media is likely to be far greater if the case is won than if it is lost.

After a long action, where the clients will often have played only a peripheral role, because the case is so often about the science and the law, rather than the direct facts of the particular client's case some sort of social gathering after the judgment is worthwhile, so that the client is given the chance to be clear about what happened, can talk in private to the legal team, and can unwind about the case, win or lose. A client who comes out a of a judgment, having seen a good deal of fraternisation between the two groups of lawyers, who has to deal with the media, and who is then left to go home alone, can become rather disgruntled and disillusioned. The lawyer should put time into ensuring that does not happen.

CHAPTER ELEVEN

THE SELLAFIELD LEUKAEMIA ACTION

1. The issues

Much has already been said about this action earlier in the book. The purpose of this chapter is to consider the judgment of Mr Justice French and draw some conclusions from the case, which may assist others in pursuing similar lengthy complex actions to trial.

The trial of the cases of Elizabeth Reay and Vivien Hope commenced in October 1992, and finished at the end of June 1993, with judgment being given in early October 1993. The trial had lasted for just short of one hundred days. Some forty-five experts had given evidence, out of 70 who had produced reports, and there were, by the end, over one hundred and fifty reports that the judge had to consider. Experts' reports continued to be handed in to the very end of the trial, as new reports were published in the scientific literature.

The basis for the action has already been set out above. The trial was entirely one about the scientific issues, the defendants having agreed to the plaintiffs' valuation of the cases, being £100,000 and £150,000. The primary issues for the judge were for him to decide whether or not he was satisfied that there was an excess of childhood leukaemias and Non-Hodgkins lymphomas (a linked solid cancer) around the nuclear reprocessing plant; whether it was caused or materially contributed to by the radiation emanating from the Sellafield plant; whether the particular cancers of the two test cases were caused by the radiation.

The cases were primarily based on the epidemiological evidence of Professor Martin Gardner, the epidemiologist, who had published a report in February 1990 showing that there was strong statistical evidence to link the excess childhood cancers with fathers who were exposed to high levels of radioactivity whilst working at the plant. The fathers of the two children whose cases formed the basis for the action, had two of the highest doses of anyone in the study.

2 Radiation Dosimetry

In the build up to the trial one of the key the issues considered in the experts' reports was the radiation doses to the workers. During the course of the discovery process it had been discovered that the dose histories produced by British Nuclear Fuels were inaccurate, because they did not take account of the poorly operating dose badges in the early years of the plants life. As a result the doses had to be reassessed for all the one hundred or so workers in the Gardner study.

Another issue was the question of the level of dose received by the children though their exposure to radiation entering into the environment from the Sellafield plant. The problem here was that despite there being strong evidence that high levels of radioactivity had escaped, the actual doses received by the children always seemed, through traditional dose modelling to be small.

In the discovery process it had been found that there were far higher releases than had been previously accepted by the operators of the plant, and the experts were attempting to determine what impact this had on the dosimetry. On this issue, the plaintiffs primarily took the view that there was little point in continuing to pursue this as a significant issue in the case, because the evidence was so strong on the occupational doses received by their fathers and, therefore, the plaintiffs' experts did not give evidence on this subject.

The discovery documents were, however put to the defendants' experts in an attempt to show how inaccurate were the defendants' analyses of the levels of exposure to the local population. The strategy worked to a minor degree in showing that the defendants' figures were not always to be trusted, but in his judgment the judge accepted a lot of what the defendants experts had said. This area became a very peripheral part of this case.

In the week after the commencement of the action the defendants agreed to have a meeting to try and see whether it was possible for the experts to agree on the doses received by the workers, and that meeting was able to attain such a compromise meaning that the judge did not have to be subjected to weeks of debate about the enormous complexities of radiation dosimetry and the general operation of the Sellafield plant over its 40 years of operating life.

3. Epidemiology

The action was always primarily about the strength of the epidemiological evidence as against the weakness of the genetic evidence. The plaintiffs' experts put all the statistical and epidemiological evidence before the judge to show that there was a very strong correlation between the excess cancers seen and fathers who worked at the plant with high doses, that such a correlation was highly unlikely to have arisen by chance, and that radiation was by far the most likely cause.

They then looked at other studies to show that although the Atomic Bomb data did not show a similar excess there were other studies looking at the children of those exposed to X Rays which did show excesses. They argued that the Atomic Bomb data should not be seen as disproving the Gardner study, because it had happened in such a different way, i.e. how could the daily exposure of workers at the Sellafield plant be compared to the one-off flash of exposure of the A Bomb victims.

In response the defendants attempted to pull the Gardner study to pieces, having gained access to all his working papers and files. They then tried to show that the study was not showing any sort of biological gradient (i.e. an increasing risk with increasing dose) and that the other X Ray studies were all either flawed or were too small to be considered any real help. Primarily they turned to the lack of excess cancers seen in the offspring of the children of the A Bomb victims as evidence that Gardner must be wrong.

In all it seemed that on the evidence available at that time, the judge was probably more persuaded by the plaintiffs than the defendants on the epidemiology.

4. Genetics

If Gardner's study was right it would have meant that the radiation, to which the workers were exposed, was genetically damaging their sperm which was leading to the ensuing child cancers. The geneticists were generally unpersuaded by Gardner.

Since the A Bomb data started to be published in the 1950s the general feeling had been that the fertilisation process was a good filter for damaged sperm, and this had been supported by mice experiments where they had irradiated the parent and looked for defects in the offspring and found very little.

The one person who had carried out directly comparable experiments with mice looking for tumours in the offspring was from a laboratory in Osaka, Japan. He had found significantly increased levels. His work had, until the Gardner study was published, been largely ignored.

The problem in this field was the very serious lack of knowledge of the experts. It is even today not clear what actually initiates a cancer, and it is by no means possible to consider a cancer and see what caused it. This lack of knowledge meant that the experts' evidence was full of holes, and simply best guesses, on both sides.

The evidence in this section of the case clearly went in favour of the defendants, which meant that at the end of the trial both parties were left wondering which side of the case had most persuaded the judge.

5. Judgment

During the latter part of the trial a number of epidemiological studies were produced by the defendants which suggested that the Gardner explanation did not by any means fit the picture that was emerging. In particular there was a study that showed that the excess seen around the immediate locality did not spread out to other areas, despite there being areas where concentrated numbers of workers lived who had been exposed to high levels of radiation. The point being that if Gardner's theory was correct it would have been expected that wherever workers with high doses lived there should be excess childhood cancers.

These studies clearly weighed heavily with the judge, when taken in combination with the genetic evidence, leading him to come down "decisively" in favour of the defendants in his judgment.

His judgment was very much based on the epidemiological evidence of the two sides, and he took the view that he was not persuaded that the plaintiffs had met the evidential burden of showing that, on the balance of probabilities the radiation had caused the cancers. The defendants had floated an alternative theory for the cause of the cancers, being that of viruses. The judge found that this theory, which had been subjected to comparatively little scrutiny in the case, was an equally plausible cause.

The judge considered very little law in the case, and his judgment, in running to five ring binders said very little other than reviewing the evidence of the experts, and in his coming down in the briefest of terms for the defendants.

Since the publication of the judgment, one study published immediately afterwards gave some support to the plaintiffs' case, but other studies moved the argument toward the defendants case, as a result of which the judge, who had been assigned to all the radiation related actions, dismissed the follow-on actions that were waiting in the wings for the test case decisions.

The trial had been a very close-fought affair, with the strengths of both sides cases ebbing and flowing. Although the judge had little scientific background, he coped well with the complexities of the action. In general, whilst the courts are in some ways a difficult forum for this type of action, this case suggested that it is possible for the most complex of toxic tort actions to be tried without the system breaking down as it has with complex fraud actions in the criminal system.

PART II: THE LAW

CHAPTER TWELVE

NEGLIGENCE

Since the snail was released from the bottle by Lord Atkin in *Donoghue -v- Stevenson* [1932] AC 562 the tort of negligence has seen tremendous development and its ambit has been considered by the appellate courts on many occasions. One senses, almost, that as negligence has thrived so nuisance has wilted.

In pollution cases negligence has the advantage that compensation for personal injuries is certainly available, and that the plaintiff need have no interest in the land to mount a claim. However, these advantages only hold good over a private nuisance, and not over public nuisance. On the other hand negligence actions have significant disadvantages; injunctions are not available; pure economic loss is not recoverable; exemplary damages are not recoverable. Another drawback is that, contrary to the position in nuisance, defendants are not liable in general for the negligent acts of their independent contractors providing that an apparently competent contractor has been selected. Finally, the plaintiff must always establish fault in the negligence action, whereas this prerequisite is somewhat diluted in nuisance actions.

1. Recent Case law

Whilst, for the above reasons, nuisance actions have been the preferred route for the toxic tort lawyer, there are nonetheless some recent cases using the tort of negligence in the environmental field. Many of these are occupational exposure cases (see for example *Thompson -v- Smiths Shiprepairers (North Shields) Ltd* [1984] 1 QB 405, a noise claim; and the many actions arising from dust, whether coal silicon brick or asbestos). These cases are not considered here as they are outside the remit of this book.

There have been notable cases of "failure to warn" leading to environmental damage. For example in *Barnes -v- Irwell Valley Water Board* [1939] 1 K.B. 21 it was held that there was a common law duty of care on a water company to warn consumers of potentially dangerous properties of water supplied and that damages were recoverable in negligence.

In 1987 a water authority was held liable in negligence for failing to warn downstream riparian owners of known chloride pollution in the river which was clearly going to be damaging to crops, (see *Scott-Whitehead -v- National Coal Board* [1987] P & CR 263).

Both these decisions have interesting implications, bearing in mind the role of other statutory and environmental agencies. It is probable that the "failure to warn" liability will be confined by the courts to cases where the defendant knows or should know that its own product or act of contamination carries a risk of harm, but it cannot be ruled out that an agency charged with a watchdog responsibility such as the NRA or HMIP would be held liable, in negligence, for failure to warn in respect of a third party's product or act where it was the watchdog's responsibility to regulate the third party. We can, however, find no reported decision where this has occurred.

In *Budden -v- BP & Shell,* (unreported, 21 May 1980 CA) actions were brought by infant plaintiffs against oil companies claiming in negligence damages for personal injury caused by the lead content of the defendants' petrol. The alleged negligence was that the company should have ceased before July 1978 to add any lead to the petrol which they refined and sold or at least should have reduced the proportion of lead in their petrol. The defendants averred that they had complied with regulations which set maximum limits for the lead content in petrol made under s75(1) of the Control of Pollution Act 1974. The defendants contended that the plaintiffs' action should be struck out on two alternative grounds: compliance with the regulations gave them an unanswerable statutory defence to the claim. Alternatively it gave them a complete answer to an allegation of fault.

The Court of Appeal was not willing to strike out the claim on the first ground but did strike it out on the second ground. The court held that the prescribed maximum lead limits in the regulations were arrived at by an independent person, empowered by parliament, having taken such advice as he regarded as appropriate to assist him in arriving at the decision which parliament had invited him to make, and which parliament, by its tacit assent to the regulations, thereafter approved.

In the circumstances the court was unable to see how a court could hold that the oil companies had breached any duty owed to the children once it was clear that they had complied with the requirements prescribed by the Secretary of State. The Court of Appeal made the point that were it to do otherwise the courts would, in effect, be laying down a permissible limit which would be determined as being of universal application and inconsistent with the permissible limit prescribed by parliament which would result in an unacceptable constitutional anomaly.

Accordingly the *Budden* case was struck out and proceeded no further. The approach of the Court of Appeal in that instance may well, however, need to be revisited. It is particularly interesting to compare the corresponding law on water pollution.

It has always been accepted that the grant of a licence to discharge polluting matter into water courses (known as a "consent") does not affect the common law rights of a riparian owner to sue a discharger even where the discharges complained of are within the limits of the consent. Clearly the fact of compliance with the consent would be a very relevant and persuasive matter on the side of the defendants in determining whether there was nuisance and/or negligence but that is very far from being conclusive of the issue.

It is however, going much further to treat compliance with the statutory standard as an automatic defence. There is certainly nothing in s75 of the Control of Pollution Act 1974 which expressly states that parliament intended to give a statutory defence to air polluters in regard to their normal common law liabilities by laying down maximum concentrations, any more than in providing the imposition of thirty mile per hour speed limits parliament intended statutory defence to negligence actions in respect of drivers travelling at 30 mph.

2. Fault

The starting point when considering the issue of fault (ie "breach of duty") is a dictum of Baron Alderson in *Blythe -v- Birmingham Waterworks Co* [1856] 11 Exch 781. He said that "negligence is the omission to do something which a reasonable man, guided upon those considerations which ordinarily regulate the conduct of human affairs, would do, or do something which a prudent and reasonable man would not do". This test refers to the standard of the reasonable man; the standard of the defendant himself is irrelevant. In the environmental context, this means the reasonable waste disposal operator, reasonable factory owner and so on. The reasonable operator will be judged objectively, but by the standards of knowledge prevailing in the relevant industry at the material time, and not at the time the case goes to trial.

There is considerable overlap here with foreseeability and the court will take a number of factors into account, including the following;

(a) the object to be attained by the defendants' conduct;

(b) the practicability of precautions. The court will look at any approved or general practice prevailing at the time of and prior to the alleged breach of duty. The fact that the defendant complied with the prevailing custom or practice will be a persuasive argument in the defendants' favour although it is not conclusive;

(c) the court will balance the practicability of any suggested precautions that the defendants could have taken against the risk of harm.

A conviction for a criminal offence, where material to the accident, can be pleaded and used in evidence in the civil compensation proceedings. This would apply for example to a public nuisance conviction. Such a conviction, notwithstanding that the stand of proof is higher in a criminal court that in a civil court, is not conclusive of the issue in the civil court. However, unless the defendant can persuade the civil court that the criminal conviction is in some material sense irrelevant or was the product of a technical irregularity (in which case the civil court would want to know why it had not been successfully appealed) the presence of a criminal conviction is likely to be conclusive on the issue of fault.

The finding of fault in the design of the operation of a plant which gives rise to toxic emissions is a matter of the most complex expert evidence and an extremely laborious discovery process. In such a case, the doctrine of *res ipsa loquitur* can assist the plaintiff. This was laid down in the case of *Scott -v- London & St Katherine Docks Co* [1865] 3 H. & C. 596:

"there must be some reasonable evidence of negligence. But where the thing is shown to be under the management of the defendant or his servants, and the accident is such as in the ordinary course of things does not happen if those who have the management use proper care, and affords reasonable evidence, in the absence of explanation by the defendants, that the accident arose from want of care".

So for example if a single incident explosion produced a poisonous gas cloud causing environmental damage it is likely that the doctrine of res ipsa loquitur could be invoked. Similarly, if there was an incident involving a leak from a waste disposal site and the emission of dangerous substances into a river. The position is likely to be different with long term, steady seepage cases where the causes tend to be multi factorial.

3. Foreseeability

The "foreseeability" test will be applied in negligence just as in nuisance cases, see *Wagon Mound* (No 2) [1967] 1 AC617. In this respect nuisance and negligence and the rule in Rylands -v- Fletcher are indistinguishable, see *Cambridge Water Co -v- Eastern Counties Leather plc* [1994] 1 All ER 53 (HL).

In that case the plaintiff Water Company had to spend a million pounds because of the spillage of chlorinated solvent over many years up to 1976 resulting from the defendant company's practice of lifting by forklift truck, and on occasions puncturing, large drums of solvent which led to the borehole from which the Water Company derived a water supply being contaminated. The Water Company sought to recover damages in negligence, nuisance and *Rylands -v- Fletcher* liability. This important decision is more fully dealt with in Chapter 22 on Land Contamination.

At first instance Kennedy J in considering the "foreseeability" test asked himself the question what the reasonable supervisor oversee-ing the operation of the plant in 1976 would have foreseen as the consequences of repeated spillages. In the judge's view, which was upheld in the House of Lords, the supervisor would not have seen that detectable quantities of solvents would find their way in the aquifer. Nor, in his view, would a reasonable supervisor in and before 1976 have believed that such spillages as the defendants were guilty of would produce any material effect upon water in the borehole. Kennedy J added:

"There must be many areas... where activities long ceased still have their impact on the environment and where the perception of such impact depends on knowledge and standards which have been gained or imposed in recent times. If... those who were responsible for those activities... should be under a duty to undo that impact... that must be a matter for parliament. The common law would not undertake such a retrospective enquiry... that there should not be an award of damages in respect of the 1991 impact of actions that were not actionable nuisances or negligence when they were committed 15 years before is to my mind not a proposition which the common law would entertain."

In applying the Wagon Mound No 2 and holding that the recovery of damages whether in private nuisance, negligence or Rylands -v- Fletcher, depends on "foreseeability by the defendant of the relevant type of damage", the House of Lords had no difficulty in ruling that, on the particular facts of the Cambridge Water case, the relevant type of damage was not reasonably foreseeable in 1976.

It would, for example, have been reasonably foreseeable at the time that regular small spills of this solvent may lead to toxic fumes, perhaps giving rise to respiratory illness, but not that the solvent would descend 30 metres into the ground and then start spreading laterally so as to affect a borehole 1.3 miles away.

In approaching foreseeability in this way the House of Lords plainly agreed with Kennedy J that foreseeability of "pollution of some kind" was not sufficiently specific for the imposition of liability. Future cases will give guidance as to degree of specificity required. For example, up to the 1950's tar works were common in industrial areas. The tar would be made in large vats. When the time came to empty or clean the vats it was typical to open the valves and let the surplus tar drain into the ground. Thus large quantities of excess tar washings were deliberately and repeatedly spread across the same area of land and, forty years later, before such land could be used for, say, residential development, it would need considerable treatment (to avoid health hazards to children playing and so forth). To take another example, "drum graves" were a typical method of "waste disposal" thirty years ago, but now, again, the drums have corroded, the toxic contents have contaminated the land, and if redeveloped for residential use major expenditure would be required to make the land safe.

In both these instances, if was perfectly foreseeable to anybody who asked themselves the question that these actions would foreseeably pollute the land. The point is, that according the standards and practices of those times, nobody ever thought to ask the question. It remains to be seen whether this will afford a defence.

A recent decision on the issue of foreseeability was the Abbeystead disaster case, *Eckersley -v- Binnie* [1988] 18 Con. L.R. 1. The Court of Appeal (with a powerful dissenting judgment by Bingham LJ as he then was) upheld the finding of liability in negligence against the defendant engineers for failing to take sufficient account of the risk of leakage of reservoir methane gas is designing a deep tunnel construction project. In consequence, inadequate precautions were taken and a methane explosion occurred killing 16 people and injuring many more. Russell LJ, giving the majority judgment, approached the question of foreseeability in this way:

"We were referred to a number of authorities dealing with the spectrum of the likelihood of events, ranging from probabilities to remote possibilities. For my part I derive most assistance from the words of Lord Reid, in *Wagon Mound No 2* [1967] AC 617. Dealing with the remote risks, he said (at 642):

"But it does not follow that, no matter what the circumstances may be, it is justifiable to neglect a risk of such a small magnitude. A reasonable man would only neglect such a risk if he had some valid reason for do so, e.g. that it would involve considerable expense to eliminate the risk. He would weigh the risk against the difficulty of eliminating it. If the activity which caused the injury to Miss Stone had been an unlawful activity, there can be little doubt that *Bolton -v- Stone* [1951] AC 850 would have been decided differently. In their Lordships' judgment *Bolton -v- Stone* did not alter the general principle that a person must be regarded as negligent if he does not take steps to eliminate a risk which he knows or ought to know is a real risk and not a mere possibility which would never influence the mind of a reasonable man. What that decision did was to recognise and give effect to the qualification that it is justifiable not to take steps to eliminate a real risk if it is small and if the circumstances are such that a reasonable man, careful of the safety of his neighbour, would think it right to neglect it."

"The test, formulated in this way, then has to be applied to the facts of the instant case. Was it foreseeable that methane would be encountered? If it was encountered, were the defendants entitled to assume that such methane was merely stress relief methane, and would not adversely affect the permanent works? Did the defendants ever consider the distinction between stress and relief methane and reservoir methane? These are the questions with which the judge had to deal."

In the *Abbeystead* case there was a vigorous dispute between experts as to whether at the date of the tunnel design a reasonable engineer would have foreseen reservoir methane gas leakage as something to be taken into account. The Court of Appeal held that the trial judge was entitled to resolve this in favour of the plaintiffs against the defendant engineers.

The comparison between *Cambridge Water* and *Abbeystead* illustrates the approach of the court to the issue of foreseeability. It also shows the wide margin of discretion enjoyed by the court on this point. Indeed the editors of Clerk & Lindsell on Tort (16th Ed. para 10-145) comment that "in this way the foreseeability test has become a cloak for the exercise of policy and discretion. It is manifestly imprecise and leaves a large element of discretion to the courts."

For those who are anxious to avoid industry having to bear stupendous costs of "clean up" as has occurred in the US under the "Superfund" legislation the *Cambridge Water* decision will provide much reassurance. No doubt this will not include the directors of Cambridge Water who are faced with having to find a million pounds in consequence of the defendants' conduct, yet without apparent remedy. The outlook for liability of contaminated land is dealt with in Chapter 23.

4. Damage

It is to be emphasised that negligence (and nuisance) are, historically, actions on the case; and accordingly in neither case is the tort complete, so that damages are recoverable, unless and until damage has been caused to the plaintiff. Pollution cases, particularly long term low level pollution cases, involve difficult questions as to when and if damage has in fact occurred. These are questions of fact and degree for the courts to determine and the answer to these questions not only governs whether or not a tort has been committed but also whether or not the limitation period has expired before proceedings were commenced.

The *Cambridge Water* case affords a good illustration. Kennedy J had stated that it was repugnant to the common law to award damages 15 years later for actions that were not actionable nuisances or negligence when they were committed. Lord Goff, in his speech in the House of Lords, felt it necessary to clarify this proposition. Since neither tort was complete unless and until damage had been caused to the plaintiff, it followed that there could not be actionable negligence or nuisance by virtue of the spillage of solvent until the spillage caused damage to Cambridge Water, ie when water available at its borehole was rendered unsaleable by reason of breach of the water quality Regulations.

Just because something is "contaminated" or even "harmful" in statute law it does not mean that the contamination amounts to "damage" for the purposes of actions in negligence or nuisance.

In *Cambridge Water* the imposition of a statutory standard which meant that *Cambridge Water* had to withdraw the borehole from use was held to constitute the actionable damage. It should be noted, of course, that the actual level of water contamination by the solvent was identical prior to the imposition of the standard but yet, at that point in time, no actionable damage would have arisen.

So far as drinking water is concerned there are a number of such statutory standards. At the present time, in relation to contaminated land, as opposed to drinking water, there are no standards with statutory force. Therefore, whether land had been "damaged", so as to constitute actionable negligence, would depend on whether, in the judgment of the court, the "damage" was "substantial".

His Honour Judge Havery QC in the context of the Docklands litigation dealing with a preliminary issue of law as to whether extensive dust soiling allegedly occasioned by negligent failure to take precautions in the building works was capable of constituting physical damage so as to found an action in the tort of negligence held that the meaning of "damage" as adopted by the Court of Appeal criminal division in *R v.Henderson and Battley* applies to the law of negligence.

In the *Henderson* case the charge was one of criminal damage to a site which had been cleared for development. The site was flat and the appellants had impudently used the site as a public tip and charged customers tipping some 30 lorry loads of soil and rubble and mud onto the site. The appellants' argument was that the site was not "damaged" because the land beneath the piles of rubbish which had been tipped upon it was in the same condition as it was before the rubbish was tipped upon it. It was argued that there must be a distinction between the cost of putting something right (because the owner had to spend about £2,000 to remove the soil and rubble and mud) and actual damage.

The court held that whether or not damage was done was a question of fact and degree for the jury. Damage can be of various kinds. In the Concise Oxford Dictionary "damage" is defined as "injury impairing value or usefulness". That, so it was held, was a definition which would fit in very well with doing something to a cleared building site which at any rate for the time being impaired its usefulness as such. In addition, as it necessitated work and expenditure of £2,000 to restore it to its former state, the value as a building site was reduced to that extent.

Other cases were relied on which had established the "impairment of usefulness" test. In one case an engine had been sabotaged, and in another case a gun spiked. Neither the engine nor the gun had been damaged as such, but both were useless until repaired. In both instances it was held that "damage" had been done. Judge Havery QC held that the deposition of dust on land "in sufficient quantities to impair the usefulness of that land" constitutes damage for the purposes of the tort of negligence and gave as an analogy the painting of graffiti on walls of railway carriages which, given labour and expense, could be cleaned off but which, nevertheless in the learned trial judge's view, constituted actionable damage. (*Patricia Hunter and Others -v- London Docklands Development Corporation*, unreported, 4th November 1994.)

In deciding whether actual damage has occurred, can the court take into account future and continuing damage? At first instance in the *Cambridge Water* case, Kennedy J answered this question, which is extremely important in the context of chronic pollution cases, in the negative.

"The damage must be substantial, and it must be, in my view, actual; that is to say the court has, in dealing with questions of this kind, no right to take into account contingent, prospective, or remote damage... so if it were made out that every minute a millionth of a grain of poison were absorbed by a tree, a millionth of a grain of dust deposited upon a tree, that would not afford a ground for interfering, although after the lapse of a million minutes the grains of poison or the grains of dust could be easily detected."

There is an arguable parallel here with the special situation of withdrawal of support. The mere withdrawal of support is not actionable in itself as a nuisance; it only becomes wrongful if and when a subsidence occurs; *Backhouse -v- Bonomi* [1861] 9 HLC 503, applied by the Court of Appeal in *Midland Bank plc -v- Bardgrove Property Services Ltd* [1992] 37 EG 126. In the Midland Bank case the bank, realising that the defendants had withdrawn support, and acting on professional advice that subsidence to their building was thereby rendered inevitable, took pre-emptive action to shore up the building at a considerable cost which it then sought to pass on the cost to the defendant who was guilty of the withdrawal of support. The Court of Appeal upholding the trial judge, dismissed the bank's claim on the grounds that until actual subsidence had occurred there was no actionable damage.

The plaintiff is caught in something of a trap here. There is an interplay between actual damage as a pre-condition to the tort being complete on the one hand and the limitation period beginning to run on the other. If the plaintiff issues proceedings and the court holds that no actual damage has yet occurred, then no tort has been committed and the action fails. If the plaintiff stays his hand in issuing proceedings until it is beyond any doubt that actual damage has occurred, then, if the court finds on a true analysis that the actual damage had in fact occurred years earlier, the plaintiff's action could be struck out on limitation (notwith-standing, perhaps, the provisions of the Latent Damage Act 1986, (see below)).

Another case to mention in this context is *Merlin -v- British Nuclear Fuels plc* a decision of Gatehouse J [1993] All ER 711. The case is dealt with in Chapter 17 (Breach of Statutory Duty). It was held that on its true construction s7 of the Nuclear Installations Act 1965 required physical damage to tangible property to be established before compensation followed, and that the ingress of radionuclides in to the plaintiff's house did not amount to physical damage to tangible property. The case is distinguishable from cases concerning the interpretation of "damage" in negligence and nuisance because, as the learned trial judge emphasised, the interpretation of the statutory provision was influenced by the fact that the statute imposed absolute liability on the defendant and a greatly extended period for the bringing of claims.

That said, the plaintiffs' argument that "property" included the air space within the walls, ceilings and floors of the house and that this had been damaged by the presence of radionuclides in the house thereby rendered less valuable as the family's home, was rejected by the judge as "far fetched".

There are already cases where measurable concentrations of methane have been discovered intruding into houses built over active landfill sites. The occupiers of such houses are in a not dissimilar position to the Merlins in that the presence of elevated levels of methane brings with it the risk or increased risk of an explosion, and this materially affects the resale value of their homes. At present there are no statutory standards prescribing maximum air/methane concentrations within private homes, and it must remain a moot point whether, absent any explosion, "damage" of an actionable kind has occurred by virtue merely of the intrusion and presence of significant quantities of the gas.

5. Limitations of Actions

Sections 14A and 14B of the Limitation Act 1980, inserted by the Latent Damage Act 1986, deal with actions in respect of latent damage. By ss(4) the limitation period is either: (a) 6 years from the date on which the cause of action accrued; or (b) 3 years from the "starting date" if that period expires later that the 6 year period mentioned at (a).

The "starting date" is the earliest date on which the Plaintiff or any person in whom the cause of action was vested before him had both the knowledge required for bringing an action and the right to bring it. Knowledge in this sense means knowledge of material facts about the damage and other facts such as causation and the identity of the defendant. It includes knowledge which the plaintiff might reasonably have been expected to acquire from facts observable or ascertainable by him or from facts ascertainable with the help of appropriate expert advice which it is reasonable for him to seek.

By s14B an overriding time limit is applied to actions for negligence not involving personal injuries: this is a period of 15 years from the date (or, if more than one, the last of the dates) on which there occurred any act or omission:

(a) which is alleged to constitute negligence; and

(b) to which the damage in respect on which damage is claimed is alleged to be attributable.

Accordingly there is a "long-stop" of 15 years from the date of the negligent act or omission after which no action can be brought in the tort of negligence. This will apply even where the cause of action in negligence has not yet accrued because no actual damage has occurred.

Suppose, for example, in *Cambridge Water* the statutory standards relating to maximum permissible levels of the solvent in question were not brought into effect until 1992, i.e. 16 years after the last spillage that could be relied on in 1976. Since there was no actionable damage for 16 years, no action in negligence could have been brought, and by the time it could properly be brought, the action would be statute barred. This long-stop does not, however, apply to actions in nuisance so that the statute of limitations would not begin to run until 1992 and the action in nuisance would be within time providing it was brought before 1998.

6. Remedies

(a) Injunctions

Injunctions are not available in a negligence claim (Denning LJ in *Miller -v- Jackson* [1977] QB 966 at 980).

(b) Damages for personal injury

Whilst general damages for personal injury in negligence actions will be assessed on the usual principles, toxic tort claims sometimes involve an additional feature of concern about late onset of illness. So, for example, in a 'toxic cloud' case the claimant may, reasonably, have (a) heightened anxiety about developing, say, cancer within the next 10 to 15 years and (b) seek compensation both for the risk of this occurring and for the expense of regular medical monitoring.

As to the heightened anxiety there is a dearth of authority on the court's approach. In *R v Hunt*, a CICB decision [1992] 1 CL 57 the Board appears to have significantly increased general damages for firemen involved in a toxic fumes fire on being satisfied that the claimants, having made a full recovery, were very anxious that they might suffer further symptoms and were not reassured that they would not do so for about 2 years after the fire.

As to the compensation for the risk of late onset, the way forward would seem to be provisional damages under s32(a) of the Supreme Court Act 1981, at least where the condition is a 'clear and severable risk', see *Willson -v- Ministry of Defence* [1991] 1 All ER 638. Annual medical monitoring ought to be recoverable as a future loss using a multiplier/multiplicand.

(c) Pure economic loss

Damages for pure economic loss, i.e. where there has been no physical damage to the plaintiff or his property, will not be awarded, (see *D & F Estates Ltd -v- Church Commissioners* [1988] 3 WLR 368 and *Murphy -v- Brentwood D C* [1991] AC 398). It should be noted that the position is different in public nuisance (see p.161,149 below) and probably in private nuisance. A good example of failure to recover pure economic loss is *Weller & Co -v- Foot and Mouth Disease Research Institute* [1966] 1 QB 569, [1965] 3 All ER 560 where loss to auctioneers was not recoverable when a market closed as a result of farmers' cattle being exposed to a virus which had escaped from the defendant's premises.

(d) Exemplary Damages

Exemplary damages are not available in the tort of negligence since it has been laid down by the House of Lords in 1964 that awards of exemplary damages should be restricted to torts which are recognised at that time as grounds in a claim for exemplary damages and, since negligence was not such a tort, exemplary damages could not be recovered, *AB and Others -v- South West Water Services Ltd* [1993] 1 All ER 609 (see a).

7. The Negligent Planner

This chapter has mainly been concerned with the negligent polluter, but suppose a plaintiff has no remedy against the polluter, can he seek redress in a negligence action against the planner who permitted the polluter to be there? The answer would appear to be no, following the decision at first instance by Judge John Newey QC sitting as an Official Referee. He held that a planning authority is not liable in negligence to a third party in respect of a grant of planning permission, see *Ryeford Homes Ltd -v- Sevenoaks DC* [1989] NLJ 255.

The plaintiffs were housing developers who sued the local authority for damages for the negligent grant of a planning permission to a company for the development of a neighbouring site.

The judge had to decide whether a duty of care arose by virtue of any proximity created by planning law between the parties. He distinguished planning from public health law in that the latter is concerned with health and safety while the former is regulatory and is concerned with ensuring the good government and planning of the authority's area as a whole with the inevitable consequence that the grant of a permission to one landowner may adversely affect others.

The judge concluded that no special relationship or proximity arose between the parties and that no duty of care was owed in respect of the grant of planning permission, alternatively he would have come to the same conclusion on the basis of public policy on the footing that the authority's duty is primarily one of good government owed to the public as a whole and that to make an authority liable for negligence as a result of granting planning permission would open the floodgates to all manner of claims. Finally, as the third basis for his decision, the judge held that even if there was liability in negligence a breach of duty would normally only give rise to irrecoverable economic loss as in the instant case, which was a further bar to a remedy.

This case bears comparison with *R -v- Exeter City Council* ex parte Thomas [1989] The Times 11 May. This was an Order 53 application for judicial review to quash a grant of planning permission to build 87 residential flats and maisonettes on a previously derelict site in Exeter. The applicants, who processed animal waste and fabricated steel, both "offensive trades", on a 24 hour a day basis were close to the site in question. The applicants reasonably anticipated that their new neighbours, once installed, would bring a nuisance action against the applicants which could well lead to the applicants being forced to close. The authority had taken these matters into account but had decided to grant the planning permission. The authority had not used its powers to seek a discontinuance of the applicants' use of land under s51 of the Town & Country Planning Act 1971 which would have involved the payment of compensation to the applicants.

The main thrust of the application to quash was that the authority was acting arbitrarily or irrationally in using the grant of planning permission to force the applicants out of business instead of paying compensation to the applicants. However the Divisional Court dismissed the application holding that the local authority had conducted a perfectly rational balancing exercise taking into account the interests of the applicant on the one hand and the interests of regenerating the area on the other hand and that unless mala fides could be shown, which it could not, the applicants had no remedy.

In general terms a negligence action against a public authority is attended by special difficulties. No action will lie against a public authority or other body exercising a statutory power for doing that which the legislator has authorised, or where the legislator has imperatively directed that the power is to be exercised in the manner complained of, see *Metropolitan Asylum District -v- Hill* [1881] 6 App CAS 193 at 213 (HL). If a public authority exercises a statutory power negligently there is no liability if the damage results from the bona fide exercise of its discretionary powers, see *East Suffolk Rivers Catchment Board -v- Kent* [1941] AC 74 1944 All ER 527. For decisions of policy no duty of care can arise unless the plaintiff has first proved that the public body was acting *ultra vires*. Where the activity of the body does not involve the exercise of discretion but the body has carried out a purely operational task negligently and in excess of its statutory power, it will be liable in negligence, see *Geddis -v- Proprietors of Bann Reservoir* [1878] 3 APP CAS 430 at 455, 456 (HL).

Accordingly where the alleged tortfeasor is a public authority the practitioner will have to consider a fresh set of principles in determining whether a claim can be mounted.

CHAPTER THIRTEEN

PRIVATE NUISANCE

1. What is Private Nuisance?

Imagine the following scenarios. A person becomes depressed through loss of sleep as a result of a nearby incinerator starting to work around the clock. Someone persistently finds surface damage to trees, or shrubs, or laundry hung out, or car body work at his/her home as a result of emissions from a nearby factory. Methane gas is leaking from an adjacent capped landfill into the foundations of nearby hotel as a result of which it has to close down whilst remedial measures are taken.

These are all potential private nuisance actions.

The actions involve compensation for property damage, loss of custom, and the remedy of injunction. They are proceedings which can be instigated by the individual citizen and for legal aid is available. Yet, the ambit of the tort and the remedies available are by no means clear. This type of action is infrequent and private nuisance has rarely come before the appellate courts in recent times. R.A. Buckley (The Law of Nuisance 1981) comments that "it is difficult to overestimate the day to day importance of the law of nuisance. The frequency with which disputes arise between neighbouring occupiers, giving rise to a need for legal advice and sometimes to litigation, is beyond question", and yet, as he points out, his book was the first to consider nuisance exclusively for more than 50 years.

In fact private nuisance has some significant advantages over its more fashionable rival, negligence. An injunction is an available remedy here, whereas this is not the case in a negligence action. Fault on the part of the defendant does not need to be established to the same extent as in a negligence action. The fact that the defendant has used "best practical means" is not an absolute defence in a private nuisance action, as it is in most statutory nuisance actions. Exemplary damages are available in a private nuisance action, whereas they are not available in an action based on negligence or breach of statutory duty.

2. The Principles

(a) Definition of private nuisance

The essence of the tort and its jurisprudential history is "unlawful interference with a person's use of or enjoyment of land, or of some right over, or in connection with it".

(b) Interest in land

It is traditionally stated that the first pre-condition of a private nuisance action is that the plaintiff must have an interest in land, and the tort focuses upon protecting the plaintiff's use and enjoyment of this interest. The leading case on the subject is the decision in the Court of Appeal in *Malone -v- Laskey* [1907] KB 141. Malone's case was an action for personal injuries. An iron bracket on the premises had been dislodged by vibrations causing the plaintiff personal injury and she sought to maintain actions in both nuisance and negligence. For reasons which are irrelevant for the present purposes (and which were reversed by *Billings v Riden* (1957)3 All ER 1 HL some 50 years later) the action in negligence was hopeless. This left the action in private nuisance, which also failed on the grounds that the plaintiff, as a mere licensee, had no interest in the property. Interestingly, none of the three members of the Court of Appeal expressed any doubt as to whether personal injuries was a recoverable head of damage in the tort of private nuisance, a proposition for which there is a dearth of authority.

Be that as it may, in the ensuing decades *Malone -v- Laskey* was relied upon as establishing that a plaintiff could not bring a private nuisance action without showing a proprietary interest in the property. It is this emphasis on ownership of an interest in land which has made private nuisance virtually valueless in redressing many complaints of environmental pollution under modern conditions. Thus spouses, children, cohabitees, lodgers who live in the property have all been denied the remedy although their interest in having their use and enjoyment of it protected, at least so far as "sensibility" claims involving noise, dust, smell and so forth are concerned, is just as important as that of an owner or tenant,

In *Khorasandjian -v- Bush* [1993] 3 WLR 476 [1993] 3 All ER 669 the Court of Appeal upheld the grant of relief in a private nuisance action in the context of harassing and abusive telephone calls at the instance of a plaintiff who was a lodger in the house, without any proprietary interest.

In the Docklands cases, which concern alleged interference with television reception and dust nuisance and where a significant number of the plaintiffs do not have a proprietary interest, the question of whether it is necessary to have an interest in the property to claim in private nuisance was heard by HHJ Richard Havery QC, sitting as an official referee, as a preliminary issue in the case. He held that a plaintiff must have an interest in property amounting to not less than a right to exclusive possession of the land, including a right shared by two or more persons to exclusive possession of it, *Hunter and Others -v- Canary Wharf Ltd* The Independent 20 December 1994.

The court found that *Khorasandjian* was an extension of the law of nuisance to cases of harassment, the connection with land was more tenuous than in traditional nuisance cases, and that private nuisance was simply a peg on which to hang a needed remedy. Malone -v- Laskey remained good law on "traditional nuisance" and this authority accordingly was applicable. The decision is the subject of an appeal.

(c) Continuous state of affairs

The general rule is that, in order to constitute nuisance, the interference must arise from a "continuous state of affairs" on land not belonging to the plaintiff, *Bolton -v- Stone* [1951] AC 850. As has recently been clarified by the House of Lords in *Cambridge Water*, the rule in *Rylands -v- Fletcher* was a development of the law of nuisance which enabled a remedy, exceptionally, to be provided for an isolated escape as opposed to a continuous state of affairs.

(d) Categories of private nuisance

There are three categories of nuisance: encroachment on the plaintiff's land, where the nuisance closely resembles trespass; physical damage to the plaintiff's land; and interference with the plaintiff's use and enjoyment of the land (which is usually referred to as a "sensibility" claim).

(e) Physical damage

The term physical damage covers damage to premises, trees, shrubs and chattel damage such as livestock on the plaintiff's land (eg *St Helen's Smelting Co -v- Tipping* [1865] 11 HL Cas 642). The term also covers damage to curtains or carbody work, (*Halsey -v- Esso Petroleum Co Ltd* [1961] 1 WLR 683). The physical damage must be material or substantial and damage is one of the essentials of nuisance. Its existence must be proved, except in those cases in which it is presumed by law to exist, see *R -v- Battsby* [1850] 16 QB 1022; *AG -v- Kingston on Thames Corporation* [1865] 34 LJ Ch 481; *Salvin -v- North Brancepeth Coal Co* [1874] 9 Ch App 705.

As to the difficult question of what constitutes "substantial damage" for the tort of nuisance, similar consideration appear to apply to those already set out in the tort of negligence, see pages125-127. Again, in relation to the overlapping topic of limitation, the matter is dealt with in that chapter and we underline that the Latent Damage Act 1986 which clearly applies to negligence actions apparently has no application in nuisance action which is a distinction of importance.

The airborne pollution "actual damage" cases have involved a number of industrial processes. The *St Helen's* case involved copper smelting. *Walter -v- Selfe* [1851] 4 De G & Sm 315 involved brick burning. *Salvin -v- North Brancepeth Coal Co* involved emissions from a coking plant and *Wood -v- Conway Corporation* [1914] 2 Ch 47 involved gas works. *Halsey -v- Esso Petroleum* involved smuts from an oil distribution dept. *Pwllbach Colliery Co Ltd -v- Woodman* [1915] AC 634 HL involved coal dust from a coal stocking depot that soiled shop produce.

In all these cases relief was granted to the persons affected by the industrial processes, notwithstanding arguments put forward by the industrial operators to the general effect that they were using best practicable means to reduce or eliminate the pollution and that they were fulfilling an important function by supplying goods and services and employing people.

(f) Sensibility claims

The third category, injury to use and enjoyment, are "sensibility" claims where no physical harm, is established, but there is injury to enjoyment caused by such things as noise, smell and dust, odour, vibration and, semble, interference with television reception *Hunter and Others -v- Canary Wharf Ltd* The Independent 20 December 1994. This is the subject of an appeal in the Court of Appeal due to be heard in July 1995.

The standard of "injury" needed to found an action in a sensibility claim is well settled. It is "inconvenience materially interfering with the ordinary physical comfort of human existence, not merely according to elegant or dainty modes and habits of living, but according to plain and sober and simple notions and habits obtaining among the English people".

Accordingly the court will not allow the hypersensitive plaintiff to impose excessive restraints on his neighbour, see *Robinson -v- Kilvert* [1889] 41 Ch D 88. It is interesting to compare the position in negligence where, of course, the defendant must take his victim as he finds him, however susceptible he may be.

In *Devon Lumber Co Ltd -v- MacNeill and Others*, New Brunswick Court of Appeal, [1988] 45 DLR (4th) 300, the plaintiff, at first instance, recovered personal injury damages in private nuisance against a cedar mill which created fine dust which exacerbated the plaintiff's allergy. On appeal the award to the plaintiff was reduced, it being held that in a nuisance action her allergy must be ignored, so damages were only recoverable using the yardstick of a normal person of ordinary habits and sensibilities.

3. The Court's Approach

The essence of the exercise is that of balancing the defendant's right to conduct his operations as he pleases, with the plaintiff's right to have the use and enjoyment of his neighbouring property without undue interference. In addressing this balancing exercise the courts take a number of matters into account in approaching the central question to be determined on the facts of each case, namely, whether the defendant is using his property reasonably or not.

In *Colls -v- Home and Colonial Stores Ltd* [1904] AC 179 Lord Halsbury said:

"What may be called the uncertainty of the test (i.e. the unreasonable user test) may also be described as its elasticity. A dweller in towns cannot expect to have as pure air, as free from smoke, smell, and noise as if he lived in the country and distant from other dwellings, yet an excess of smoke, smell and noise may give a cause of action, in each of such cases it becomes a question of degree, and whether in each case it amounts to a nuisance which will give a right of action."

While numerous circumstances are taken into account in the balancing exercise the cases show that the three factors most commonly given weight are locality, whether the defendant has used best practical means to minimise interference, and the social value of the defendant's operation.

(a) Locality

Locality is clearly a factor. Lord Halsbury's famous allusion to Bermondsey and Belgravia has been given recent emphasis in the decision by Buckley J in *Gillingham -v- C.V. Medway (Chatham) Dock Co* [1992] 3 WLR 449 [1992] 3 All ER 923.

In that case a former naval dockyard was given planning permission to operate as a commercial port. Access to the port was limited to two residential roads. Very quickly heavy traffic was using the road for 24 hours a day causing great disturbance to the local community.

When the planning application had been made, however, the local authority had been aware that an increase in heavy traffic was likely to take place. The defendant had in fact estimated that some three to four hundred lorry movements would occur per day, thus increasing noise levels, particularly at night. Planning permission had been granted because of the economic benefit of having a commercial port which were considered to outweigh the environmental disadvantages.

In 1990, no doubt faced with many complaints by residents, the local authority commenced an action under s222 of the Local Government Act 1972 seeking an injunction to prevent traffic movement between 7 pm and 7 am on the grounds of public nuisance, (on this point public and private nuisance are indistinguishable). The trial judge ruled that the effect of the grant of planning permission was to change the character of the neighbourhood to the extent that a nuisance action has to be considered in the light of the existing environment, not the one that existed in the past. The local authority's action was dismissed. There was no appeal from this decision, which is perhaps unfortunate since it is far from clear that the principles and reasoning would have been upheld in the Court of Appeal.

Although, in his judgment, Buckley J explicitly approves the proposition that planning permission is not a licence to commit nuisance and that a planning authority has no jurisdiction to authorize nuisance, the basis of his decision, namely that a planning authority can, through its development plans and decisions, alter the character of a neighbourhood so as to render lawful, on the facts, what would otherwise constitute a nuisance is perilously close to achieving the same end by another means.

So far the courts, where the opportunity has arisen, have declined to follow the lead of Buckley J. In *Wheeler and Another -v- J.J. Saunders Ltd and Others*, Court of Appeal, The Times 4th January 1995, planning permissions had been granted for two pig rearing houses. The plaintiffs subsequently brought a successful nuisance action as a result of the smells from the units. The simple question on appeal was whether the planning permission provided a good defence for such an action. The Court of Appeal considered the *Chatham Docks* case and rejected any interpretation giving rise to a wider proposition that a planning decision automatically authorised any nuisance which would inevitably result from it, and dismissed the appeal in *Wheeler's* case upholding the trial judge's award of damages and injunction.

Nonetheless, Lord Justice Peter Gibson in distinguishing the *Chatham Docks* case on the basis that it concerned a major redevelopment with wide consequential environmental affects where the local authority could have been expected to weigh up all the balancing interests was prepared to allow that, in such circumstances, the grant of a subsequent injunction following a nuisance action would not be in the public interest, although he appears to have left open the question of an award of damages. The judge went on to emphasise that it did not follow that such a principle should apply to the grant of every single planning permission: "The court should be slow to acquiesce in the extinction of private rights without compensation as a result of administrative decisions which could not be appealed or were difficult to challenge."

In the Docklands litigation, the defendants sought to rely on Chatham Docks but HHJ Havery QC was not prepared to hold that the planning permission conferred an immunity or unavoidable interference, and this decision is the subject of appeal.

(b) Best practicable means

A second factor which will be taken into consideration is whether the defendant is using best practicable means to eliminate or reduce the inconvenience caused to the plaintiff. The finding that the defendant is not using best practicable means, though not conclusive, may well render the defendant liable in nuisance. On the other hand, the fact that the defendant has used best practicable means is by no means conclusive in the defendant's favour, save in building and construction cases (see section 5 below).

(c) Social Value

The third factor to be brought into account is the social value of the defendant's operation. The "social value" of the defendant's activity is only a factor, but not a conclusive one, in the balancing exercise. For example in Shelfer's case (*Shelfer -v- City of London Electric Lighting Co* [1895] 1 Ch 287) Lindley LJ said "neither has the circumstance that the wrongdoer is in some sense a public benefactor (e.g. a gas or water company or a sewer authority) ever been considered as sufficient reason for refusing to protect by injunction an individual whose rights are being persistently infringed." This dictum was applied by the Court of Appeal in *Kennaway -v- Thompson* [1981] QB 88 where the claim succeeded for an injunction restraining noisy speedboat racing.

4. Foreseeability

In a damages claim in private nuisance the plaintiff must first establish "unreasonable user" by reference to the foregoing factors, and, if he does so, must then establish foreseeability of damage of the relevant type at the date at which the acts or omissions complained of were carried on, *Cambridge Water -v- Eastern Counties Leather*. This is more fully considered in Chapter 22. The ambit of the phrase "damage of the relevant type" is considered in the chapter on Negligence at page 118.

5. Defences

In the standard works the defences of Prescription, Grant of Rights,

Act of God and Act of Trespasser are dealt with. In toxic tort claims however the defence of most importance and that which has seen the most recent development in the case law is the defence of statutory authority.

(a) Statutory Authority

This defence has been the subject of consideration by the House of Lords in three cases in the last decade, *Allen -v- Gulf Oil Refining Ltd* [1981] AC 1001, *Tate & Lyle Industries Ltd -v- GLC* [1983] 2 AC 509 and *Department of Transport -v- North West Water Authority* [1984] AC 336.

In the *Allen* case the residents of a previously quiet village sought to bring nuisance proceedings in respect of the Milford Haven Oil Refinery development. The action was struck out. The House of Lords construed the special Act authorising the construction of the refinery as conferring immunity on the Company provided they could prove it was inevitable that despite their using all reasonable care the local residents would still sustain the harm about which they were complaining. The court was unable to award any damages to the plaintiff as no compensation for that harm was directly given by the Act. The plaintiffs' only remedy was to the extent that the actual nuisance exceeded that for which such immunity was conferred, i.e., to the extent that the Company did not use reasonable care.

Thus, once nuisance has been established, the burden is effectively transferred to the company to show that it has exercised all reasonable care to minimise the nuisance. To the extent that it is able to do so, immunity has been conferred by the courts.

This was well illustrated in *Tate & Lyle -v- GLC*. This action, as in the case of *Allen,* was based on public nuisance, although on this point there is no distinction between public and private nuisance. The GLC, acting with statutory authority, constructed ferry terminals at Woolwich. Because of the faulty design and construction of the ferry terminals the river bed became heavily silted which meant that the plaintiffs had insufficient depth of water to gain access to their jetties. The plaintiffs had to spend more than £500,000 dredging the river to regain access. It was held that the defendants should bear three quarters of this cost and the plaintiffs one quarter on the footing that due diligence by the defendants would still have left the plaintiffs with some dredging to do (hence conferring an immunity) but that, to the extent that the design and construction by the defendants was faulty, no such immunity was conferred.

Whilst it is quite plain that a special Act authorizing a development confers statutory authority and invokes the above principles, it is by no means clear whether lesser instruments are capable of having the same effect. In *Hunter -v- Canary Wharf Ltd,* the docklands action for interference with their television reception, the defendants claimed the Canary Wharf development, being a development undertaken pursuant to Enterprise Zone consents which were in turn expressly authorised by parliament pursuant to the 1980 Local Government Planning and Land Act in which s136(1) has as its object the regeneration of the area, together operated to confer the defence of statutory authority on the defendants' development. HHJ Havery QC rejected this, The Independent 20 December 1994, and the ruling is the subject of an appeal.

It has been held that the grant of a planning permission cannot operate in law to confer the defence of statutory authority, *Wheeler -v- Saunders* (CA) The Times 4 January 1995.

It would be a matter of great concern if there was to be any judicial extension of the special Act principle affording developers and industry a licence to commit what would otherwise be an actionable nuisance. In the planning or licensing stage it is not possible to see all the ramifications of the project. Therefore the plaintiff should not be shut out from taking proceedings based on how the project works out in practice because of a preceding grant of a permission or licence based on how it would work out in theory.

Further, such an extension of this principle would result in many more contests over the grant of permissions and licenses than now take place. The applicants will put forward their hypothesis, and the local residents will put forward their responding arguments. The decision maker will then be left in the somewhat unrealistic position of conferring extensive and long last immunities based on a evaluation of competing hypotheses. It is reassuring, in respect of these observations, to find Lord Justice Peter Gibson expressing the view, in *Wheeler -v- Saunders,* that "the court should be slow to acquiesce in the extinction of private rights without compensation as a result of administrative decisions which could not be appealed and were difficult to challenge."

Another attempt to obtain what the Americans call "statutory pre-emption", ie an immunity providing a compliance with a statutory scheme can be demonstrated, occurred in the context of a local authority certificate for noisy construction works pursuant to s60 of the Control of Pollution Act 1974. In *Lloyds Bank -v- Trollop & Colls* [1986] 35 BLR 34 the Court of Appeal held that the fact that a local authority, exercising its powers under s60 of the Control of Pollution Act 1974, had granted a certificate allowing certain working hours for a construction site did not confer an immunity on the developer from injunction proceedings in private nuisance at the instance of a private party seeking further and greater restrictions on the hours that could be worked than those laid down in the s60 Certificate.

Under the Environmental Protection Act 1990 there is an extensive system for the licensing of scheduled industries involving a far more exacting scrutiny of the applicant's activity than has ever previously been the case. It may well be that the defendant will try to use the existence of an operating licence or permit granted by a statutory authority as a defence against any nuisance action. This point remains to be tested in English courts.

(b) Reasonable precautions taken

Where the defendant is the creator of the nuisance the fact that the defendant has taken reasonable precautions to reduce or prevent the nuisance will not constitute a defence, *Cambridge Water -v- Eastern Counties Leather* reaffirming established law, for example Lord Symonds in *Read -v- Lyons* [1947] AC 156: "If a man commits a legal nuisance, it is no answer to his injured neighbour that he took the utmost care not to commit it. There the liability is strict."

If, on the other hand, the defendant is not the creator of the nuisance, but is a "continuer" in the sense that he comes into ownership or occupation of the land and subsequently has knowledge actual or constructive that a nuisance is being caused, then the fact that he has used all reasonable means to reduce or prevent the nuisance continuing does constitute a defence to a nuisance action see *Goldman -v- Hargrave* [1967] 1 AC 645, [1966] 2 All ER 989, *Leakey -v- National Trust for places of historic interest or natural beauty* [1981] All ER 17, [1982] WLR 65, and the *Cambridge Water -v- Eastern Counties Leather*. The significance of this distinction is developed further in chapter 22 on land contamination.

In this context, however, the practitioner should beware if the proposed defendant is a statutory undertaker exercising powers rather than duties. Public authorities have special responsibilities which mean their liabilities have to be considered in the light of statutory functions, see for example *Dear -v- Thames Water* [1993] 4 Water Law 116.

(c) Coming to the Nuisance

It is commonly thought that it is a defence that the plaintiff "comes to the nuisance." It is not. The Court of Appeal so held in *Miller - v- Jackson* [1977] QB 966 where the plaintiffs moved to a new residential estate which bordered a longstanding cricket pitch from which balls were intermittently hit into the plaintiffs' garden. In so doing the Court of Appeal affirmed the old authority of *Bliss -v- Hall* [1838] 4 Bing NC 183. The exception to this rule is where a right has been acquired to any easement by prescription, i.e. for more than a 20 year term. We know of no reported cases in which a prescriptive right has been upheld as a defence to nuisance action.

(d) One of many

It is also sometimes assumed that a company defending a nuisance action will succeed by saying that the company was "one of many." Again this is wrong. "One of many" does not constitute a defence. It was so held in the water pollution case of *Blair -v- Deakin* [1887] 57 LT 522 where several manufacturers, having their works upstream, caused nuisance to a riparian owner below. it was held no answer in a nuisance action brought by the riparian owner against one of the manufacturers for such manufacturer to say that the share he contributed to the nuisances was infinitesimal and inappreciable. It should be emphasised, however, that this was an application for injunction. It was by no means clear the same approach would be taken in a damages action, although *Graham v. Rechem* has established that it would be, (see Chapter 23).

6. Remedies

a) Injunctions

An injunction is one of the most significant of the available remedies in private nuisance actions. For example in *Crump -v- Lambert* [1867] LR 3 Eq 409 an injunction was granted which would have had the effect of closing a factory in Walsall in a "sensibility" case. This was notwithstanding the point that Walsall was an industrial locality, and an acceptance that the factory served the public interest in conferring economic benefit on the community. In *Allison -v- Merton Sutton and Wandsworth Area Health Authority* [1975] CLY 2450 an injunction was granted where the noise from a hospital boiler kept the plaintiff awake at night resulting in feelings of depression although not psychiatric illness. In *Halsey -v- Esso Petroleum Co Ltd* [1961] 1 WLR 683 an injunction in private nuisance was granted in respect of noise from the boilers, the Esso plant generally, and from Esso's vehicles. In *A.G. -v- Gastonia Coaches* [1977] RTR 219 the judge granted a suspended injunction where a firm's coaches emitted diesel fumes and "revved" their engines in a residential street. The general principles of an injunctive relief are dealt with in Chapter 18.

b) Compensation for property damage

It is settled law that damages are recoverable in respect of property damages (*St Helen's Smelting Co -v- Tipping* [1865] 11 HL Cas 642) and chattel damage *(St Helen's Smelting and Halsey)*. The property and chattel must, of course, be connected with the plaintiff's land, for example the livestock in *St Helen's Smelting* and the washing hanging on the line in *Halsey*. By contrast, in the *Halsey* case where the car was parked, not on the plaintiff's property, but in the road between the plaintiff's house and the factory, the bodywork damage from oil smuts was not recoverable in private nuisance. It was, however, held to be recoverable in public nuisance. Had Mr Halsey had a driveway to his house in which he habitually parked his car, then the damage to his car would have been recoverable as a private nuisance.

c) Compensation for Personal Injury

Surprisingly, so far as damages for personal injury are concerned, there does not appear to be any authority directly in point. Some academic authors take the view that personal injury damages are recoverable as long as they are consequential upon the invasion to property, eg a respiratory illness would be recoverable in a nuisance action based on air pollution (see Street, Tort p329, Clerk and Lindsell on Torts 16th ed p1366) Fleming, Law of Torts (7th ed p412). On the other hand Buckley (The Law of Nuisance) thinks that the better view is that an allegation of negligence is generally essential.

On the one hand it seems odd that you can recover damages for injury to your cat but not to yourself in a private nuisance action based on the same industrial emissions. On the other hand, as Buckley points out, it seems anomalous to create a special class of plaintiff who, by virtue of having an interest in land, does not have to prove negligence to recover damages. The arguments are finely balanced and no doubt the courts will be called upon to determine the issue. An opportunity certainly arose in *Malone -v- Laskey* [1907] 2 KB 141 where the Court of Appeal dismissed a private nuisance action claiming compensation for personal injury on the grounds that the plaintiff had no interest in the property. None of the members of the court expressed any misgivings in relation to the claim for personal injury damages in any action brought in private nuisance.

The only relevant judicial utterances in recent times are obiter dicta in some of the speeches in *Read -v- Lyons* [1947] AC 156, a decision on *Rylands -v- Fletcher* liability in a claim involving personal injury. Lord Macmillan said:

"Whatever may have been the law of England in early times I am of the opinion that as the law now stands an allegation of negligence is in general essential to the relevancy of an action of reparation for personal injuries."

It is difficult to reconcile these dicta with settle authority for liability for breach of statutory duty in injury cases, although this case law has emerged since *Read -v- Lyons*.

Although Lord Goff in his speech in *Cambridge Water* explicitly declined to address the recoverability of personal injury damages in nuisance actions, in other respects Lord Goff cited with approval Professor Newark's appeal for orthodoxy in the law of nuisance in respect of which Professor Newark proclaimed personal injury compensation to be a heretical remedy in a nuisance action and appealed for the courts to follow the lead given by Lord Macmillan in *Read -v- Lyons*.

d) Quantum in "sensibility" claims

In property damage and personal injury claims quantum will be determined on principles and precedents which are fully set out in McGregor on Damages and Kemp and Kemp on Quantum. However the principles and precedents in respect of quantum in sensibility cases are a good deal more difficult to locate.

The only guidance from the Court of Appeal in recent times was in the case of *Bone -v- Seale* [1975] 1 WLR 9. The defendant owned a pig farm from which offensive smells emanated from time to time giving rise to an actionable nuisance intermittently over a period of some 12 years. At first instance the judge calculated the damages at £500 per annum making a total of £6,000 (current equivalent £27,500). The Court of Appeal allowed the defendant's appeal on quantum and substituted a figure of £1,000 (current equivalent £5,000). The court stated that damages in personal injury cases may provide a loose analogy not involving "anything approaching a precise or accurate comparison" but simply looking at the injury cases and keeping them "at the back of one's mind" in arriving at the figure for the nuisance suffered by the plaintiff. Accordingly damages should not exceed in nuisance actions the general damage scale for personal injuries awards. As the Court of Appeal pointed out in Bone, in the money of the day £6,000 was the value of "a serious and permanent loss of amenity as the result of a very serious injury" and therefore too high for a transient and intermittent nuisance.

In *Halsey -v- Esso Petroleum Co Ltd* [1961] 1 WLR 683 Veale J awarded £200 (current value £2,300). This award was in respect of a nuisance broadly put on two bases: pollution of the atmosphere and noise. The pollution took the form of smells and of acidic deposits and oily smuts (laundry and car body damage being recoverable in a separate special damage claim), and the noise comprised noise from boilers pumps and vehicles; the vehicles consisting of tankers passing very close to the plaintiff's house at intervals throughout the night giving decibel readings of about 83 decibels. It is plain from the judgment that in making the award the court had in mind 3 years of "very considerable discomfort" for the plaintiff since the introduction of the night shift at the end of 1957.

In *Bone -v- Seale* [1975] 1 WLR 9 the Court of Appeal approved the award of damages which the judge had made in Halsey.

In *Emms -v- Polya* [1973] 227 EG 1659 Plowman J awarded £350 general damages for 1 year's disruption resulting from building works taking place on the other side of a party wall. The actionable nuisance consisted of intermittent hammering, banging, drilling and the falling of rubble. The current equivalent of this sum is £2,300. This decision does not seem to have been considered in Bone.

In summary, and using current values, the reported awards have been £2,300 for 1 year (Emms), £2,300 for 3 years (Halsey) and £5,000 for 12 years (Bone). It is not as difficult to reconcile these awards as it may at first appear. Emms was the most continuous interference and Bone was very intermittent. Furthermore, there is bound to be a discount for past years in a case such as Bone where the nuisance has gone on for many years.

Other guidance may be obtained from damages levels in cases where tenants have suffered discomfort arising from a landlord's failure to repair. A good starting point in *Watts -v- Morrow* [1991] 1 WLR 421. Probably less useful, because they are cases in contract, are the "holiday" cases, but, again, they may offer some assistance.

e) Loss of profits

Although we can find no decided case in which a plaintiff has recovered pure loss of profits as such in a private nuisance action this head of damage is recoverable in public nuisance and should also be recoverable in private nuisance.

We would distinguish the negligence cases on irrecoverability of pure economic loss on two grounds.

First, that line of cases is primarily concerned with the question of foreseeability of loss which is relevant to a negligence action but not to nuisance where, once the wrong is established, liability is strict. It is this point which aligns private with public nuisance.

Secondly, the line of cases culminating in *Murphy -v- Brentwood District Council* [1991] 1 AC 398 does not apply to claims for direct damage and a loss of profit claim arising from a pollution incident will probably be held to be direct damage.

In any event it is settled law that damages for "diminution in value" of the premises which are the victim of the nuisance are recoverable in private nuisance and this claim will usually involve a loss of profit claim. For example in the typical case of a hotel's trade being impaired by a neighbour's negligently conducted construction operations then the consequential loss of trading profit is reflected in the balance sheet (viz. lower retained profits of the business) and is thus recoverable as diminution in value of the hotel business.

That said, following *Caparo Industries plc -v- Dickman* [1990] 2

AC 605, the principle consideration is "policy" and it becomes a question of judicial discretion whether pure economic loss is recoverable in private nuisance. We predict that the court will allow such recovery where the damage is properly foreseeable and consequential in the sense expressed by the Privy Council, particularly Lord Reid, in *Wagon Mound No.2.*

It should also be emphasised that an injunction to restrain, say, a nuisance building development is generally unlikely to be granted, (because for example of consequent injury to third party rights), and in such an instance, absent the right to loss of profit the plaintiff will have no remedy.

f) Exemplary Damages

Exemplary damages are available in private nuisance, but confined to those cases of private nuisance where there is deliberate and wilful interference with the plaintiff's rights of enjoyment of land where the defendant has calculated a profitable benefit for him will exceed will the damages he may have to pay, see *AB -v- South West Water Services Ltd* [1993] 1 All ER 609, at 621 . Sir Thomas Bingham MR in the same case seems to have considered that exemplary damages were available in private nuisance without being confined to any particular class of private nuisance.

7. The award must not exceed extent of nuisance

A note of caution should be sounded particularly to practitioners in the "all or nothing" world (contributory negligence apart), of negligence claims.

Where in a nuisance claim the defendant incurs liability because his otherwise lawful activity causes excessive interference with the plaintiff's use or enjoyment of land, the court will ensure that the defendant is only required to pay compensation for the extent to which his interference is unreasonable and hence actionable. Thus in many cases there will be a discount because of the effect on the plaintiff of those activities which the defendant could lawfully have carried on.

This limiting principle is likely to be of particular relevance in construction works cases. Indeed in the leading case, *Andreae -v- Selfridge* [1938] Ch 1, where the plaintiff succeeded in proving that a nuisance had been caused by the defendants as a result of noise and dust produced during their building operations it was emphasised that a lesser degree of interference would not have been actionable, and, in reducing damages which had been awarded at first instance, Sir Wilfred Greene MR said:

"... one must be careful not to penalise the defendant company by throwing into the scales against it the loss.. caused by operations which it was legitimately entitled to carry out. It can be made liable only in respect of matters, in which it has crossed the permissible line."

8. Building and Construction Operations

Construction and building operations, including demolition, almost invariably cause some disturbance through noise, dust and vibration to the local residents. By their very nature such works are temporary, although in the case of a huge project, such as the London Docklands development, temporary can mean many years. Faced with the need to respect the public interest in regeneration, redevelopment and restoration the courts have evolved special principles for dealing with this category of cases.

The law is well settled and was restated by the Court of Appeal in *Andreae -v- Selfridge & Co* [1938] Ch 1 by Sir Wilfred Greene MR dealing with a case of demolition in the West End of London as follows:

"The Judge found that "by reason of all three operations, there was a substantial interference with the comfort of the plaintiff in the reasonable occupation and use of her house, such that, assuming damage to be established, an actionable nuisance would be constituted. But it was said that when one is dealing with temporary operations, such as demolition and re-building, everybody has to put up with a certain amount of discomfort, because operations of that kind cannot be carried on at all without a certain amount of dust. Therefore, the rule with regard to interference must be read subject to this qualification, and there can be no dispute about it, but in respect of operations of this character, such as demolition and building, if they are reasonably carried on and all proper and reasonable steps are taken to ensure that no undue inconvenience is caused to neighbours, whether from noise, dust or other reasons the neighbours must put up with it."

In construction cases, therefore, nuisance is effectively put on the same footing as negligence, with one significant difference. Whereas in a negligence action it is for the plaintiff to establish fault on the defendant's part, in a construction nuisance case, once the plaintiff has established the *prima facie* actionable nuisance arising from the construction works, the burden shifts to the defendant to show non-negligence in relation to prevention and abatement of nuisance. This latter distinction is however more apparent than real. A plaintiff would still need the reassurance of technical evidence which would probably rebut such a defence before launching his or her proceedings.

In determining whether the defendant has or has not taken all reasonable precautions it will not avail the defendant, in general terms, to advance the propositions either that a particular precaution would cost him more, or, (as in the case of a restriction of hours of working, e.g. at night) would delay the termination of works. Yet again, however, there is a balancing exercise here. The court is most unlikely to bankrupt the project at the instigation of local residents temporarily affected.

So, for example, in *Hart -v- Aga Khan Foundation* (unreported Court of Appeal 13 February 1981 Bar Library Transcript 1980 M4893) the plaintiff, who lived in Thurlow Place, brought injunction proceedings in respect of the construction of the Ismaili Cultural Centre opposite the Victoria and Albert Museum in the Cromwell Road. Lawson J granted injunctions relating to the type of equipment to be used, and restricting the hours of work. The Court of Appeal substantially set aside the injunction on the grounds that the restricted hours would rise to a cost over-run of the order of £1.2 million. However all major construction projects have built in timescales underpinned by financial penalties and involving third party obligations and it remains to be seen how far the courts will permit the contractual structure to limit the plaintiff's ability to obtain relief in nuisance.

In the Hart case Stephenson LJ thought it right to require greater precautions to be taken when the temporary work of demolition and rebuilding is likely to take a matter of months or years rather than only weeks or days. If this principle of proportionality is invoked by the courts huge projects taking 5 years or more would call for state of the art techniques to minimise dust, vibration and noise. This should mean that the courts will not just consider equipment available on the English market, but what is available world-wide.

Time restrictions and the introduction of best equipment costs money and the residents actions will always be met with the "injury to profits" defence. Nonetheless, in the instance of a long term construction project the balance ought to favour the resident. Construction projects lasting days or weeks usually enhance the amenity of the neighbourhood because they involve refurbishment and restoration so that, at the price of temporary inconvenience, the plaintiff will see some long term benefit. In the case of a long term project however, the impact is usually a permanent and radical alteration of the neighbourhood, involving the destruction of a community sometimes of very long standing and the relocation of many of its members. In this instance there is little if any long term enhancement for the plaintiff to balance against the years of injury to amenity whilst construction is undertaken. In every sense, the profit, social and environmental gain will belong to persons other than the long standing residents.

CHAPTER FOURTEEN

PUBLIC NUISANCE

To understand the principles behind public nuisance it is again helpful to consider typical scenarios. A whole community is up in arms because of the repeated and foul stench from an animal waste processing business. A neighbourhood complains *en masse* when a papermill which had worked a 12 hour day now works a 24 hour day giving rise to night time noise and lorry movements, forklift trucks and bailing machines. A village downwind of an old quarry, long disused, is concerned to find that the quarry is now being filled with thousands of tons of fibrous asbestos waste. The population of a given area finds the supply of drinking water has been contaminated making it temporarily unfit for human consumption.

These are all potential public nuisance claims. There is a lot of common ground between public and private nuisance, and in many instances claims can be made good in both. However, there are significant differences, particularly in relation to remedies, most notably that damages for personal injury are definitely available in public nuisance. Indeed public nuisance where particular damage can be shown (see below) is a formidable weapon in the hands of the private citizen who seeks a remedy for an environmental wrong and it is surprising that it has not received more attention and more use.

1. Principles

Public nuisance is one which inflicts damage, injury or inconvenience on all the Queen's subjects or on all members of a class who come within the sphere or neighbourhood of its operation. However, it may affect some to a greater extent that others.

There are many statutory provisions which impose penalties for nuisances affecting public health, morals and comfort. However, the common law liability remains, and any person who by any act unwarranted by law or by any omission to carry out a legal duty endangers the life, health, property, morals or comfort of the public commits a criminal offence known as public nuisance.

Stephens Digest of Criminal Law (9th edn, p179) describes public nuisance in this way:

"Every person is guilty of an offence at common law, known as public nuisance, who does an act not warranted by law, or omits to discharge a legal duty, if the effect of the act or omission is to endanger the life, health, property, morals, or the comfort of the public, or to obstruct the public in the exercise or enjoyment of rights common to all her Majesty's subjects."

By way of recent example the South West Water Authority was convicted of public nuisance in the Crown Court at Exeter arising out of the Camelford Water contamination incident in 1988. The criminal conviction for public nuisance was pleaded in the civil claim for compensation for personal injury arising out of the water pollution incident.

The essential ingredients are:

(i) an actionable wrong and (ii) material effect on a large number of people.

As to the second point, the wrong may affect some members of the public to a greater extent than others. The question whether the number of persons affected is sufficient to constitute a class is one of fact. Not every member needs to be affected in the neighbourhood. The leading case on the point is *Attorney General -v- PYA Quarries Ltd* [1957] 2 QB 169 in which Romer LJ said (at p184):

"It is, however, clear in my opinion that any nuisance (public) which materially affects the reasonable comfort and convenience of life of a class of Her Majesty's subjects. The sphere of the nuisance may be described generally as "the neighbourhood"; but the question whether the local community within that sphere comprises a sufficient number of persons to constitute a class of the public is a question of fact in every case. It is not necessary, in my judgment, to prove that every member of the class has been injuriously affected; it is sufficient to show that a representative cross-section of the class has been so affected for an injunction to issue."

This passage was adopted by HHJ Havery QC sitting as an Official Referee in ruling, in the context of the Docklands claims in nuisance based on interference with the reception of television broadcasts, that 600 plaintiffs constituted a class of the public sufficient to found a case of public nuisance.

2. Who May Bring Proceedings in Public Nuisance

Public nuisance actions, in modern times, are usually brought by local authorities. Importantly, where certain specific matters can be established, individual citizens can bring public nuisance actions and this is also considered below. Finally, the Attorney General still has a jurisdiction, now rarely exercised, and we make reference to this.

(a) Local authorities: statutory nuisance

s.222 of the Local Government Act 1972 allows local authorities to institute civil proceedings "in their own names".

A good example of the local authority system at work in this field is *Shoreham By Sea Urban District Council -v- Dolphin Canadian Proteins Ltd* [1972] LGR 261. The defendants owned a long established factory in an industrial area. The factory produced feeding stuffs, fertiliser and tallow from boiling down chicken feathers, chicken offal, fats, bones and other forms of offal. Emission of unpleasant smells arising from his processing was a nuisance to local inhabitants.

The evidence of nuisance was compelling, consisting of, for example, the fact that school situated about 100 yards away from the factory occasionally had to keep the windows closed in summer such that the children were so hot they were unable to pay attention to what they were doing. Another nearby factory found that on occasion its workers could not eat their lunch because the smell from the defendants' premises affected their stomachs, and, of course, there were numerous complaints from local householders who had to keep their windows closed and could not sit out in their gardens in the summer. Mr. Justice Donaldson as he then was reminded himself that this was a "sensibility" case and that this was an industrial area. The local inhabitants were not entitled to expect to sit in a sweet smelling orchard. He was not however satisfied the best practicable means to abate had in fact been employed ("there is no profit in anti-pollution measures"), and he would have granted an injunction.

In fact the defendant company gave undertakings to abate the nuisance within 9 months, but breached the undertakings. The local authority then moved for leave to issue a writ of sequestration against the defendant company for contempt of court. The court stayed its hand and substituted a heavy fine for contempt.

Nowadays the local authority would bring such proceedings by way of statutory nuisance under s79 of the Environmental Protection Act 1990, and particularly s79(1)(d): "any dust, steam, smell or other effluvia arising on industrial, trade or business premises and being prejudicial to health of a nuisance". It is however a complete defence under s80(7) of the Act to show that best practicable means were used to prevent or counteract the effects of the nuisance.

However, a citizens action based in common law nuisance (see below) has a better prospect of success, because, whilst the use of best practicable means will be a factor to be taken into account by the court in looking at the reasonableness of the defendant's conduct, it is not conclusive. Accordingly parliament has conferred a statutory defence on an alleged polluter facing local authority proceedings in statutory nuisance which the polluter will not enjoy if the citizen brings a common law nuisance action.

When a neighbourhood action group, suffering substantial inconvenience from an industrial operation, having exhausted negotiations with the industrial operator, then goes to the local environmental health officer the two legal remedies which the local authority will have at the forefront of its mind will be statutory nuisance proceedings under Part III of the Environmental Protection Act 1990 and common law public nuisance. Where the local authority is prepared to act, this may well save the aggrieved citizen much time and trouble.

It must be said that the local authority will not always act and even when it does there are very clear limits to what such an action can achieve for the aggrieved individual. In the first place a local authority common law public nuisance action may only achieve an injunction to stop the nuisance. It cannot achieve compensation and damages for the aggrieved citizens. Whilst for most citizens the abatement of the nuisance will be more significant than the money, in circumstances where abatement is impossible money compensation is at least a mitigating factor.

Further where the nuisance has gone on for a long period and has affected a lot of people, the compensation claim could be worth a substantial amount of money. In any case the local authority may decide that any injunction is unlikely to be awarded or, in an interlocutory case, that it is unwilling to give a cross-undertaking in damages. Although it should be noted that the Crown and other public authorities seeking to enforce the law have been held to be exceptions to the usual rule on undertakings as to damages *Kirklees BC -v- Wickes Building Supplies Ltd* [1992] 3 WLR 170.

Every local authority has a finite budget and it is bound to prioritise in terms of the number of industrial processes it is prepared to take on in the courts in any given period. This means, inevitably, some meritorious cases may not be taken up by a local authority.

(b) Citizens' public nuisance actions

Accordingly there will be cases where, for the above and a myriad of other possible reasons, the local authority will not be willing to act and, if any remedy is to be sought, it must by the citizen or, more likely, citizens group perhaps with the help of the local law centre.

A private individual may bring an action in his own name in respect of a public nuisance when, and only when, he can show that he has suffered some particular, foreseeable and substantial damage over and above that sustained by the public at large, or when the interference with the public right involves a violation of some private right of his own.

As to the requirement of foreseeability, this has recently been reaffirmed by the House of Lords in the *Cambridge Water* case. What remains unclear is the degree of specificity with which the type of damage complained of must be foreseen, see the discussion on this point in chapter 13.

The other pre-condition is that in order to bring public nuisance proceedings the individual citizen will have to satisfy the court that he or she suffers "particular damage" over and above that sustained by the public at large.

Ordinarily this ought not to be a hard test to fulfil. So, for example, in *Tate & Lyle -v- GLC* [1983] 2 AC 509, it was held that the interference with the public right of navigation of the river was a public nuisance and the fact that the plaintiffs could not use their jetties was a particular damage enabling the plaintiffs to bring their own action successfully in public nuisance.

In *Halsey -v- Esso Petroleum* [1961] 1 WLR 683, the smuts descending on vehicles in the public street were held to a public nuisance but the damage to the plaintiff's car was particular damage entitling the plaintiff to claim damages in public nuisance. In the same case the defendants were held liable in public nuisance for the noise of their lorries entering the plant at night in respect of which the plaintiff had suffered particular damage in that his sleep was disrupted.

In the Docklands nuisance claims for interference with television reception the defendants contended, as a preliminary issue, that the plaintiffs in those proceedings failed the "particular damage over and above" test. HHJ Havery QC declined to deal with that point as a preliminary issue, ruling that he would need to hear the evidence before giving judgment.

However, the defendants took an additional point, claiming that the "particular damage" not only had to be "over and above" that sustained by the public at large, but also "different in kind" from that suffered by the public at large. They sought to rely principally on *Ricket -v- Metropolitan Railway Co.* [1867] LR 2 Hl 175. In relation to obstruction of a highway, Lord Chelmsford LC said (p190):

> "It is doubtful whether the owner of the house sustained any injury different in kind, though it might be greater in degree, from that of the rest of the public; and therefore it is questionable whether he could have maintained an action if the distinction had been created without the authority of parliament."

Again, HHJ Havery QC ruled that he needed to hear the full facts on this point. He commented that the concept of difference in kind is not sufficiently precise for it to be desirable for the court to make a pronouncement on the point in the absence of facts.

Whilst therefore in certain instances establishing "particular damage" may involve difficulty, once the pre-condition has been satisfied, the individual citizen is in as good a position as the local authority to sue in public nuisance for damages and injunction.

(c) The Attorney General

The unique constitutional position of the Attorney General has long been recognised. In *Gouriet -v- Union of Post Office Workers* [1978] AC 435 it was regarded as settled that he alone stands as *parens patriae* and therefore normally only he can bring a public action in respect of "public wrongs". Unfortunately the Attorney is not seen very often, partly because the local authorities now do his work, partly because he is not often asked and partly because, when asked he wants to know where the money is coming from to underwrite the legal costs of his intervention.

All civil proceedings brought in respect of public nuisance other than a private action by an individual who has suffered particular damage or by a local authority in its own name to protect the inhabitants of its area must therefore be brought with the sanction and in the name of the Attorney General. If, therefore, a citizen, or group of citizens, was unable to satisfy the "particular damage" test and was unable to persuade the local authority to bring public nuisance or statutory nuisance proceedings to protect the inhabitants of the areas, the citizen or group of citizens could nonetheless apply to the Attorney General who would have jurisdiction to bring the proceedings, notwithstanding that no "particular damage" could be established.

3. Establishing public nuisance

In terms of establishing the nuisance the court will take into account similar factors, ie "locality", "best practicable means" and social value as in sensibility claims and private nuisance where the conduct or misconduct of an industrial operation is concerned. Defences to a claim in public nuisance are also similar, notably the defence of statutory authority, the defence which was used with partial success in the Tate & Lyle case (*Tate & Lyle -v- GLC* [1983] 2 AC 509).

In general terms, unless specifically decided otherwise, private nuisance principles apply to public nuisance because, as Sir Thomas Bingham MR put it, "public nuisance is private nuisance writ large" *AB -v- South West Water Services Ltd* [1993] 1 All ER 609 (627G). In the context of that case Sir Thomas Bingham did point to two significant distinctions, namely that public nuisance is a criminal offence, and that public nuisance is likely to lead to many complaints and therefore many plaintiffs.

From the standpoint of the practitioner who is considering possible proceedings, the two most important distinctions between public nuisance and private nuisance are probably these:

(i) do not need an interest in property to bring an action in public nuisance;

(ii) personal injury damages are definitely recoverable in public nuisance.

4. Remedies

a. Personal Injury

The importance of using public nuisance, where it is an available remedy, is further enhanced by the fact that some remedies which are questionable in private nuisance are available in public nuisance. In particular it seems well established that damages for personal injuries are recoverable in public nuisance, see *Castle -v- St Augustine's Links Ltd* [1922] 38 TLR 615, in which the plaintiff road user recovered damages in public nuisance when blinded in one eye by a golf ball misdriven from the tee on the defendant's golf course.

We consider that the recoverability of personal injuries in a public nuisance action is so well settled that it is likely to survive. That said, the question of the recoverability of damages for personal injury in the tort of nuisance as a whole must be regarded as due for a full reconsideration by the courts in the light of some parts of Lord Goff's speech in *Cambridge Water -v- Eastern Counties Leather* in which, in certain respects, Lord Goff endorsed Professor Newark's treatise on the law of nuisance, *Cambridge Water -v- Eastern Counties Leather* [1994] 1 All ER 53 at 69 and 70.

b. Economic loss

It seems clear that pure economic loss is recoverable in public nuisance (e.g. traders loss of profit) where it is not recoverable in negligence. In *Harper-v-Haden* [1933] 1 Ch D 298, the defendants erected scaffolding on a pavement which caused the plaintiff shop owner to lose custom. The trial judge found the defendant liable in public nuisance and awarded damages to the plaintiff for loss of custom, (successfully appealed on another point).

c. Exemplary damages

Exemplary damages are not available as a remedy in the tort of public nuisance. In *AB -v- South Water Services Ltd* [1933] 1 All ER

609 the Court of Appeal held that since it had been laid down by the House of Lords in 1964 that awards of exemplary damages be restricted to torts were recognised at that time as grounding a claim for exemplary damages and, since public nuisance was not such a tort, the exemplary damages could not be recovered by a plaintiff for particular damage resulting from public nuisance.

d. Other heads of damage

Compensation may be awarded in public nuisance for damage to property and chattels, and for injury to sensibility, just as in private nuisance claims.

e. Injunction

It is plain that injunctions may be awarded in public as in private nuisance (but not negligence). The principles of Injunctive relief in environmental cases are set out in Chapter 18.

CHAPTER FIFTEEN

RYLANDS -v- FLETCHER

In the mid nineteenth century a mine owned by the plaintiff was flooded when independent contractors employed by the defendant failed to block off underground shafts leading to the mine before filling the reservoir with water. The flooding had occurred without any fault on the part of the defendant but he was held liable on the ground that anyone who brought onto his land or collected there something likely to cause damage if it escaped, was under a duty to prevent an escape. If the person failed in that duty, he was strictly liable to any person suffering loss or damage as a natural consequence of the escape.

Blackburn J. said:

"We think that the true rule of law is, that the person who for his own purposes brings on his lands and collects and keeps there anything likely to do mischief if it escapes, must keep it in at his peril, and if he does not do so, is *prima facie* answerable for all the damage which is the natural consequence of this escape. He can excuse himself by showing the escape was owing to the plaintiff's default; or perhaps that the escape was the consequence of vis major, or the act of God; but as nothing of this sort exists here, it is unnecessary to enquire what excuse would be sufficient. The general rule, as above stated, seems on principle just. The person whose grass or corn is eaten by the escaping cattle of his neighbour, or whose mine is flooded by the water from his neighbour's reservoir, or whose cellar is invaded by the filth of his neighbour's privy, or whose habitation is made unhealthy by the fumes and noise and vapours of his neighbour's alkali works, is damnified without any fault of his own; and it seems both reasonable and just that the neighbour, who has brought something on his property which was not naturally there, harmless to others so long as it is confined to his own property, but which he knows to be mischievous if it gets on his neighbour's, should be obliged to make good the damage which ensues if he does not succeed in confining it to his own property. But for his act in bringing it there no mischief could have accrued, and it seems but just that he should at his peril keep it there so that no mischief may accrue, or answer for the natural and anticipated consequences. Upon authority, this we think is established to be the law whether the things so brought be beasts, or water, or filth or stenches."

Rylands -v- Fletcher [1866] LR 1 ex 265 (at 279 - 280) in the House of Lords, Lord Cairns adopted his judgment, but he also introduced an element of discretion, and certainly opened the door to judicial policy making, by restricting the rule to circumstances where the defendant had made "a non-natural use" of the land (*Rylands -v- Fletcher* [1861 - 73] All ER REP 1.

In *Cambridge Water Co -v- Eastern Counties Leather Plc* [1994] 1 All ER 53 the House of Lords reviewed in depth *Rylands -v- Fletcher*, and restated the principles, holding, in effect, that *Rylands -v- Fletcher* had not introduced any radical new departure from the well settled principles of nuisance, but was an extension of the law of nuisance to deal with "one-off escapes". In other words the law of nuisance generally requires the presence of a "state of affairs" amounting to an unreasonable user. It was the extension, approved in *Rylands -v- Fletcher*, that enabled the law of nuisance also to be applied, given certain preconditions, to one-off incidents.

It follows that in future text books Rylands -v- Fletcher may well not be given a chapter of its own, but relegated to a section of the chapter on nuisance where liability for one-off escapes is specifically considered.

1. Things likely to do mischief

The rule in *Rylands -v- Fletcher* applies only to things likely to do mischief if they escape. A wide variety of things have been held to come within the rule, for example water, sewage, fires deliberately made or brought onto the land or arising accidentally in a dangerous object which is likely to catch fire easily or to do damage if it escapes, gas, electricity, gas oil, acid smuts, fumes, explosives, and decayed wire rope, colliery spoil, trees, vibrations, a flagpole, a chair-o-plane, and even caravan dwellers who committed nuisances, see Halsbury's Laws 4th Ed vol.34 para 341 for case references.

The rule has been held not to apply to the branch of a tree liable to fall on the highway, an aeroplane, an oil can, a boiler without a safety valve, a cricket ball driven out of the ground, and the tipping of "swarf" into barges, see Clarke & Lindsell on Torts 16th Ed para 25-03 for case references.

In view of the dangers inherent in the production or use of atomic energy, nuclear installations and liability in respect of radiation emitting or waste discharge from them are regulated by statute, ie. the Nuclear Installations Act 1965. This provides for strict liability for damage and personal injury, but the word "damage" has been narrowly construed, *Merlin -v- British Nuclear Fuels Plc* [1993] All ER 711.

(a) Non-natural use of land

Blackburn J said the rule only applied to a thing "which was not naturally there"; in the House of Lords Lord Cairns added that the defendant is only liable if, in bringing it there, he is making a "non-natural" use of the land.

Over the years the courts repeatedly construed "natural" use of land very broadly indeed in favour of industrial defendants, such that, for example, munitions or explosives factories in wartime were regarded as natural. Indeed, this freedom of interpretation threatened to emasculate the rule altogether.

However, in the Cambridge Water case the House of Lords held, obiter, that storage of substantial quantities of chemicals on industrial premises is an almost classic case of non-natural use of land even in an industrial complex. In differing with the Judge at first instance on this point, the House of Lords has breathed new life into the rule and many industrial operations will now be regarded as "non-natural" notwithstanding that they take place in an industrial area, increase public wealth, generate employment and so forth. The many cases on "non-natural" use e.g. those cited in Clarke & Lindsell on Torts 16th Ed para 25-06, need to be reconsidered in the light of Lord Goff's speech in Cambridge Water with which all the other members of the House agreed.

(b) Escape

The rule in *Rylands -v- Fletcher* only applies where the thing which does the damage has escaped. For the purposes of the rule, "escape" means escape from a place where the defendant has occupational control over land to a place which is outside his occupational control, *Read -v- Lyons* [1947] AC 156 [1946] 2 All ER 471 HL. It seems that the rule does not apply to an escape from a ship: the *Wagon Mound No. 2* [1963] 1 Lloyds Rep 402 (NSW) a case in which the appeal was allowed on different grounds.

(c) Remoteness of damage

Foreseeability of damage of the relevant type as well as an escape from the land of things likely to do mischief is a pre-requisite of liability. Accordingly, strict liability for the escape from their land of things likely to do mischief only arises if the defendant knew or ought reasonably to have foreseen, applying standards and knowledge of the date of the acts or omissions complained of, that those things might if they escaped cause damage, *Cambridge Water -v- Eastern Counties Leather* [1994] 1 All ER 53 (HL). In this sense foreseeability has been made a pre-requisite of liability in *Rylands -v- Fletcher* just as it is in the law of nuisance and in the law of negligence.

Difficulty may be caused, however, in assessing the degree of specificity of the "type of damage" which needs to be foreseeable for liability to attach. This is discussed in the chapter 13 on negligence, see pages. It is plain however that the fact that "a pollution" of some kind is foreseeable is not sufficiently specific for liability to be imposed.

(d) Defences

The rule in *Rylands -v- Fletcher* does not apply where the escape is caused by an act of God. Nor does it apply if the escape was due to the act of a stranger of whose acts the defendant has no control and which was not an act which the defendant ought reasonably to have anticipated and guarded against, *Perry -v- Kendricks Transport* [1956] 1 All ER 154 [1956] 1 WLR 85 CA. Once the defendant has proved that the escape is caused by the act of a stranger he avoids liability unless the plaintiff can go on to show that the act which caused the escape was an act of the kind which the defendant could reasonably have anticipated and guarded against, see *Perry -v- Kendricks Transport*.

The rule does not apply where the escape was due to some act or default of the plaintiff nor where the plaintiff has consented to the presence of the thing which escapes, *A. Prosser & Son -v- Levy* [1955] 3 All ER 57, [1955] 1 WLR 1224 CA. In many cases in which this exception operates the thing is kept on premises for the common benefit of the plaintiff and the defendant and if, in some cases, the consent and common benefit have been regarded as too separate and independent exceptions to the rule. However it seems that the true basis of this exception is consent and the common benefit is only an element in showing implied consent. This exception is chiefly exemplified in cases concerning water, but there is no reason in principle why it should be confined to such cases.

As to common benefit, it would be wrong to take the view that the finding of "general benefit to the community" always excludes the application of the rule. The rule has been applied to gas companies, see *North Western Utilities Ltd -v- London Guarantee and Accident Co Ltd* [1936] Ac 108, water companies, see *Charing Cross Electricity Supply Co -v- Hydraulic Power Co* [1914] 3 KB 772, tram companies, see *West -v- Bristol Tramways* [1908] 2 KB 14, railway companies, see *Jones -v- Ffestionnog Railway* [1868] LR 3 QB 733, and colliery companies, see *Rylands -v- Fletcher* itself.

A whole series of cases suggests that the use of the land for the general benefit of the community is not enough to exclude the application of the rule. The dictum of Lord Moulton in *Rickards - v- Lothian* [1913] AC 263 relating to general benefit of the community is as follows:

"It must be some special use bringing with it increased danger to others and must not merely be the ordinary use of the land or such a use as is proper for the general benefit of the community" (p280).

If the general benefit of the community is construed as supplying some local employment and if this were to be held conclusive of the issue, then the rule has unquestionably been emasculated out of all practical existence. It is however plain that each case must be decided on its own facts and the real test will come in an "escape" case from a specially hazardous large scale operation, such as a toxic waste landfill site or a toxic waste incinerator. No doubt the defendants will always refer to the benefit to society of being able to dispose of its hazardous waste in defence of their action. On the other hand policy developments at international, regional and national level make it clear that a clean and healthy environment is for the "general benefit of the community". What may have to be tested is what is meant by the "public", particularly in cases where hazardous waste is imported from other regions and other countries in order to make the business profitable.

When a dangerous thing is used under statutory authority it is generally necessary to prove negligence in order to establish liability, see *Geddis -v- Proprietors of Bann Reservoir* [1878] 3 APP CAS 430. Where a thing is brought onto the land under the authority of a statute which provides that there is liability for a nuisance caused by the exercise of the statutory power, in the absence of negligence, under the rule in *Rylands -v- Fletcher*, there is no liability for an escape, see for example *Smeaton -v- Ilford Corporation* [1954] Ch450, [1954- 1 All ER 923; *Dunn -v- North Western Gas Board* [1964] 2 QB 806, [1963] 3 All ER 916 CA. This is another example which shows that where the prospective defendant is a statutory undertaker the practitioner must take special precautions to ensure that the claim can be properly founded, because statutory undertakers acting with statutory powers are generally in a special position.

2. Remedies

On the footing that *Rylands -v- Fletcher* is an extension of the law of nuisance, then the "nuisance" remedies of compensatory damages and/or injunction are available.

(a) Damages for personal injuries

It has been accepted in several cases that under the rule damages can be recovered in respect of personal injuries: *Miles -v- Forest Rock Granite Co (Leicestershire) Ltd* [1918] 34 TLR 500 CA; *Shiffman - v- Venerable Order of the Hospital of St. John of Jerusalem* [1936] 1 All ER 557; *Hale v- Jennings Brothers* [1938] 1 All ER 579, CA; *Perry -v- Kendricks Transport Ltd* [1956] 1 All ER 154, [1956] 1 WLR 85 CA.

However in *Read -v- Lyons* [1947] AC 156, [1946] 2 All ER 471 some members of the House of Lords, notably Lord McMillan, expressed doubts as to whether the rule does extend to cover personal injuries, doubts which were vigorously endorsed by Professor Newark in the article on the law of nuisance which, in other respects, was adopted and endorsed by Lord Goff in the *Cambridge Water* judgment.

The law here appears to be well settled, i.e. that damages for personal injuries are available under the rule in Rylands -v- Fletcher but, in the light of some of the observations in the Cambridge Water decision, the issue of whether damages for personal injuries are available in nuisance actions, including the extension of nuisance to cover single incidents under the rule in *Rylands -v- Fletcher*, may require detailed review.

(b) Economic Loss

The rule cannot be applied at the suit of a plaintiff who has no interest in land menaced by the escape and whose only damage is financial loss. In *Cattle -v- Stockton Waterworks* [1875] LR10 QB 453 the plaintiff could not recover where the escape of water made it more expensive for the Plaintiff to construct a tunnel; again, the plaintiff, who was a cattle auctioneer, failed to recover in a loss of profits claim where the escape of a virus from the defendant's research instituted damaged a third party's cattle and severely affected the profitability of the plaintiff's business, *Weller -v- Foot & Mouth Disease Research Institute* [1966] 1 QB 589, [1965] 3 All ER 560.

(c) Exemplary Damages

It has been impossible to locate any decided case in which exemplary damages have been awarded under the rule and, indeed, it would seem to be a contradiction in terms. Exemplary damages are awarded to punish gross misconduct (as defined in *Rooks -v- Barnard* [1964] 1 All ER 367) whereas in cases where the rule in *Rylands -v- Fletcher* is invoked the purpose, and the effect, is that the defendant's conduct does not require investigation for the purposes of determining negligence or fault since his liability is strict once the rule operates.

On the footing that the rule is an extension of the law of private nuisance, then exemplary damages are not available, see *AB -v- South West Water Services Ltd* [1993] 1 All ER 609 CA.

CHAPTER SIXTEEN

BREACH OF STATUTORY DUTY

UK statute law and EEC law impose a large number of duties in environmental matters. In some instances where a person has suffered damage in consequence of a breach of a such a duty the law affords civil remedy to that person by reason of the breach, and in some instances it does not. In drafting the statute the legislator sometimes expressly states that a breach of the statutory duty will confer a civil remedy, and sometimes expressly states that it will not. More usually the instrument will be silent on the question, which means that it will be left to the court to determine the intention of the legislator. Where the breach is by a statutory undertaker, the leading case is now *X-v- Bedfordshire CC* (HL) The Times 30th June 1995.

This chapter looks at examples of all three situations. Since the majority of statutory duties in the environmental field are now (and in the future) sourced in EC law and particularly in EC directives one should have in mind the special rules for construction/application of the provisions of EC Directives.

1. Statute expressly provides for civil liability for breach

(a) Waste on Land

s73 (6) of the Environmental Protection Act 1990 provides as follows:

"Where any damage is caused by waste which has been deposited in or on land, any person who deposited it, or knowingly caused or knowingly permitted it to be deposited, in either case so as to commit an offence under s33 (1) or s63 (2) above is liable for the damage except where the damage

(a) is wholly due to the fault of the person who suffered it; or (b) was suffered by a person who voluntarily accepted the risk of damage being caused; but without prejudice to any liability arising otherwise than under this sub-section".

s.73 (8) defines "damage" as including death and personal injury.

These sections, which are not yet in force, substantially reproduce ss. 88 and 105 of the Control of Pollution Act 1974. There have been no reported decisions in which the civil liability of these sections in the 1974 Act has been considered.

S.33 of the 1990 Act creates the basic offence of depositing controlled waste without a licence. "Controlled Waste" means household, industrial and commercial waste (s75 (4)). S.63 in effect makes it an offence to fly tip waste which is not controlled waste (e.g. from mines and quarries and agriculture).

The effect of s73(6) is therefore to impose strict liability on persons involved in the unlawful deposit of waste for any damage caused by it, though not where it was the plaintiff's own fault, or the plaintiff voluntarily assumed the risk. It will not be necessary to show that the waste disposer has been prosecuted or convicted for offences under ss33 or 63 (although it will make the task much easier if this is the case). It will be sufficient to show that the offences have been committed, irrespective of whether they have been prosecuted.

So, for example, in a case where an industrial operator uses a hole in the ground to store toxic waste in order to save the costs of proper disposal, and his neighbours' land is subsequently affected by the waste seepage, the operator will be strictly liable pursuant to this provision for damage caused. The disposal must, of course, be of "waste" so that, for example, an operator who caused underground contamination because drums of new solvent were moved and damaged by forklift trucks would not be liable under this section.

(b) Nuclear Installations

Section 12 of the Nuclear Installations Act 1965 gives a right to compensation where any injury or damage has been caused by a breach of statutory duty under the Act. The Sellafield childhood leukaemia claims were pursued under this Act.

The ambit of the provision relating to damage to property was considered by Gatehouse J in *Merlin -v- British Nuclear Fuels plc* [1990] 3 WLR 383. There, the plaintiffs discovered that their house had been contaminated with radio nuclides emanating from the defendants nuclear reprocessing plant at Sellafield. They decided to move because of the health risk. They put their house on the market. They were commendably frank with prospective purchasers with the result that eventually the house had to be sold at auction, fetching at least £30,000 less than it would have done in an uncontaminated condition (it was sold to a Sellafield worker).

Section 7 (1) of the 1965 Act imposes a statutory duty upon the defendants to secure that no occurrence involving nuclear matter or emission of radiation caused injury to any person or damage to any property. The issue for determination was whether the diminution in value caused by the contamination fell within the definition of "damage to property" under s7.

The Judge held that damage to property meant physical damage to tangible property and did not accordingly include diminution in value. The implication of the decision is that, in the event of large scale evacuation caused by a nuclear plant failure, the local population, temporarily evacuated, could neither claim their relocation expenses, nor for the diminution in value of their properties that the blight would no doubt provoke. This position is made all the worse because most insurance policies exclude claims related to damage resulting from radiation damage.

(c) Oil Bulk Carriers

Civil liability is imposed on the owner of a ship carrying a bulk cargo of oil where there is an escape or persistent discharge of the oil from the ship, under the provisions of the Merchant Shipping (Oil Pollution) Act 1971. The owner is liable for any damage caused in the United Kingdom including the cost of measures reasonably taken to prevent or reduce the damage, and for damage caused by any such measures taken.

This Act is comprehensively dealt with by M Forster in Civil Liability of Ship Owners for Oil Pollution (1973) JBL23. Three statutory defences are provided relating to wars, exceptional natural phenomena (i.e. acts of God) and, also, wrongful or unforeseeable acts of a third party such as negligence of an authority in its function of maintaining navigational aids. The Act, it should be noted, abolishes liability under the common law.

(d) Defective Products

Under the Consumer Protection Act 1987 (which implemented EEC product liability Directive 85/374/EEC) where any damage is caused wholly or partly by a defect in a product the producer of the product and sometimes the importer and supplier shall be strictly liable for all damage caused including personal injury brought about by the defective product.

Practitioners should be alert to the use of this important statute in environmental matters. The definition of "product" expressly includes electricity and gas and may well be wide enough to include water supplied for human consumption. Where, therefore, unwholesome drinking water is supplied the producer is strictly liable to those injured through drinking it under the Consumer Protection Act.

Other products in the environmental field that could be "products" for the purposes of this Act are pesticides and fertilisers. An interesting question concerns "by products" which are part of the manufacturing process of products, such as hazardous wastes whether in liquid or solid form or in the form of particulate matter escaping from a chimney into the atmosphere and then being deposited in surrounding areas. The courts may well have to grapple with the question of whether such by products fall properly within the definition of product under the Consumer Protection Act 1987, thereby giving rise to civil remedies based on strict liability.

2. Statutes expressly excluding civil liability for breach

The principal example is s100 of the Water Resources Act 1991 which excludes any right of action in civil proceedings in respect of any contravention of the water pollution provisions of the Act. Two points should be noted. The exclusion is limited, in effect, to offences of polluting controlled waters (Part III of the Act). Secondly, s100 expressly states that common law rights are unaffected, so that nuisance and negligence actions may still be taken even where a discharger is complying with a consent granted under Schedule 10 to s88 of the Act.

It is odd, on the face of it, that the legislature should have excluded civil liability for breach of statutory duty in respect of river quality provisions. It may well be in breach of Community law. There are a number of provisions of Community environment directives which have direct effect in respect of river quality and it is settled law that Member States have the responsibility to incorporate provisions of Community environment legislation into national law in such a way that their application is effectively ensured. This includes providing for legal consequences (sanctions) in the event of a provision not being respected. These sanctions must be effective and appropriate and be equivalent to legal consequences applying to contravention of comparable national provisions.

In effect, the United Kingdom is taking the position that the criminal sanctions for river pollution under s85 of the Water Resources Act 1991 are a sufficient and effective compliance with community law. Criminal sanctions however leave the individuals affected, such as Angling Associations, without remedy by way of an injunction (to restrain the pollution) or by way of financial compensation for damage arising from it. This, on the face of it, is a derogation of the entitlement to the effective remedy on his or her own behalf which Community law requires an individual citizen to have. This point will no doubt be tested, and the issue will probably be the extent to which the remedies in common law negligence and nuisance are an adequate substitute for the lack of remedy based on breach of statutory duty.

3. Statute silent as to civil liability for breach

Where the statute is silent, the general rule is that the plaintiff must show that Parliament intended breach of the relevant statutory duty to be actionable in damages by an individual harmed by the breach, see *R -v- Deputy Governor of Parkhurst Prison Ex parte Hague* [1991] 3 WLR 340.

There are a number of tests that the courts have traditionally applied in order to divine parliamentary intention in this respect.

a) The injury of which the plaintiff complains must fall within the ambit of the statute. If a statute requires something to be done with a view to avoiding one particular form of harm, then if non-compliance with the statute results in another form of damage, the plaintiff will have no basis for a claim for breach of statutory duty. A good example, although on a different subject matter, is that of the Building Regulations. Their purpose is to protect public health. A claim under the Regulation by developers suffering from economic loss did not succeed, (see *Peabody Donation Fund (Governors) -v- Sir Lindsay Parkinson* [1985] AC 210).

b) Another important test is to ask whether the duty under the statute is owed primarily to the state as representing the community at large, or to a limited class. Where the statute imposes a duty towards the community at large no action will lie for breach of statutory duty, see

Monk -v- Warbey [1935] KB 75. In that case it was held that a duty imposed by the road traffic acts on all vehicle owners to insure their vehicles was imposed for the benefit of all road users. On the other hand the safety provisions of the Factories Act 1961 and the Offices Shops & Railway Premises Act 1963 are examples of provisions where a limited class of persons are envisaged i.e., employees, and therefore individual employees were held to be entitled to damages for breach of these statutory duties.

c) Usually a statutory duty is imposed to prevent some particular form of harm, and in order to succeed in establishing damages for breach of statutory duty it must be shown that the damage suffered was within the scope of the injury contemplated by the statutory provision.

In *Gorries -v- Scott* (1874) LR 9 Ex 125 a sheep was washed overboard when carried as deck cargo without proper pens. An action was commenced on the basis that the defendants had contravened a statute. The claim failed on the basis that the statutory provision was intended to prevent the spread of contagious disease and not to safeguard the cargo from perils of the sea.

Similarly the plaintiff could not recover damages from a water company which had failed to maintain a certain pressure of water in their pipes when his house was destroyed by fire *Atkinson -v- Newcastle Waterworks Co* (1877) 2 ExD 441; nor could the plaintiff recover for damage suffered from purchasing diseased figs which had been sent to market in contravention of regulations designed to avoid infection of cattle *Ward -v- Hobbs*) (1878) 4 App Cas 13.

d) A further factor which the courts take into account is whether a statute prescribes sanctions. The broad rule is that if a statute creates a duty but imposes no civil or criminal remedies for its breach there is a presumption that a person who is injured thereby will have a right of action; for otherwise "the statute would be but a pious aspiration" *Cutler -v- Wandsworth Stadium* [1949] AC 398 at 407, per Lord Symonds. The fact that criminal sanctions are prescribed is, however, not conclusive against the imposition of damages for breach of statutory duty, [for example there are criminal sanctions in the Factories Act but there is civil liability for breach].

The approach to be adopted when considering this question was recently considered by the House of Lords in *Lonhro Ltd -v- Shell Petroleum Co Ltd* (No 2) [1982] AC 173. In that case Lonhro sought compensation from Shell who were their competitors in the oil trade. They alleged they had suffered loss because they had complied with Orders in Council prohibiting trade with Rhodesia whilst Shell had allegedly flouted these Orders. Rejecting their claim, Lord Diplock with whom the rest of the House concurred, stated the general rule was;

"where an Act creates an obligation and enforces the performance in a specified manner.. that performance cannot be enforced in any other manner". However, he went on "where the only manner of enforcing performance for which the Act provides is prosecution for failure to perform the statutory prohibition there are two classes of exception to this general rule;

(i) where on the true construction of the Act it is apparent that the obligation or prohibition was imposed for the benefit or protection of a particular class of individuals, as in the case of the Factories Act and similar legislation and (ii) where the statute creates a public right (ie a right to be enjoyed by all those of Her Majesty's subjects who wish to avail themselves of it) and a particular member of the public suffers particular direct and substantial damage other and different from that which was common to all the rest of the public."

The House went on to hold that the purpose of the Orders in Council was to bring down the illegal regime and not to benefit traders such as Lonhro and further that the Orders in Council did not create any public right to be enjoyed by all those who wished to avail themselves of it. Accordingly Lonhro could not benefit by the second exception either. Lonhro and Cutler were both considered recently in *X -v- Bedfordshire CC* (HL) The Times 30th June 1995.

(e) There is a traditional reluctance on the part of the courts to impose liability for breach of statutory duty on public authorities where the duty in question is a general statutory responsibility for the public welfare. Hence it has been held that no action lies against the Minister of Education for breach of his duty "to promote the education of the people of England and Wales" *Watt -v- Kesteven CC* [1955] 1 QB 408 and an action against the Minister of Health for failing to provide an efficient and comprehensive health service failed *R -v- Secretary of State for Social Services ex p Hincks* (1973) 123 SJ 436. There are many such general statements of duty to be found in the environmental legislation.

(f) The plaintiff must establish and define the specific duty owed to him personally rather than to society at large. An example is to be found in

Thornton -v- Kirklees MBC [1979] QB 626 where the plaintiff succeeded in an action against the local authority who had failed to house him as required by the Housing (Homeless Persons) Act 1977. It was held that the duty imposed on the authority was intended to benefit individuals who found themselves homeless and it was therefore more than a general statement of the "political" duties of the local authority. That said, where a public authority is concerned, the correct remedy will more usually be an urgent application for judicial review. A damages action in tort may well be struck out on the principle set out in *O'Reilly -v- Mackman* [1983] 2 AC 237.

(g) It was to be hoped that where English environmental law is reinforced by EEC law, mindful of its obligations to provide an effective remedy under Community law, British courts would be more willing to provide a remedy in damages for a wrong committed by a public authority, but in *Bourgoin SA -v- Minister of Agriculture* [1986] 1 QB 716 the Court of Appeal was unwilling so to do. Whether Bourgoin would be decided (or argued) the same way since the House of Lords decision in *Factortame Ltd v Secretary of State for Transport* (No 2) [1991] AC 603 and the European Court of Justice in *Francovich v Italian Republic* (joined cases C-6/90 and C-9/90) is however open to doubt.

Summary

For toxic tort purposes the main lesson which emerges from the above review of the factors which the courts take into account seems to be this. Where the duty is defined in concrete terms and can be characterised as directed at the plaintiff personally, as, for example for the protection of his or her health, the court will probably give a remedy in damages for the breach of statutory duty. An example in the toxic tort field is *Read -v- Croydon Corporation* [1938] 4 All ER 631, which was the test case on liability resulting from the Croydon typhus epidemic which led to the deaths of more than 40 people from drinking unwholesome water supplied by the defendants as statutory water undertaker. The court held that s31 of the Water Act 1945, which imposed a duty on the water undertaker to supply wholesome water was for the protection of the plaintiff and such as to found an action in damages in breach of statutory duty. The leading case on determining whether breach of statutory duty by a local authority gives rise to a private law cause of action is now *X -v- Bedfordshire CC* (HL) The Times 30th June 1995.

CHAPTER SEVENTEEN

CRIMINAL LIABILITY

A successful prosecution may well fortify compensation proceedings in tort. Further, the prosecution is often a prelude to, or runs in tandem with, remediation measures taken by the prosecuting authority who then uses its statutory power to recover the remediation costs from the defendant, which can therefore constitute a very substantial civil law liability.

For these reasons there is a significant overlap between civil law liability for environmental wrongs and criminal liability, and, for reasons set out below, this is likely to become more important when the proposed statutory framework for land contamination is put in place. It is therefore necessary for the practitioner in the field of civil liability to have a reasonable understanding of liability in criminal law for pollution.

It should also be noted that where the proper authority decides not to proceed with a criminal prosecution, in certain circumstances a private prosecution may well be considered as an alternative to, or in conjunction with, civil proceedings.

Environmental legislation has given rise to the creation of a large number of statutory offences of which the following are currently the most prominent.

1. Specific Offences

a. Freshwater

Section 85 of the Water Resources Act 1991 makes it a criminal offence to cause or knowingly permit any poisonous, noxious or polluting matter or any solid waste matter to enter any controlled waters or to breach the conditions of any consent to discharge. A conviction in the Magistrates Court gives rise to a term of imprisonment not exceeding 3 months or to a fine not exceeding £20,000 or both, and a conviction in the Crown Court gives rise to imprisonment for a term not exceeding 2 years or to an unlimited fine or both.

b. Air Pollution

Section 23 of the Environmental Protection Act 1990 makes it an offence to carry on a prescribed industrial process falling within Part I of the EPA, except under an authorisation and in accordance with its conditions. Conviction in the Magistrates Court gives rise to a fine of up to £20,000 whilst conviction in the Crown Court results in an unlimited fine or imprisonment for up to 2 years or both.

The offence appears to be one of strict liability, and ignorance that a condition was being contravened would not provide a defence. Nor is there any defence of "reasonable excuse", such as applies to some of the other offences. There are about five thousand scheduled processes related to this section involving complex and major installations. This calls for scientifically qualified inspectors under Her Majesty's Inspectorate of Pollution (HMIP).

c. Noise, Smoke and Smell

Emissions of noise, smoke, dust and smell from all unscheduled processes (i.e. any industrial operation however small not requiring an authorisation under Part I of the EPA) is dealt with under Part III of the EPA. Part III of the EPA (sections 79-85) came into force on January 1st 1991 and deal with statutory nuisances, clean air, and controls over offensive trades. In relation to statutory nuisances ss79-82 of the EPA replace the provisions of the Public Health Act 1936 and the Public Health (Recurring Nuisances) Act 1969 with a more streamlined system of summary procedures.

Since the proposed statutory framework to deal with contaminated land (see chapter 22) will follow the Part III statutory nuisance procedure it is worth setting out the steps, as follows:

i) local authority satisfied that statutory nuisance exists or is likely to occur or recur;

ii) service of abatement notice;

iii) person served may appeal to magistrates within 21 days;

iv) failure to comply with abatement notice is an offence and local authority may abate nuisance and recover expenses.

A failure to comply with a court order in respect of abatement of the nuisance without reasonable excuse will result in a fine not exceeding £20,000 together with a further daily fine for each day that the offence or failure to abate continues.

As to the meaning of "statutory nuisance" these are set out in s79 EPA which, in broad terms, refers to smoke, fumes or gases, dust, steam, smell or other effluvia, and noise which are "prejudicial to health or a nuisance".

d. Waste Disposal

Under s33(1) of the EPA, which came into force on 1st May 1994, it is an offence to deposit waste, or knowingly cause or knowingly permit waste to be deposited except with a licence, and, further, it is an offence to treat keep or dispose of waste or knowing cause or knowingly permit waste to be treated kept or disposed of except in accordance with the conditions of the licence. In the Magistrates Court the maximum fine is £20,000 or 6 months imprisonment or both. In the Crown Court the Court can order an unlimited fine or 2 years imprisonment or both. If the waste is special, i.e. particularly hazardous, rather than merely "controlled" waste, the maximum prison sentence is 5 years.

Under s34 of the EPA which came into force on April 1st 1992 any person who fails to comply with the "duty of care" as respects the production, transmission, treatment or disposal of waste is guilty of an offence. The criminal sanctions are somewhat less, namely, in the Magistrates Court a fine of up to £20,000, and in the Crown Court an unlimited fine. There is no power of imprisonment. The "duty of care" as respects waste was first enacted in the EPA and flows from various calls for enhanced responsibility on the part of the persons producing or having control of waste. Accordingly, under s34, it is no longer possible for the producer of waste to rid himself of responsibility for it simply by consigning the waste to any agent or contractor. The responsibility is primarily focused on the control of waste prior to transfer and the steps and precautions to be taken on transfer. In other words the producer of waste who disposes of it at a knock down price through a "cowboy" contractor now does so at his peril.

Finally, the specific reference should be made to s33(1)(c) which is also in force, and was a new enactment in the EPA. This makes it an offence for anyone (whether licensed or not) to treat, keep or dispose of controlled waste (i.e. waste other than household waste for practical purposes) "in a manner likely to cause pollution of the environment or harm to human health". The words "pollution of the environment" have not previously appeared in any enactment involving a sanction and, as defined in the EPA, seem capable of having a wide meaning.

e. Contaminated Land

During the course of 1995 a new Part IIA will be inserted into the EPA giving powers to the new Environmental Agency and the local authorities to require remediation of contaminated sites. Remediation notices can be served on the persons who caused or knowingly permitted the pollution and also (in certain circumstances) the owner or occupier for the time being of the site in question.

The person served with the remediation notice can appeal against its terms to the Magistrates Court (see the statutory nuisance procedure set out above) but if the Magistrates Court does not vary or revoke it, then failure to comply with the remediation notice constitutes an offence attracting financial penalties in the Magistrates Court and Crown Court. If the work is not carried out in compliance with the remediation notice so that the agency or local authority is empowered to do the work itself and recover the cost against the appropriate person.

A more detailed analysis of these proposed enactments is to be found in chapter 22 on land contamination.

2. The Use of Criminal Sanctions

In the past, criminal proceedings have only rarely been taken mainly because the environmental regulatory agencies believed that collaboration rather than coercion was the best approach. This mood is undergoing change. Criticism of the "cosy" relationships between watchdog bodies and those under supervision; the specific separation of "poacher" from "gamekeeper" in the Water Act 1989 and similarly in respect of the Waste Disposal regime in the EPA have all led to a different culture.

The National Rivers Authority has certainly taken a much more vigorous approach to prosecuting offenders. Further, HMIP hinted in 1991 that it will be more willing to look for penal sanctions in the future. The new waste regulation authorities, given their independent status, may also be expected to flex their muscles. In terms of prosecution policy overall, it remains to be seen what effect the bringing together of the various agencies, most particularly the NRA and HMIP, under the new Environmental Agency will achieve.

Companies do not like to be prosecuted. It tarnishes their corporate reputation which, given the increased public awareness of environmental matters, is increasingly significant. Further, in the Crown Court at least, fines are starting to become expensive. In 1990 Shell was fined one million pounds for an oil spill in the Mersey and in 1991 British Steel Corporation was fined two hundred thousand pounds for a twenty tonne oil spill in the Severn Estuary. Finally, the "character" of the corporation and of individual directors is now material to the granting of new licences and permits. So, for example, in the waste disposal regime in Part II of the EPA the concept of "fit and proper person" to hold a waste disposal licence has been introduced, and any previous convictions, particularly for environmental offences, will be taken into account in deciding whether to grant licences.

Up to the present time virtually all environmental prosecutions have been against the company, rather than individual officers of the company. Under s217 of the Water Resources Act 1991 and s157 of the EPA it is expressly provided that where a company is guilty of an offence which is proved to have been committed with the consent or connivance of, or to be attributable to any neglect on the part of, any director, manager, secretary or other similar officer of the company, then that person, as well as the company, is also guilty of the offence.

Accordingly the preconditions for personal criminal liability are either consent, connivance or neglect. Consent means that the individual knows that is going on and agrees to it. Connivance means knowing what is going on and turning a blind eye to it. Neglect is, of course, the widest of the three standards and implies some act or omission or at least a failure to perform a duty which a person knows or ought to know.

In *R-v- City Equitable Fire Insurance Co Ltd* [1925] Ch40 Romer J pointed out that in ascertaining the duties of a director it is necessary to consider the nature of the company's business and the manner in which its work is reasonably distributed between the directors and other officers. If a director has properly delegated his duties to another person he will not be guilty of neglect.

Up to now the regulatory authorities have been reluctant to prosecute individuals in addition to companies. For example, in *Wrothwell -v- Yorkshire Water Authority* [1984] Crim LR 43 a director who deliberately poured herbicide, known to be toxic to fish, into a drain with the result that a large number of fish were killed, was not indicted as a co-defendant when the company was prosecuted.

This mood may well change. The feeling exists that the presence of individual directors in the dock facing terms of imprisonment will have a marked impact on their colleagues in industry and lead to a more vigorous and intrusive approach by top level management in respect of the company's environmental responsibilities.

3. Private Prosecutions

Section 6 of the Prosecution of Offenders Act 1985 provides that any person may institute and conduct any criminal proceedings save where a statute expressly limits this right. The point needs to be made that in all private prosecutions both the Attorney General and the Director of Public Prosecutions (DPP) have a right to take over and either continue the prosecution themselves, or close down the prosecution. It is very rare for either course to be taken by the Attorney General or DPP.

A recent example of the DPP taking over a prosecution arose out of the Camelford water pollution. The Anglers' Co-operative Association initiated a private prosecution in respect of damage to fish under s4 of the Salmon and Freshwater Fisheries Act and s32 of the Control of Pollution Act 1974. The DPP took it over, added the public nuisance charge, and prosecuted South West Water to conviction. It would be interesting to know whether the DPP would have acted but for the ACA's initiative.

Neither the EPA nor the Water Resources Act 1991 (WRA) contains any express restriction on private prosecutions, but wherever a private prosecution is contemplated, it will be necessary to check the enactment. It is rare for there to be prohibition on private prosecution. Where it occurs, the restriction will normally involve seeking the consent of the DPP to the prosecution.

The first private prosecution for freshwater pollution appears to be that of *Wales -v- Thames Water Authority* (unreported) in 1987. There, a private prosecution was successfully instituted by the

Anglers Association under s34(5) of the Control of Pollution Act 1974 in respect of various breaches of the discharge consents from a sewage plant.

More recently Greenpeace prosecuted Albright and Wilson, a chemical company, for breaches of its consent limits for zinc, chromium, copper and nickel (discharges into the Irish Sea). The defendant company vigorously contested this prosecution but on August 31st 1991 was convicted by the Whitehaven Justices and fined £2,000. It was further ordered to pay costs of £20,000.

We can find no cases on private prosecution in relation to air pollution and waste disposal (see the specific offences outlined above). There are, of course, numerous instances of private prosecutions in Magistrates Courts for statutory nuisances, particularly noise.

A major difficulty in pursuing a private prosecution is that Legal Aid is not available. It is however possible that legal expenses insurance may cover such a prosecution. In cases where funding is available to mount a prosecution there are two good reasons why this may be an appropriate route as part and parcel of the strategy of seeking redress for an environmental wrong. Interlocutory procedures involving discovery, particulars and interrogatories are not generally so cumbersome in prosecutions as can be the case in environmental civil litigation, with the result that criminal cases tend to come to trial sooner and are less expensive than civil proceedings.

The second advantage is that there may be cases in which it is felt that it would be more desirable to have a jury considering the case than a judge. A jury will very rarely be available in a civil action, but where the justices commit a prosecution to the Crown Court in criminal proceedings, which is highly likely in any case of unusual gravity or complexity, then a jury will determine the issue. This is, of course, always subject to the judge's power to consider at the close of the prosecution case whether there is sufficient *prima facie* evidence against the defendants for the jury to consider.

A conviction in a criminal court is admissible as evidence in a civil court and may therefore be used to advance a claim for damages in nuisance or negligence, see s11 of the Civil Evidence Act 1968.

The conviction is not conclusive of the issue in the civil

proceedings, even where the issue is the same, but, unless the defendant can establish that the conviction was in some material sense irrelevant, or arrived at on the basis of irregularity (in which case the civil judge will expect it to have been successfully appealed), it is highly unlikely that the civil judge will arrive at a finding inconsistent with it, particularly taking into account that the standard of proof upon which the defendant has been convicted in the criminal court is significantly higher than the standard of proof in the civil court.

4. "Causing or Knowingly Permitting"

The word "causing" where it appears in the context of s85 of the WRA namely "cause or knowingly permit any poisonous, noxious or polluting matter or any solid waste matter to enter any controlled waters...." was considered by the House of Lords in *Alphacell -v- Woodward* [1972] AC 824 in which the House of Lords determined that a defendant "causes" the pollution if he takes some active part in it and it not necessary to demonstrate that the defendant knew of the pollution, nor that he was in some sense culpable or negligent in respect of it.

Alphacell remains the leading case but, very recently, there have been a series of decisions revisiting the vexed question of "causation".

It is necessary to review these authorities not just because of the importance in the field of water pollution law, but because, in the proposed Part IIA of the EPA dealing with the remediation of contaminated land the expression "caused or knowingly permitted" has been borrowed from the WRA, and will therefore become the cornerstone for both criminal liability and, perhaps even more importantly, liability under the Agency's powers to recover remediation costs from the appropriate person.

The focus of attention is the extent to which mere ownership of the land, absent involvement in the operations that take place on the land, can result in a liability for "causing" pollution.

It remains the position that the leading case is the HL decision of the *Alphacell -v- Woodward* [1972] AC 824. Lord Wilberforce stated that "causing" .... "must involve some active operation or chain of operations involving as a result the pollution...". *Alphacell* decided that an operation could include the design and installation of a facility which, in certain circumstances including breakdown, discharges polluting substances into controlled waters. In other words, according to *Alphacell*, it is important to consider the background circumstances, the whole complex operation, and not just the immediate polluting event itself.

In *Wychavon District Council -v- National Rivers Authority* [1993] 2 All ER 440 (DC) Wychavon was the sewerage agent for the statutory undertaker with day to day responsibility for the operation and maintenance and repair of sewers in its area, and was informed by the NRA that raw sewage was discharging into a river from a storm overflow. Wychavon failed promptly to take preventative action by unblocking the system which was causing the raw sewage discharge. In the result a significant amount of additional pollution occurred and it was prosecuted for causing water pollution. The Divisional Court held that the pollution was not caused by any "positive or deliberate act" on the part of Wychavon, hence it did not cause the pollution. Wychavon may have passively looked on, but there was no "active operation" by Wychavon which caused the pollution.

In *NRA -v- Welsh Development Agency* [1993] ENV LR 407 the WDA developed and then leased factory units on an industrial estate. The drainage system on the estate was designed built and maintained by the WDA. One night caustic soda entered the drains from one of the factory units and was thereby discharged into controlled waters. The WDA was prosecuted for causing water pollution. The Divisional Court found that the case was distinguishable from Wychavon and held that neither the design nor the construction of the drain played any part in the discharge and hence there was no positive act of causation by the WDA.

In *NRA -v- Yorkshire Water Services* [1995] 1 All ER 225 (HL) Yorkshire Water (YW) was prosecuted by the NRA for causing polluting matter to enter controlled waters. An unidentified YW industrial customer had discharged an unconsented polluting substance (Iso-octonal) into YW's sewers with the result that it had passed through YW's sewage works (which, absent specific notification, were not equipped to screen out Iso-octonal) and having, thus, been "treated" in YW's sewerage works were discharged into controlled waters.

The Justices convicted YW. The Crown Court acquitted them. The Divisional Court convicted them. The House of Lords acquitted them, allowing the appeal on the basis of statutory defence which sewerage undertakers have under s108(7) of the WRA. For our purposes this statutory defence is not relevant. What is relevant is that absent to statutory defence the HL would have convicted YW, applying *Aphacell*, as causing the pollution because:

"Although the water authority was not responsible for the presence of the Iso-octonal in the effluent discharged into the river and beck, by setting up a system for gathering effluent into its sewers and thence into its sewerage works for treatment, the arrangement deliberately intended to carry the resulting treated effluence into controlled waters, it had "caused" poisonous noxious and polluting matter to enter controlled waters accordingly, on the facts it would, without more, have been guilty of the offence."

In Attorney General's reference No. 1 of 1994 the criminal division of the Court of Appeal found that where a party had undertaken the day to day running and maintenance of a sewerage system, and then failed properly to maintain it and carried on running it in an unmaintained state, with the result that there was a blockage in the system, a secondary pump failed, and a pollution incident subsequently arose, the party could properly be convicted of "causing" pollution.

Lord Taylor, the Lord Chief Justice, began by stating the general legal principles concerning the offence of causing pollution that could be derived from the case law, summarised as follows:

i) it was a question of fact in each case whether a defendant could be said to have "caused" the entry of the polluting matter into the water;

ii) while the second limb of the offence related to "knowingly permitting" the entry of such matter, the word "knowingly" did not qualify the offence of causing pollution, and it was a true strict liability offence;

iii) the word "causes" should be given its plain meaning;

iv) the word "causes" involved active participation in the operation or chain of operations which resulted in the pollution in question;

v) mere standing by and looking on was insufficient to amount to "causing".

It is difficult to reconcile the finding by the Court of Appeal criminal division that mere standing by and looking on in the sense of running a system in an unmaintained state could amount to "causing" on the one hand with the decision of the Divisional Court in *Wychavon* that the failure promptly to unblock the system so that additional raw sewage pollution occurred could not constitute a "causing" of pollution on the other.

It is difficult to reconcile the *Yorkshire Water Services* decision that the ownership and operation of a works into which an unknown person without the owner's knowledge passes polluting matter nonetheless constitutes a "causing" of pollution by that owner on the one hand with the decision in the WDA case that ownership and control of the site as landlord, where a tenant discharges polluting substances down the drains on the site, does not constitute "causing" pollution by the landlord on the other.

We think that the last word has not been said on this issue. In particular, in the context of contaminated land remediation and the potentially astronomical financial liabilities which they may occasion, the Agency will have a duty under the proposed new Part IIA of the EPA to serve a remediation notice in the first instance on the person who "caused or permitted" the pollution of the land.

It is of vital importance, therefore, for owners and landlords and others who own these facilities but do not take an active part in the day to day operations on them to feel that they are not in the first line of fire as persons who "cause or knowingly permit". On the basis of *Wychavon* and *WDA* they are probably not in the first line of fire, but on the basis of *Yorkshire Water Services* they may well be. No doubt there will be further developments.

CHAPTER EIGHTEEN

INJUNCTIONS

1. Introduction

The most powerful and flexible weapon in the armoury of the court in environmental litigation is the injunction, which is usually in the form of a prohibitory injunction, i.e. an order restraining the commission or continuance of some wrongful act or omission, although, exceptionally, a mandatory injunction may be granted, see *Redland Bricks Ltd v Morris* [1970] AC 652.

The injunction is available in the High Court in all divisions (Supreme Court Act 1981 s37). It is important to note, however, that in the Chancery Division an application for an interlocutory injunction will be heard in open court, whilst in the Queen's Bench the application will be in Chambers. Thus, the question of whether publicity is sought to be gained or avoided can have a bearing on the choice of division.

Injunctions are available in the County Court (s.38 County Courts Act 1984) and the old rule that in the County Court there is no jurisdiction for the grant of an injunction unless ancillary to a damages claim was abolished in 1977. It is not, incidentally, a precondition of the grant of an injunction that a plaintiff has suffered a loss which is quantifiable as damages, see *Attorney General v Acton Local Board* (1882) 22 ChD 221. It is not generally permissible to bring a personal injuries claim in the Chancery Division. A nuisance action is generally brought in the Chancery Division, although see the White Book 36/1-9/13 which suggests that claims in nuisance and environmental claims should now be transferred to the Official Referee.

An injunction is speedily available and exceptionally effective. It has proved particularly useful in river pollution cases and the prominent role of the Anglers' Cooperative Association during the last 30 years, since 1955 when, in *Martell v Consett Iron Co* [1955] Ch 363 the activities of the Association in financing nuisance cases was held not to constitute maintenance. Their activities have been the best example in recent times of how citizens can play a really effective role in using injunctions to police the environment. Under RSC O.15 r.12 "an injunction may be granted on behalf of representatives of an unincorporated association, or other groups whose members have a sufficiently common interest", providing, of course, the representatives qualify for relief on the principles set out below.

2. Causes of action in which the injunction is available

The injunction is available in all private nuisance actions to anyone with an interest in land whose use or enjoyment of the land is being interfered with or affected.

An injunction is available in the tort of public nuisance in the following instances. The Attorney General may seek an injunction, acting on behalf of a section of the community, see for example *Attorney General v Gastonia Coaches* [1977] RTR 219. A local authority may seek an injunction, pursuant to its powers under s222 of the Local Government Act 1972, see for example *Shoreham UDC v Dolphin* [1972] 71 LGR 261. By contrast, the individual citizen has no locus standi in a public nuisance case unless he or she can show "particular damage" over and above that caused to the community at large by the public nuisance (see Cahpter 14 p. 159). Where the private citizen can show particular damage he or she has locus to bring an action for both damages and injunction in public nuisance, see *Boyce v Paddington Corporation* [1903] 1 Ch 109, and this can be highly effective, as was the case in *Halsey v Esso Petroleum* [1961] 1 WLR 683.

In negligence actions the remedy is not available, see *Miller v Jackson* [1977] QB 966.

In an action for breach of statutory duty the scope for the grant of injunctions probably depends on the context. Where the action is against a governmental or public authority in public law for breaching its statutory duty then an injunction is plainly available as one of the remedies which may be granted in judicial review proceedings. Where, on the other hand, the statutory duty is imposed on a private person, as for example a duty of care in respect of waste disposal under s34 of the Environmental Protection Act 1990, and the action is a writ action, for example for damages for careless waste disposal, then it is by no means clear that an injunction would always be available in a writ action. Where the action was based on an interest in land, by analogy with nuisance injunctive relief will probably be available. Where, by contrast, the action is based on personal injury, then the position would seem to be more akin to the negligence action and an injunction would not be available. The position here would then resemble a claim for personal injuries for negligence and breach of Factories Act statutory duty in the health and safety at work context, and it has not been possible to locate any decided case in which an injunction has been granted for a breach of statutory duty under the Factories Act.

Even where, as in the public law context, there can be no doubt of the availability of an injunction, for the private citizen there may well be a bar to proceedings for want of *locus standi*. For example in ex parte *Rose Theatre Trust Co*, [1990] 1 QB 504, a company limited by guarantee was formed by individual citizens with the object of protecting the site of the Rose Theatre in Southwark. This was held at first instance to lack standing to obtain an interim injunction restraining the site's owner from carrying out any development work on the site. Although this decision has alarmed many practitioners, this concern may well be over-stated.

Firstly, it ought in most cases to be possible to find an applicant who is likely to be directly affected by the unlawful act or omission complained of, who would certainly have locus to bring the proceedings. Secondly, it should be noted that in Rose Theatre the claim failed on the merits. We think it unlikely that in a claim which is likely to succeed on the merits that the court will deny the remedy on the ground of lack of standing. Finally it is worth emphasising that Rose Theatre was not appealed so that the question of locus in this context has yet to be examined by the appellate courts.

In certain instances regulatory bodies have powers, and sometimes, arguably, duties, to seek injunctions. The following are illustrations:

(a) Statutory nuisance.

Local authorities have duties both to monitor their areas for the presence of statutory nuisances and to investigate any complaints concerning possible nuisance (s79 EPA 1990). By s80 EPA 1990 where the local authority is satisfied that a statutory nuisance exists it shall serve an abatement notice which is the first step in the statutory nuisance procedure. By s81(5) local authorities can take proceedings for injunction in the High Court where a nuisance prosecution would "afford an inadequate remedy". It is, therefore, necessary for a local authority to have actively considered whether the Magistrates' Court abatement proceedings would afford an adequate remedy, but it is not necessary for the local authority to have actually exhausted these procedures, see *Hammersmith LBC v Magnum Automated Forecourts Ltd* [1978] 1 WLR 50.

(b) Licensing of large plants: EPA Part 1.

Under Part I of the Environmental Protection Act 1990, by virtue of s24, either HMIP or the local authority are given powers to use the High Court to enforce Enforcement Notices (s13) or Prohibition Notices (s14).

(c) Water pollution.

The National Rivers Authority has the responsibility for ensuring compliance with water quality objectives and for prosecuting water pollution offences. There is no express power in the Water Resources Act 1991 which authorises the NRA to seek injunctions to restrain pollution of controlled waters. It is, however, arguable that the NRA has powers to seek an injunction under its general power to do anything which is calculated to facilitate or is conducive or incidental to the carrying out of the Authority's functions.

(d) Land use and planning.

By s187(b) of the Planning and Compensation Act 1991 local authorities may use or seek injunctions where it is "necessary or expedient" for the enforcement of any actual or prospective breach of planning control. It is expressly provided that this power is exercisable whether or not any other statutory enforcement powers have been or are proposed to be used.

3. Types of injunction

It is necessary to distinguish between final injunctions, interlocutory injunctions and the grant of an injunction "quia timet".

(a) Interlocutory injunctions

An interlocutory injunction means an injunction granted to afford temporary relief to the plaintiff pending trial. Since the House of Lords decision in *American Cyanamid Co v Ethicon Ltd* [1975] AC 396 the plaintiff need not, any longer, show a *prima facie* case and a threat of substantial and irreparable injury. The test is not so high, and the approach is broader. For an interlocutory injunction to be granted the court must be satisfied:

(i) that there is a serious triable issue as to whether a final injunction should be granted, and

(ii) that the balance of convenience favours the grant - e.g. that there is a likelihood of serious environmental harm if the activity is unrestrained, which outweighs in the court's view the damage to the defendant if the activity is restrained.

An undertaking as to damages will normally be required. There may be exceptions to this rule where the applicant is:

i) a local authority, see *Kirklees Borough Council v Wickes* (HL)1992 3 All ER 717;

ii) an impecunious legally aided citizen, see *Allen v Jambo Holdings Ltd* [1981] 1 WLR 1252;

iii) an established environmental protection group bringing a public interest case raising issues of enforcement of environmental statute, which is a point not tested in UK but in the Australian Land and Environment Court Pearlman J so held, see *Byron Shire Businesses v Byron Council* reported in Environmental Law and Management December 1994 201.

(b) Injunction Quia Timet

Usually a tort has to have been committed before an action will lie for an injunction to restrain a continuation or repetition. However an injunction may in certain circumstances be sought "quia timet" where interference is apprehended but has not yet occurred. The plaintiff must surmount three hurdles, all of them difficult (see *Fletcher v Bealey* [1885) 28 Ch 688):

(i) imminence (of danger);

(ii) near certainty of substantial damage (from the apprehended danger if it arises);

(iii) impossibility of protecting the plaintiff in any other way other than by granting the injunction.

A recent example of a successful application was *Hooper v Rogers* [1975] Ch 423, a decision of the Court of Appeal. There the defendant bulldozed a track around the plaintiff's farmhouse, exposing the farmhouse to a process of soil erosion that would eventually lead to support being withdrawn and collapse. The court held that a mandatory injunction could be awarded compelling the defendant to reinstate the ground, although in fact, the Court of Appeal awarded damages in lieu. See also *Midland Bank v Bardgrove* (Chap. 12 p.128) where the CA thought that a *quid timet* injunction might have been successfully sought.

A *quia timet* will fail if fear (of imminent danger) cannot be shown to have secure scientific or rational basis. In the late 19th century there were a number of actions concerning the siting of hospitals for infectious diseases which illustrate this principle, and fall either side of the line. In *Metropolitan Asylum District v Hill* [1881] 6 App Cas 193 a *quia timet* was granted against the erection of a hospital for contagious diseases in a particular place. On the other hand, in *Attorney General v Manchester Corporation* [1893] 2 Ch 87, an injunction to restrain the building of a smallpox hospital on the grounds of fear of infection was refused. Incidentally, these cases serve also to illustrate the important point that a public authority can expect no preferential treatment from the court when it comes to the grant or denial of injunction.

4. Grant of final injunction: general principles

The principles covering the grant or refusal of an injunction are the same in public law (Order 53) as in private law. The test is elastic: whether it is "just and convenient" to make the grant, (s37 of the Supreme Court Act 1981). The grant of the remedy is discretionary and will depend on all the circumstances of the case.

In general, a plaintiff who proves a continuing violation of his rights such that damages would be an inadequate remedy will be granted a perpetual prohibitory injunction as a matter of course, see the nuisance cases of *Imperial Gas Light & Coke Co v Broadbent* [1859] 7 HL Cas 600 (air pollution) and *Pride of Derby and Derbyshire Angling Association v British Celanese Ltd* [1953] Ch 149 (water pollution). The violation must be more than trifling and it must be continuous rather than intermittent, both matters being questions of fact and degree for the court.

In the light of EC Directives which impose limit values on air and water quality and have been incorporated into English law it may now be arguable that a plaintiff, qua citizen of Europe, can seek an injunction because there has been a "continuing violation" of his or her rights to air or water quality in accordance with the statutory limits, and damages would be an inadequate remedy.

So, for example, the possibility arises of, say, cyclists who regularly use the streets of a particularly polluted city bringing proceedings on the basis of air quality tests which show breaches of quality limits although a pre-condition would be damage either actual or imminent. Needless to say this will be a difficult hurdle to surmount (causation again) but, if surmounted, on the basis of the doctrine of direct effect there would seem no reason in principle why an action for injunction should not lie against the member state.

5. Public interest

There has been some conflicting authority as to the extent to which public interest in the activity complained of may be held by the court to outweigh an individual's right to be entitled to protection by way of injunction. The old law was clear, namely that the interests of the public cannot override the rights of the individual, see *AG v Birmingham Corporation* [1858] 4 K&J 528 and *Manchester Corporation v Farnworth* [1930] AC 171. However, in *Miller v Jackson* [1977] QB 966 two members of the Court of Appeal refused to grant an injunction to stop cricket being played, although the cricket amounted to a nuisance, on the grounds of public interest. In *Kennaway v Thompson* [1983] WLR 361 the Court of Appeal disapproved of the dicta on the public interest point in *Miller*, so the old law would appear to be restored.

CHAPTER NINETEEN

NOISE POLLUTION

1.Introduction

Noise pollution tends to receive relatively little publicity when compared with other forms of environmental damage. However, according to the records ofthe Environmental Law Foundation noise nuisance complaints make up the majority of the pollution complaints tackled. Noise pollution is a relatively complex area of law and the statutory controls are of paramount importance. The legal framework is intertwined with the science of noise measurement.

Ideally a noise nuisance should be measured objectively to enable a court to determine whether or not a given level of noise amounts to a nuisance either under statute or at common law. Often the noise problem will be an ongoing one which the plaintiff will wish to restrain. The choice of remedy and forum are therefore of particular importance. This chapter sets out to demystify the science of noise measurement and considers the range of remedies available in both the Magistrates' Court and in the Civil Courts.

2. An outline of the statutory provisions

Part III of the EPA 1990 largely replaces the noise control provisions of the Control of Pollution Act 1974 (the "CPA 1974"). Sections 58-59 of the CPA 1974, which used to govern statutory noise nuisance in the whole of Great Britain, now only apply to Scotland. The key statutory provisions are now contained in the EPA 1990 and in particular section 79 (as amended by Noise and Statutory Nuisance Act 1993) which makes noise emitted from premises so as to be prejudicial to health or a nuisance a statutory nuisance. The enforcement of the prohibition on statutory nuisances is primarily carried out by Local Authorities (section 80), although individuals may bring proceedings in a magistrates' court under section 82.

The Control of Pollution Act 1974

The CPA 1974 remains in force in relation to noise in the streets (section 62) and noise on construction sites (sections 60 and 61).

Section 60 gives a local authority power to serve a notice on any person carrying out construction works imposing requirements as to the way the works are carried out and requiring them to use the "best practicable means" (as defined in section 72) to minimise the noise. A person intending to carry out construction works may apply to the local authority for a consent under section 61 and the authority may impose conditions in such a consent.

Section 62 (as amended by the Noise and Statutory Nuisance Act 1993) prohibits the use of a loud-speaker in a street between the hours of 9 pm and 8 am for any purpose and at any other time for the purpose of advertising any entertainment, trade or business.

Sections 63-67 provide for the designation of "noise abatement zones" by a local authority and a register of noise levels. A noise abatement order may apply to the whole or part of a local authority's area (the zone) and will specify the classes of premises to which it will apply. The authority must give publicity to the proposed order before it is made and objections must be considered. The level of noise is then measured from premises within the zone and are recorded in a noise level register. It is then made an offence for the noise level recorded in the register to be exceeded without the consent of the authority. If the authority refuses consent there is a right of appeal to the Secretary of State.

If a notice is served under s60 (control of noise on construction sites), s61 (prior consent for work on construction sites) or s66 (reduction of noise levels) of the CPA 1974 that notice may be appealed to the Magistrates' Court under the Control of Noise (Appeals) Regulations 1975. The grounds of appeal depend upon the notice being appealed but broadly speaking the grounds are that:

(a) notice is not justified by the section under which it is served;

(b) defect or error in the notice;

(c) requirements of the notice are unreasonable;

(d) times within which notice is to be complied with are unreasonable;

(e) notice should have been served on some person other than the appellant;

(f) notice might have been served on some person in addition to the appellant being a person who is carrying out the works required. On hearing the appeal the court may (i) quash the notice; (ii) vary the notice in favour of the appellant; or (iii) dismiss the appeal.

Codes of practice

There are a number of codes of practice which have been approved by the Secretary of State (under s71 of the CPA 1974) aimed at minimising noise nuisance. Their legal effect is equivocal, but where they have been breached they may assist a Plaintiff in establishing that a noise amounts to a nuisance.

Noise and Statutory Nuisance Act 1993

The 1993 Act covers noise in the street; operation of loud speakers in the street; and audible intruder alarms. Section 8 of the Act governs the consent of local authorities to the operation of loudspeakers in streets or roads. Section 9 empowers the local authority to control noise nuisance from audible intruder alarms.

Civil Aviation Act 1982

It is worth noting that under section 76 of the Civil Aviation Act 1982 no action shall lie in respect of trespass or in respect of nuisance, by reason only of the flight of an aircraft over any property at a height above the ground which is reasonable. However, there is the possibility of the public authority carrying out insulation works pursuant to the Land Compensation Act 1973 s20 and the Noise Insulation Regulations 1975, s19 which are considered below. Aircraft noise is controlled under the Air Navigation (Noise Certification) Order 1990 and the Aeroplane Noise (Limitation on Operation of Aeroplanes) Regulations 1993.

Land Compensation Act 1973

Section 20 of the Land Compensation Act 1973 provides that the Secretary of State may make regulations imposing a duty or conferring a power on responsible authorities to insulate buildings against noise caused or expected to be caused by the construction or use of public works or to make grants in respect of the cost of such insulation.

The Noise Insulation Regulations 1975 impose duties to upon authorities to carry out insulation work and to make grants. Under reg 3 where the use of a highway to which the Regulations apply is expected to cause noise at a level not less than $L_{10(18\ hour)}$ 68dB the appropriate highway authority shall carry out or make a grant in respect of the cost of carrying out insulation work in dwellings and other residential buildings within 300 metres of the highway (see reg. 7).

Under reg. 5 grants may be made where the works for the construction or alteration of the Highway are expected to cause noise nuisance. If an offer to carry out insulation work or make a grant is not made an occupier who claims that the authority are under a duty under reg. 3 may make an application for an offer under reg. 13. If that request is refused the authority must give written reasons for their refusal.

Construction Plant etc (Harmonisation of Noise) Regs 1988

Regulation 3 of the Construction Plant and Equipment (Harmonisation of Noise Emission Standards) Regulations 1985 provides that no person shall on or after 26 March 1986 market any item of construction plant or equipment unless s/he has an EEC type-examination certificate and a certificate of conformity has been issued and an EEC mark has been placed on it.

An EEC type-examination certificate is a certificate that the equipment conforms to the directives adopted by the Council of the Communities relating to the permissible sound power level of compressors, tower cranes, welding generators, power generators and powered hand-held concrete breakers and picks. Under Reg. 7 the periodic check of construction plant or equipment may be carried out by the body approved by the Secretary of State. If the requirements are not met the approved body may issue a notice specifying: (a) the respects in which items do not conform; (b) that unless steps not taken to ensure such items do conform within a specified period the certificate will be withdrawn; (c) if the approved body thinks fit the certificate will be suspended immediately.

Under reg. 9 any person who, without reasonable excuse, contravenes or fails to comply with Reg. 3 shall be guilty of an offence and liable to a fine not exceeding £2,000.

3. Defining noise: a glossary of terms

Most of us have a subjective idea of what constitutes an acceptable level of noise. However, a noise which one person considers unacceptable may be tolerated by another. Whether or not we consider a noise intrusive depends upon a number of factors including its intensity, pitch, duration, the time of day and ultimately our own sensibilities. In order to present a noise nuisance case to a court accurately and objectively reference a scientific approach is required.

Sound

To understand actions related to sound it is important to understand some of the terms. **Sound** is a periodic fluctuation of air pressure and sound pressure is the amount by which the air pressure fluctuates.

The **Frequency** is the rate at which the air pressure fluctuates. The higher the frequency the higher pitched the sound. The human ear responds to frequencies between 20 Hertz (Hz) and 20,000Hz The **loudness** of sounds depends upon sound pressure level and frequency.

The unit of measurement is the **decibel** (dB) which is commonly "A weighted", and therefore expressed as dB(A). The A weighting is an agreed frequency response similar to that of the human ear.

Although the audible range is about 20-20,000Hz, the human ear's response to sounds at low and very high frequencies is not as good as it is to mid-range sounds. It is therefore usual, when making noise measurements, to incorporate an electrical filter in the measuring system in order to give the system a response similar to that of the human ear. The filter that is most frequently used is the **A-weighting** and noise measured using this weighting results is expressed as so many dB(A). As well as filtering out those frequencies to which the human ear is less sensitive and which cannot therefore be intrusive, noise measurement needs to take account of any fluctuations in noise level over time. In other words it may be time weighted.

The indicator on a sound level meter does not show the instantaneous level of sound pressure on at the microphone since that level is subject to rapid fluctuation. The value shown a meter is an average known as the root-mean-square (r.m.s.) level expressed in decibels. There are four standard **time weightings**: peak; impulse; fast; and slow. The peak weighting will indicate the maximum instantaneous air pressure at the microphone i.e. the noise level at its momentary peak. The other three weightings will result in the dB level corresponding to the r.m.s. value of the sound signal averaged over 35ms, 125ms, or 1000ms respectively.

Statistical parameters - L_{A10} or L_{A90}

The fact that noise level at any particular point will probably vary from time to time makes it difficult to arrive at a figure for the "level" of noise. A common approach to resolving this problem is to determine the noise level which is exceeded for a stated percentage of the measurement period. Thus L_{A50} is the level exceeded for 50% of the measurement period. L_{A10} is the level exceeded for 10% of the time. It is therefore an indicator of how high the noise level rises. $L_{10(18\ hours)}$ is used as an index of road traffic noise. L_{A90} is the level exceeded for 90% of the time. It is therefore an indicator of how low the noise level falls. It is specified in BS4142:1990 as the background noise level.

The equivalent continuous noise level (LEQ) of a fluctuating noise is the level of a notional steady sound which, at a given position and over a defined period of time, would have the same A-weighted acoustic energy as the fluctuating noise. Thus L_{EQ} gives a form of average noise level.

The sound exposure level (LAE) is a form of L_{EQ} which enables L_{AEQs} for different periods of noise to be compared. L_{AE} is the continuous level that would in 1 second result in the same energy being emitted as is represented by the noise energy emitted over the actual period.

Sound sources cannot simply be added together. Two sound sources each emitting 50 dB do not equate to 100dB. If two sound sources are acting together and the difference between them is greater than 10dB the higher level is the one that should be taken. If the two sources are the same then 3 dB is added thus in the above example given the total of 2 sources emitting 50dB would be 53dB (see Control of Noise (Measurements Etc) Regulations 1976 and Noise Levels (Measurements and Registers) (Scotland) Regulations 1982.

Aircraft noise consists of a build up to a peak level and then fall off and occurs at intervals. The level of nuisance caused depends on peak perceived noise levels and on the number of aircraft heard in the period.

Noise from aircraft engines is concentrated in certain frequency bands. Measurements in dB are made in a number of the frequency bands and from these a total level is calculated emphasising the predominant components.

Construction site noise is covered by BS 5228 1975 and is measured in Leq.

Noise may include vibration (see the Control of Pollution Act 1974 s73). **Vibration** is the oscillation of an object about a reference point. It is measured using a piezoelectric accelerometer, or vibration meter.

4. Noise level tables

The table below sets out the sound level in $dB_{(A)}$ of some familiar sounds.

Noise levels

Noise	SoundLevel $dB_{(A)}$
Pain threshold	140
Pneumatic road breaker	130
Supersonic flight path within 5 miles of take off	125
High Speed Train at 2 metres	105-110
Heavy Lorry at 3 metres	90
Kerbside of busy street	80
Moderately loud radio in domestic room	70
Loud speech at 1 metre	65
Restaurant or Department Store	60

Changes in noise levels

The decibel scale is not linear but logarithmic, so whereas 100 metres is twice as far as 50 metres, 100dB(A) is not twice as loud as 50dB(A). Changes in the average level of fluctuating sound, such as traffic noise, need to be of the order of 3dB(A) before becoming definitely perceptible to the human ear and a change in sound level of 10dB(A) is experienced by the average listener as a doubling or halving of loudness.

Band of Change in Sound Level dB(A)	Subjective Impression	Description
0 - 2	imperceptible change in loudness	marginal
3-5	perceptible change in loudness	noticeable
6-10	up to a doubling or halving of loudness	substantial
16-20	up to a quadrupling or quartering of loudness	substantial
21+	more than a quadrupling or quartering of loudness	very substantial

5.When does a noise amount to a nuisance?

The question for the civil courts is whether or not the noise is such that it interferes with the plaintiff's reasonable enjoyment of his property (see for example *Halsey v Esso Petroleum Co. Ltd* [1961] 2 All ER 145). In the magistrates courts the question is whether the noise amounts to a statutory nuisance within the meaning of s 79(g) of the EPA 1990 (noise emitted from premises so as to be prejudicial to health or a nuisance).

Whether or not a noise constitutes a common law nuisance or a statutory nuisance will depend upon a number of factors including the loudness of the noise, its character, the nature of the locality, and time of day or night and the length of time for which it persists.

Whilst there are no express statutory noise limits the following are worth noting: The Wilson Report (Noise, Final Report Wilson Committee on the Problem of Noise (1963, Cmnd 2056) HMSO) proposed 2 criteria: (i) 75dB(A) in urban areas near main roads and heavy industrial areas; and (ii) 70 dB(A) in rural, suburban and urban areas away from main road traffic and industrial noise. The value of 75 dB(A) was also proposed as a guide in the original (1975) edition of British Standard 5288. The current version of that standard (1984) makes no explicit recommendation with regard to daytime noise.

In *Halsey v. Esso Petroleum Co Ltd* Veale J. observed at 156:

"The scale of decibels from nought to 120 can be divided into colloquial descriptions of noise by the use of words: faint, moderate, loud, and so on. Between 40 and 60 decibels the noise is moderate, and between 60 and 80 it is loud. Between 80 and 100 it is very loud and from 100 to 120 it is deafening."

As far as night time noise is concerned, the standard is normally taken as the avoidance of sleep disturbance. The guidelines vary from the World Health Organisations suggested maximum of 35 dB to Rice and Morgan of the Institute of Sound and Vibration who suggest that sleep disturbance would not be expected to become significant provided the external L_{Aeq} does not exceed 55 dB.

6.Evidence

The starting point for any toxic tort is the collation of good anecdotal evidence. The following categories of primary evidence will need to be obtained:

(i) anecdotal evidence of the plaintiff;

(ii) anecdotal evidence of others eg. neighbours;

(iii) a noise notebook/diary should be kept by the plaintiff and by neighbours. It should detail the date, time, duration and source of the noise and indicate its character and the perceived loudness;

(iv) where the character or pattern of the noise is important a tape recording of the noise should be obtained. It should be stressed that a tape recording cannot be used as evidence of the loudness of the noise which is the province of the decibel meter. Tape recorders may be useful to give some idea of the character of the noise, where it has a particularly irritating pattern;

(v) If the loudness of the noise is to be measured objectively a decibel meter must be used. Although there is no formal requirement for this sort of evidence it is advisable for a plaintiff to adduce it rather than simply rely on his own (or his neighbours) perception of the noise. It is important to record not just the measured level of noise but the point at which the reading was taken.

Evidence from witnesses setting out the nature of the perceived time always carries weight and a prospective plaintiff will wish to have as many witness as possible to describe the source and character of the noise and the interference it causes. This anecdotal evidence will be all the more important where it is not dependant on the vagaries of the witnesses' memories but is recorded contemporaneously in a diary. In the case of *Tetly v Chitty* [1986] 1 All ER 663 (discussed below) the trial judge specifically referred in his judgement to both the witness evidence on the character of the noise, and the technical evidence of the noise meter readings.

Whilst much of the initial evidence may be gathered by the individual or individuals affected, it should be remember that the local authority may well be better placed (and better equipped) to investigate a noise complaint.

Once the primary evidence has been obtained consideration should be given to instructing an expert to prepare a report which addresses the level of noise experienced by the plaintiff and sets out the level which the plaintiff alleges would be reasonable. With the evidence in place an informed decision can be made on the merits of commencing proceedings.

7.Choice of forum: Magistrates Court or Civil Courts?

A prospective plaintiff or complainant has a choice of bringing proceedings in the Magistrates' Court or in the Civil Courts. The choice of forum will depend upon the nature of the nuisance and on the means of the plaintiff. Broadly speaking where the primary remedy sought is the cessation of the noise (rather than compensation) and where dispute is relatively simple where for example neighbours are in dispute the informality of the Magistrates' Court may be preferred (particularly where the complainant does not qualify for legal aid). Conversely, where the nuisance arises on industrial or trade premises the availability in the Magistrate's Court of the defence of BPM means that civil proceedings may be preferred although they are generally more expensive.

The following table should enable legal advisers to identify the appropriate forum:

	Magistrates' Court	County Court/High Court
Legal Aid	No	Yes
Defence of Best Practical Means	Yes	No
Remedy	Abatement	Injunction
Remedy if nuisance persists	Fine for breach of abatement	Contempt of Court Proceedings
Compensation	Compensation order unlikely	Damages

8. Remedies in the civil courts

Any action in the civil courts will be based on private or public nuisance the principles of which are discussed in detail elsewhere in this work. The cases set out illustrate how the civil courts apply general principles of nuisance in cases of noise pollution.

The courts take account of any benefit to the public. Thus noise caused by building works is not a nuisance if the works are carried out with reasonable skill so as to reduce the noise as much as is practicable. In *Andreae v Selfridge & Co* [1938] Ch 1 (CA) the plaintiff was the proprietor of a hotel on part of an island site. The defendant company demolished various properties on the remainder of the site and the plaintiff complained that the defendant had conducted its building operations in such a way as by noise and dust to interfere with the reasonable and comfortable enjoyment by her of her premises. The trial judge found damages alleged proved and assessed them at £4,500. See also Chapter 13 p.151.

On appeal the Court of Appeal held:

(i) that no cause of action arises in respect of operations such as demolition and building if they are reasonably carried on and all reasonable precautions and proper steps are taken to ensure that no undue inconvenience is caused to neighbours;

(ii) that the evidence showed that the plaintiff was inconvenienced by the dust and noise, but in estimating damages the court must be careful not to penalise the defendant company by throwing into the scales against it losses caused by operations which the defendant company was legitimately entitled to carry out. Order of the trial judge varied by reducing damages to £1,000.

The courts take into account the length of the nuisance. In *Metropolitan Properties v Jones* [1939] 2 All ER 202 the plaintiffs leased a flat to the defendant who assigned the lease to S. S. absconded and the defendant re-entered the flat. The plaintiffs installed heating in the flat above during S.'s tenancy and this incorporated an electric pump.

For a period of 3 weeks the noise from the electric pump amounted to a nuisance. The plaintiffs brought an action to recover rent and the defendant counterclaimed for damages for nuisance. It was held: (i) that the noise was not one of a merely temporary character but would give rise to a cause of action; (ii) the person liable was the landlord who had installed the apparatus; since the defendant was an original lessee who had assigned his interest in the legal estate he could not maintain a counterclaim for nuisance. Had damages been recoverable Goddard LJ indicated that he would have assessed them at £21.

Consideration will be given to the area in which the noise has taken place. In *Sturges v Bridgman* (1879) 11 ChD 852 a confectioner's mortars and pestles created a noise in an area consisting primarily of the consulting rooms of medical practitioners. Thesiger L.J said at 856:

"whether anything is a nuisance or not is question to be determined, not merely by an abstract consideration of the thing itself, but in reference to its circumstances: what would be a nuisance in Belgrave Square would not necessarily be so in Bermondsey; and where a locality is devoted to a particular trade or manufacture carried on by the traders or manufacturers in a particular and established manner not constituting a public nuisance, judges and juries would be justified in finding, and may be trusted to find, that the trade or manufacture so carried on in that locality is not a private actionable wrong."

That said if the noise level is sufficiently high it will probably amount to a nuisance. In *Rushmer v Polsue & Alfieri Limited* [1907] AC 121 (HL(E)) The plaintiff had from 1887 carried on business as a dairyman and resided at premises in Gough Square, Fleet Street. The district was then devoted to printing and allied trades and the defendants carried on business as printers in premises adjoining the plaintiff's. In 1904 the defendants set up machinery which the trial judge found caused a serious disturbance at night time to the plaintiff. The Trial Judge granted an injunction restraining the defendants from so working their machines and so carrying on their printing works that they caused a noise nuisance. The Defendants appealed. The House of Lords approved the following statement of the law:

"It does not follow that because I live, say, in the manufacturing part of Sheffield I cannot complain if a steam hammer is introduced next door, and so worked as to render sleep at night almost impossible, although previous to its introduction my house was a reasonably comfortable abode, having regard to the local standard; and it would be no answer to say that the steam-hammer is of the most modern approved pattern and is reasonably worked."

The courts will not protect a sensitive use of land, but acts done with the intention of actually causing annoyance will be a nuisance. In *Hollywood Silver Fox Farm v Emmett* [1936] 2 KB 468 the defendant was held liable in nuisance for deliberately firing guns to cause vixens to abort. But in *Rattray v Daniels* (1959) 17 DLR (2d) 134 there was no liability for bulldozing close to a mink farm in the whelping season where there was no intention to harm and no negligence.

The owner or occupier of property will be liable for nuisance caused by activities to which he has expressly or impliedly consented. In *Tetly v Chitty* [1986] 1 All ER 663 the defendant council granted permission to a go-kart club to develop a go-kart track on land belonging to the council. The council granted a 7 year lease to the club with the express purpose of using and developing the site as a go-kart track. The plaintiffs who lived near the track brought an action against amongst others the council claiming damages for noise nuisance and an injunction restraining the use of the track.

It was held that:-

(i) the council were liable in nuisance because the noise generated by the go-karting activities was an ordinary and necessary consequence or a natural and necessary consequence of the operation of go-karts on the council's land, and the council as landlords had given express or at least implied consent to the nuisance;

(ii) damages were an insufficient remedy and the plaintiffs were entitled to a permanent injunction restraining the council from permitting the continuation of go-karting on the land;

(iii) damages of £750 to the first and second plaintiffs and £500 to the third based upon the nuisance lasting for 5 weeks.

Often the plaintiff in an action for noise pollution will be less concerned with damages than having the quiet enjoyment of their property restored and it should be remembered that the court will, in appropriate circumstances, grant an interim injunction. In *Kennaway v. Thompson* [1981] QB 88 the Court of Appeal granted an injunction to restrain a motor boat club from causing noise nuisance to an adjoining property. The courts will not allow a nuisance to continue simply because the wrongdoer is able and willing to pay for the injury he might inflict. The table below sets out further examples of noise nuisances that have been considered by the courts.

Case	Noise source
Broder v Saillard (1896) 2 Ch.D 692	Stables
Colwell v St. Pancras Borough Council [1904] 1 Ch 707	electric Station
Dunton v Dover District Council (1977) 76 LGR 87	playground noise
Hawley v. Steele (1877) 6 Ch. D 521	rifle range
Inchbald v Robinson (1869) LR 4 Ch 388	circus
Leeman v Montagu [1936] 2 All ER 1677	crowing cockerels
Newman v Real Estate Debenture Corp. [1940] 1 All ER 131	banging doors

Soltau v De Held (1851) 2 Sim (NS) 133	bells
Vanderpant v Mayfair Hotel Co [1930] 1 Ch 138	hotel kitchen

9.Remedies in the Magistrates' Court

As we have already noted the statutory controls are of paramount importance in the field of noise nuisance. Under s79(1)(g) of the EPA noise emitted from premises so as to be prejudicial to health or a nuisance is a statutory nuisance. An individual may make a complaint to a Magistrates' Court under s82. A Local Authority may serve an abatement notice under s80.

Individuals

In proceedings brought under s82 the complainant must give 3 days' notice of intention to start proceedings. If the court is satisfied that a noise nuisance exists or is likely to recur it will make a noise abatement order. Failure to comply with that order is an offence punishable by a fine of up to £5,000.

Local Authorities: the noise Abatement notice

Section 80 of EPA 1990 provides where a local authority is satisfied that a statutory nuisance (s79(1)(g) and exists, or is likely to occur or recur, in the area of the authority, the local authority shall serve a notice ("an abatement notice") imposing all or any of the following requirements-

(a)requiring the abatement of the nuisance or prohibiting or restricting its occurrence or recurrence;

(b)requiring the execution of such works, and the taking of such other steps, as may be necessary for any of those purposes,

and the notice shall specify the time or times within which the requirements of the notice are to be complied with. The form of the notice is particularly important since if it is defective it may be appealed to a Magistrates' Court under Statutory Nuisance (Appeals) Regulations 1990 (SI 2276).

The abatement notice shall be served on the person responsible for the nuisance or where the nuisance arises from any defect of a structural character, on the owner of the premises; or where the person responsible for the nuisance cannot be found or the nuisance has not yet occurred, on the owner or occupier of the premises. s80(3) provides that a person served with an abatement notice may appeal against the notice to a magistrates' court within the period of twenty-one days beginning with the date on which he was served with the notice.

Section 80(4) provides that if a person on whom an abatement notice is served, without reasonable excuse, contravenes or fails to comply with any requirement or prohibition imposed by the notice, he shall be guilty of an offence. By 80(7) and (8) it shall be a defence to prove that the best practicable means were used to prevent, or to counteract the effects of, the nuisance where it arises on industrial, trade or business premises.

A conviction under s80 for failing to comply with an abatement notice without reasonable excuse carries a maximum penalty for nuisances on business premises of £20,000 and on other premises of £5,000.

Defences under Section 80(4)

The meaning of the words "without reasonable excuse" was considered by the High Court in relation to the pre-cursor of this section, section 58(4) of the Control of Pollution Act 1974, in *A Lambert Flat Management v Lomas* [1981] 2 All ER 281 it was held that reasonable excuse included special difficulties in complying with a notice such as illness. Skinner J said at p284d:

"A comprehensive right of appeal is given by s58(3) which was not available under the 1960 Act. Regulation 4(2)(a) of the 1975 regulations permits an appeal on the ground that the notice is not justified by the terms of s.58. In my judgement an excuse cannot be "reasonable" under s58(4) if it involves matters which could have been raised on appeal under 58(2) unless such matters arose after the appeal was heard or, if there was no appeal, after the time for appeal had expired."

Regulation 4(2) of the 1975 Regulations (SI 2116) is broadly similar to regulation 2(2) of the Statutory Nuisance (Appeals) Regulations

1990 (SI 2276) and it is submitted that courts would be likely to hold that an excuse cannot be "reasonable" under s.80(4) if it involves matters which could have been raised on appeal under 80(3).

Where a local authority is of the opinion that proceedings for an offence under section 80(4) above would afford an inadequate remedy in the case of any statutory nuisance they may take proceedings in the High Court for the purpose of securing the abatement, prohibition or restriction of the nuisance.

Under s81(3) where an abatement notice has not been complied with the local authority may, whether or not they take proceedings for an offence under section 80(4) abate the nuisance and do whatever may be necessary in execution of the notice.

The following cases provide useful illustrations of the principles applicable to statutory noise nuisance and in particular the potential pitfalls which should be avoided when drafting abatement notices.

In *R v Clerk to Birmingham City Justices, ex parte Guppy* JP Vol 152, 159 the applicant occupied premises from which a loud noise made by amplified music was emitted. The local authority served an abatement notice which prohibited the recurrence of the nuisance, required immediate termination of the use of the equipment creating the nuisance and required all other steps necessary for that purpose to be taken. On application by the occupier for judicial review it was held in dismissing the application that where a notice requires the abatement of a nuisance and/or the execution of works or the taking of other steps, a time for compliance must be specified but it is inapt to interpret a prohibition on recurrence as something which is to be complied with within a specified period.

In *McGillivray v Stephenson* [1950] All ER 942. The respondent kept pigs in such a manner as to cause a statutory nuisance. The local authority served an abatement notice requiring him to abate the nuisance and "for that purpose to remove the whole of the pigs from the premises, clean up the effect of their past presence and cease for the future to allow the premises to be used for pig keeping at all".

The respondent failed toed comply. In dismissing the notice one of the grounds relied on by the justices was that the abatement notice was void as it required the respondent to abate the nuisance in a specific manner. It was held on appeal that the abatement notice was a good notice since its operative part was the request to abate the nuisance and the steps whereby the abatement might be effected could be regarded as mere surplusage.

In *Myatt v Teignbridge District Council* 20 June 1994 (Garner). The Divisional Court held, in dismissing an appeal by way of case stated from a conviction under EPA 1990 for failure to comply with an abatement notice served under the EPA 1990 s80, that the notice should specify the works to be executed or the steps to be taken to abate the nuisance. The appellant Mrs. Myatt had kept as many as 17 dogs in 2 small properties. The council served an abatement notice upon her which merely stated that the nuisance was "the keeping of dogs" and did not specify the nature of the nuisance nor the steps to be taken to abate it. However, on the facts the Divisional Court found against the appellant on the basis that where a person keeps a number of dogs in 2 properties it "really requires one to have an exceptionally technical approach to say that they do not know of the matter causing the nuisance and the steps to be taken to abate it."

It would seem that the courts do not wish to adopt an over technical approach and that whilst the notice should specify the nature of the nuisance and the steps to be taken to abate it however the amount of information required will necessarily be a matter of fact and degree.

That decision must be considered in the light of *Network Housing Association Ltd v. Westminster City Council* The Times 8 November 1994 (Queen's Bench Divisional Court). In that case a tenant complained of an invasion of his flat by noise from the flat above which arose from the second flats ordinary residential use. A notice was served requiring the landlord to make alterations so as to reduce the noise to a certain level of decibels without indicating the work to be carried out. It was held that the notice was defective as it did not state what work was to be put in hand.

In *R -v- Fenny Stratford Justices Ex parte Watney Mann (Midlands) Ltd* [1976] 2 All ER 888 residents complained of noise made by a juke-box in a public house situated in a building containing residential flats. The residents applied under to the justices to make a nuisance order requiring the applicants to abate the nuisance. The justices made an order that the level of noise should not exceed 70 decibels.

It was held that although it was helpful of the justices in the instant case to attempt to provide specific guidance, they did not specify where the noise level was to be recorded. The term of the order specifying the noise level was imprecise and therefore void for uncertainty. Lord Widgery CJ said at p892h:

"Of course it is open to those who draft the summons, the order or the notice (which can be relevant under these provisions) to describe the nuisance in general terms as a nuisance and to require its abatement in general terms".

In *Wellingborough District Council v Gordon* [1991] JPL 874. the defendant was prosecuted for playing loud music at his address in contravention of a noise abatement notice served some 3 years previously. The court held that:

(i) to establish noise nuisance it was not necessary to adduce evidence from a neighbouring occupier that he had actually suffered interference with his reasonable enjoyment of his property and that justices were entitled to infer from the evidence of the police officers that a nuisance by noise had been created

(ii) the fact that the noise was made on a birthday could not amount to reasonable excuse (under the precursor of s80(4)).

Bristol City Council v Higgins The Times 9 September 1994. Mr. Higgins played music for up to 14 hrs per day in his bedroom. For 3 years council officers attempted to prevent noise nuisance including 2 seizures of equipment and 2 prosecutions under EPA 1990. Mr. Higgins continued to play the music and the council obtained an injunction to restrain nuisance under s81(5) EPA 1990. Mr. Higgins ignored the injunction and was jailed for 3 months.

CHAPTER TWENTY

FRESHWATER POLLUTION

1. Introduction

The lawyer approaching a freshwater pollution case is faced with a number of legal and evidential issues which are not raised by other toxic tort cases ranging from identifying riparian rights to assessing damages for the loss of the pleasures of trout fishing. This chapter examines the principles governing recovery in this area and the directions in which they are likely to evolve. At the end of the chapter we consider the application of these principles to a typical river pollution case.

In June 1992 the Royal Commission on Environmental Pollution reported that the quality of Britain's rivers had deteriorated over the past decade and that there is now extensive pollution of the nation's aquifers - the layers of rock or soil which hold underground water. This underlines the continuing problems of pollution in Britain's watercourses, a problem not only for the NRA, as the enforcement authority, but also for those who use watercourses for employment or recreation, and those who enjoy the amenity that the water environment offers in a healthy and unpolluted state.

2. The mechanism of pollution

The pollution of water can arise from a "point" source or can be "diffuse". Point pollution is the discharge of polluting matter from a single source or more than one source in close proximity, for example an factory discharge outlet. Diffuse pollution, as the word suggests, signifies pollution entering watercourses from a wider area and such pollution may be from more than one source.

The way in which the effluent is discharged can vary from persistent discharges to a single gross discharge. The former will often cause long-term damage to the receiving water and to the ecology of that water. The latter is more likely to have the effect of wiping out the whole or part of plant and animal life in the receiving water although the long-term impact on water quality may be minimal.

The type of the pollution that is present will be relevant to the common law remedy to be applied. For example, an injunction will be the likely remedy for persistent discharges (together with a claim for damages), whereas a damages claim alone is more appropriate to a single discharge.

3. Types of Watercourse

Water is present in the environment in different forms, and the remedies which are available depends, to some extent, upon the type of water involved.

Percolating Water

Water not flowing in a known and defined channel is not capable of ownership. Percolating water or water that has gathered temporarily will not be subject to the common law (riparian) rights set out below. Thus an owner of land can abstract percolating water from his land even if this results in the exhaustion of the supply of water to a neighbour's well (see, for example, *Bradford Corporation v. Pickles* [1895] AC 587). However, it is a nuisance to pollute water not flowing in a defined channel if the pollution escapes onto another's land (see *Ballard v. Tomlinson* [1885] 29 Ch.D 115 considered by the House of Lords in the *Cambridge Water* case).

Tidal Water

The land lying beneath coastal waters and the foreshore (i.e. between ordinary high and low water marks) is vested in the crown, unless there is evidence that there has been a grant of rights by the crown.

Artificial watercourses

Riparian rights as explained below do not automatically accrue to artificial watercourses as they do to natural watercourses. Artificial watercourses are those which owe their existence to some act of man, such as canals or drainage ditches. To establish such riparian rights it is necessary to show a presumed or actual grant of rights, (see *Rameshur Pershad Narain Sing v Koonj Behari Pattuk* (1874) 4 App. Cas. 121).

4. Riparian Rights: Common law rights in water

Riparian rights is the term used to describe the bundle of common law rights enjoyed by the proprietor of land which abuts a watercourse. Such a proprietor is often described as the riparian owner. Fundamental to the concept of riparian rights is the idea of rights to use water rather than ownership of the water. Indeed flowing water has been described as *publici juris* (see *Embury v. Owen* (1851) 6 Ex. 353) in that all those who have a right of access to it may reasonably use it and a person may only have property in a particular portion of the water which he has chosen to extract and take into his possession.

Riparian rights over natural watercourses are enjoyed automatically and do not rely on any grant. They exist in relation to all forms of water subject to the exceptions mentioned above. Thus they will attach to all water flowing in a defined channel whether above or below ground level. Although there has never been a decided case on the specific point it is likely that similar rights will exist in favour of owners of lakes ponds or pools.

A riparian owner is an owner of land which abuts a watercourse. Such an owner will, as of right, acquire riparian rights. The rights which the environmental practitioner is likely to find himself concerned with are likely fall into one of two categories: positive and negative rights. Positive rights allow the riparian owner to do certain acts for example to abstract or obstruct the flow of the water. In the sense that they permit a riparian owner to do certain things without liability to an adjacent owner with similar rights (freedoms to interfere).

The case of *McCartney v. Londonderry Lough Swilly Railway Co* [1904] AC 301 provides a useful illustration of the operation of positive rights. It identifies three ways in which a riparian owner may use the water to which his rights attach:

(i) "ordinary" such as domestic purposes or ordinary use of an agricultural holding. Use of water for such ordinary purposes may be enjoyed notwithstanding the effect which such use has on a lower owner (this use is permitted);

(ii) for an extraordinary purpose, but in a way that does not cause sensible damage to another riparian interest (this use is also permitted);

(iii) extraordinary use which damages a lower riparian owner (this use is not permitted by riparian rights).

Negative rights concern the riparian owners right to freedom from interference, for example, pollution. Again reference to the case law is instructive. In *Young John & Co. v. Bankier Distillery Co.* (1893) All ER Rep [1891-4] 439 HL, Lord Macnaghten said:

"A riparian proprietor is entitled to have the water of the stream, on the banks of which his property lies, flow down as it has been accustomed to flow down to his property, subject to the ordinary use of the flowing water by upper proprietors, and to such further use, if any, on their part in connection with their property as may be reasonable under the circumstances. Every riparian owner is thus entitled to the water of his stream in its natural flow, without sensible diminution or increase, and without sensible alteration in its character or quality. Any invasion of this right causing actual damage, or calculated to found a claim which may ripen into an adverse right, entitles the injured party to the intervention of the court."

The protection offered to riparian interests is therefore substantial. The protective approach adopted by the courts is underlined by the fact that the discharge of polluting matter into a watercourse is considered an extraordinary use of land, and is therefore permissible only to the extent that it does not cause damage.

Whilst other rights arise from ownership of land adjoining watercourses, the abovementioned comprise the rights the breach of which will give rise to a claim as a consequence of toxic damage to the water environment.

In addition to freehold ownership riparian rights can be acquired by virtue of a lease being granted of land including the banks of a river pond or lake. A proprietary interest can also arise from the grant of legal rights over water. Most commonly this right will be the right to take and carry away fish which is a profit á prendre i.e. a grant of rights appurtenant to the land rather than a disposal of the land itself.

A person who is not the riparian owner, but who enjoys a lesser interest and will not, therefore, have a cause of action. In particular a licence will not amount to a proprietary interest. The law states (see for example *Inwards v. Baker* [1965] 2 QB 29) that a licence is merely permission to do something that would otherwise be unlawful (see also the Scottish case of *East Lothian Angling Association v Haddington Town Council* 1980 SLT 213). This case decided that the Association was not entitled to recover damages following a pollution of its waters. It will be a question of fact in each case whether a plaintiff is a mere licensee or not. In the case of *Mason v Clarke* [1955] AC 778 it was decided that an oral agreement, in this case to catch rabbits on another's land, was sufficient to establish a right in equity.

5. Rights of Action

There are a number of potential causes of action for breach of riparian rights and inevitably there will be some degree of overlap between them. With the exception of claims brought in negligence and public nuisance, which are discussed below, it is essential to establish that the potential plaintiff is the riparian owner in respect of the watercourse which has been polluted to enable a potential plaintiff to bring a claim for damages or an injunction.

The primary torts relevant to toxic damage to the water environment are: (i) private nuisance; (ii) *Rylands v Fletcher*; (iii) trespass; (iv) negligence; (v) public nuisance.

Actions in private nuisance, *Rylands v. Fletcher* [1865] LR 1 Ex 265 and trespass require, as a condition precedent, an interference with the rights or interests described above. Actions in negligence or public nuisance by contrast do not (although proof of damage will be a precondition).

Private nuisance

Nuisance is the principal tort adopted in water pollution cases. It will apply both where the damage occurs as a result of a single toxic discharge or a persistent one. A nuisance is committed in relation to waters in respect of which riparian rights are enjoyed where it can be shown that those waters have been altered by another so as to interfere with the owners use and enjoyment of its land or physical damage has been caused to the land. It is necessary to prove damage before a claim in nuisance can be brought, but in practice this is unlikely to be a problem in water pollution actions. The general principles of nuisance actions are set out in Chapters 13 and 14.

Rylands v. Fletcher

In the case of *Pride of Derby Angling Association v. British Celanese Ltd* [1953] Ch 149 Lord Denning suggested that the treatment and disposal of sewage would not amount to a non-natural use of land. In *Cambridge Water* the House of Lords held that *Rylands v Fletcher* was only a specific application of the law of nuisance and therefore foreseeability of relevant damage was a prerequisite to recovery. Lord Goff thought that the storage of substantial quantities of chemicals on industrial premises should be regarded as an almost classic case of non-natural use. He found it very difficult to think that it should be thought objectionable to impose strict liability for damage caused in the event of their escape.

"Let it be assumed that ECL was well aware of the possibility that PCE, if it escaped, could indeed cause damage, for example by contaminating any water with which it became mixed so as to render that water undrinkable by human beings. I cannot think that it would be right in such circumstances to exempt ECL from liability under the rule in Rylands v. Fletcher on the ground that the use was natural or ordinary.

Trespass

The tort of trespass has not so far been mentioned in this book. Applied to freshwater claims it involves the introduction of polluting matter into the aggrieved party's water by the wrongdoer. It may well be that a trespass to water rights will occur when the pollution results in the deposition of solid matter in the plaintiff's water, and is thus more limited in scope that nuisance. However Wisdom's Law of Watercourses (5th Ed.) cites *Courtney v. Collet* (1697) 12 Mod Rep. 164 as authority for the proposition that causing water to overflow into another person's fishery will be a trespass.

One potential advantage of an action in trespass is that it is not necessary to prove damage to bring a claim. Whilst in most cases a claim is initiated in response to the infliction of damage, there may be situations where a persistent discharge has not yet caused palpable damage, but will do so if it is not abated. This may be particularly relevant in the case of discharges that are high in suspended solids for example from abandoned mines. The leading case on trespass to waters is *Jones v Llanwrst Urban Council* [1911] Ch 393.

Negligence

The usual principles of negligence apply to pollution of water, see chapter 13. Negligence is an important remedy in the area of water pollution for three reasons. Firstly, statute may relieve a statutory body from liability in nuisance as, for example, in the case of sewage effluent. Secondly, factual situations may make it impossible to prove one of the elements of the torts of strict liability (nuisance; *Rylands v. Fletcher*; and trespass). For example, for a defendant to be liable in nuisance it is necessary to show that he has caused or allowed polluting matter to enter a watercourse. However, a situation may arise where negligent design results in failure of a treatment process, so that blame will attach to a person other than the owner of the site from which the polluting matter escaped. Thirdly there may arise situations where an aggrieved party does not have sufficient interest in the watercourse to establish a cause of action in a tort of strict liability. As set out above, whereas it may be essential to establish a proprietary interest in land to bring a claim in torts of strict liability, an action in negligence is based on the neighbour principle.

Negligence may therefore provide a cause of action to persons other than the riparian owner. If, for example, discharges of sewage or industrial effluent represent a serious health risk or amenity loss to local residents there seems no reason in principle why a resident, or group of residents, should not be able to bring an action in negligence. Such an action would of course be subject to the other requirements of a negligence action set out in Chapter 13.

7. Defences

The primary statutory and common law defences are: (i) prescription; (ii) grant of rights; (iii) act of God; (iv) act of a trespasser; and (v) statutory authority.

Prescription

A right to discharge effluent into water or to abstract can be acquired by prescription. The usual rules as to the acquisition of such rights applies. As the right will constitute an easement it must have been enjoyed for the relevant period without force, without secrecy and without the consent of any third party. This defence is subject to the important qualification that a person claiming such an easement must be able to prove that the abstraction or pollution in question has been constant over the period over which the prescriptive right is claimed. Thus for example in the case of *Cargill v. Gotts* [1981] WLR 441 a defendant was unable to rely on prescriptive right as a defence where he sought to abstract a far greater quantity of water for a different purpose than had previously been the case.

Grant of rights

A grant of rights can be made by one landowner to another to do something that would otherwise be unlawful e.g. to discharge effluent.

Act of God

This defence is most commonly adopted in cases of exceptional meteorological conditions. Extreme drought conditions may be relevant in an action involving abstraction. Equally excessive rain may be alleged as the effective cause of a pollution if it causes slurry to be lifted from a tank. The burden lies on the Defendant to show that there were exceptional conditions which cased the damage. Meteorological evidence can be obtained from the Met. Office or from experts. In practice it is difficult to run this defence effectively, given the vagaries of weather conditions in this country!

Act of Trespasser

The classic application of this defence is where pollution has occurred due to an act of vandalism. The burden of proof again falls on the defendant.

Statutory Authority

This defence was considered in detail Chapter 13 in relation to undertakers carrying on operations pursuant to special Acts who have a defence of statutory authority in respect of unavoidable nuisances necessarily incidental to their operations. However, in the context of water it is important to consider first the abstractor or discharger who has a defence if he has been granted a "consent", ie. a statutory licence.

The availability of the defence depends on whether water has been abstracted or effluent has been discharged. In the case of the abstraction s.59 of the Water Resources Act 1991 provides that where a person has been granted an abstraction licence by the NRA then, provided the abstraction is made in accordance with that licence, it will operate as a defence to a common law action.

In the case of discharges of effluent, consent for which has been given by the NRA pursuant to s.88 and Schedule 10 of the Water Resources Act, consent only acts as a defence to criminal proceedings under s.85 of the Act and not as a defence to a common law action. Thus a downstream owner can bring a common law action for pollution damage even though the discharger is operating within its consent. An example is *Cook v South West Water* (Plymouth County Court, Judge Cox, 15 April 1992, unreported): The plaintiff obtained damages of £2,500 and £1,500 costs against the Water Company for allowing discharges resulting in frothy foam which damaged the plaintiff's trout · and salmon "beats". The plaintiff succeeded notwithstanding that neither the consent nor the river quality objections were breached.

It is a defence that an act is being carried out pursuant to statutory authority. This most commonly arises in the case of sewage discharges where the statutory undertaker is not only authorised but also obliged to accept and treat sewage effluent. In each case it is necessary to look at the statute in question to determine the extent of the statutory authority that has been given. It is not therefore a blanket defence. As a general rule the defence of statutory authority will not be available where the wrongdoer has been guilty of negligence, see Chapter 13.

Other sources of pollution (a "non-defence")

It is worth adding that it is not a defence to plead that another source of pollution is present in a watercourse. Liability for pollution is joint and several. It may however be relevant to a claim for damages to determine an apportionment of liability where two tortfeasors are responsible for one pollution.

8. The NRA

The NRA has extensive powers under section 161 of the Water Resources Act 1991 to regulate pollution where it considers that

(i) any poisonous, noxious or polluting matter;

(ii) is likely to enter or be present in or have been present in controlled waters; or

(iii) then it can carry out works to prevent such entry, remove or dispose of such matter, remedy or mitigate any pollution which has occurred and restore flora and fauna.

Once works have been completed the NRA can recover its costs from the person who caused or knowingly permitted the matter in question to be at the place from which it was likely to enter controlled waters or to be present in them.

This is a good example of strict liability imposed by statute. There is apparently no limitation period after which a party is no longer at risk of being required to clean up. However, the limitation is that the NRA may only recover once the work is done. This is a large disincentive to undertaking costly clean up work where there is uncertainty as to the relevant party or the only party liable is financially weak.

9. Statutory Compensation: Water Industry Act 1991

Para 2(3) of schedule 12 of the Water Industry Act 1991 provides that where any damage to, or injurious affection of, any neighbouring land is attributable to the exercise by a undertaker of any power to carry out pipe-laying works on private land, the undertaker shall pay compensation in respect of that damage or injurious affection to any person entitled to an interest in that land. Paragraph 3 provides for the assessment of compensation and the reference of disputed compensation to the Lands Tribunal in such circumstances.

Plainly this covers physical damage to the property but in the authors' view the scope of compensation for injurious affection is more uncertain, particularly with regard to loss of profits although in principle the proper measure of compensation should reflect the appropriate to damages in tort. However, application of the McCarthy rules (see: *Metropolitan Board of Works v McCarthy* (1874) LR 7 HL 243) would suggest that the injurious affection must be the consequence of the lawful exercise of statutory powers and if not, then the appropriate remedy would be by action in the courts in the usual way.

10. Evidence

As with all litigation the cornerstone of success is good quality evidence, and it is worth making one or two comments on the acquisition of information and samples, and the use of experts in the field of freshwater pollution.

Whether proceedings are for damages or an injunction the principal source of information will be the NRA. The NRA have a statutory obligation to maintain a public register under the Water Resources Act 1991. This register contains the analysis of all samples taken of effluent discharged pursuant to a discharge consent. It also contains analysis of samples of water other than effluent. Furthermore the register contains copies of all consents to discharge and applications pending.

As well as this data the NRA will usually have a good deal more information as to water quality as a result of biological and chemical surveys that have been undertaken. Even if these surveys have not been made available to the public the NRA will generally supply copies provided they are satisfied that they are seen to be impartial and reasonable charges are paid for the information. Similarly the NRA hold information relating to water resources an hydrogeological data including all licences to abstract.

The NRA will generally, on reasonable request, make officers available for interview. If such officers are required to give evidence it will normally be necessary to serve *subpoenas*.

Whilst liability will often not be in dispute in the case of one-off toxic discharges, it will be in disputes relating to long-term discharges where injunction proceedings are to be brought. Expert evidence will be crucial to the success of any such proceedings. The elements to be proved and which an expert will have to address can be summarised as follows:-

(i)The nature and extent of the suspected pollution;

(ii)whether the pollution is causing the damage complained of; and

(iii) the extent to which extraneous factors, such as water levels and other toxic effluent are affecting the watercourse in question.

The expert will need to have made available all material information. Much of this, as indicated above, will be available from the NRA but it may well prove necessary to undertake further site specific survey work. In that case consideration needs to be given to the scope of such survey work. It should include quantitative and qualitative surveys of plant and animal life in the affected water and some survey work upstream of the suspected source of the pollution to establish the causation and extent of the damage.

11. Heads of Damage and evidence on damage.

A claim arising from toxic damage to water may raise the heads of damage: (i) restocking; (ii) loss of amenity; and (iii) loss of profit.

Restocking of fisheries

A watercourse may take tens of years to recover in the absence of restocking and the cost to a defendant of compensating for loss of sport in the interim period is likely to be a much more expensive option. Calculation of restocking claims is generally straightforward as the NRA will in the majority of cases have prepared an assessment of the restocking required to reinstate the fishery. If necessary an independent expert can be approached to advise on restocking and fish suppliers to provide estimates of the cost of replacement.

Where an accurate assessment has not been provided by the NRA it is generally accepted that a multiplier is applied to the number observed to have been killed to arrive at the number of fish needed to reinstate. This multiplier will depend on the type of water and the circumstances of the pollution.

Some types of pollution will pass through a stretch of water quickly causing no long-term damage to the ecology of the water course. In other cases insect and plant life will have been damaged, and it may be necessary to reinstate the ecology and the cost of doing so should be included in the claim see *Marquis of Granby v Bakewell Urban District Council* (1921) 87 J.P. 105.

A final word should be said about fish kills in migratory river. Many rivers running into the North, and Irish Seas and the Atlantic Ocean contain primarily stocks of salmon and sea trout. These fish breed in the river and their progeny spend between one to three years in the river and going to sea, for again one to three years. They then return as adults to spawn and die. The value of the fishing to netsmen and anglers lies primarily in the adult fish returning up the river. A kill of fish in a migratory river, will therefore result in a loss of fish not only in the year of the kill but also in the years when the progeny of the fish killed would otherwise have returned to the river. Restocking is not a straightforward option in these cases. Expert evidence will often be needed to assist in arriving at an accurate assessment of loss.

Loss of amenity

This part of the claim is intended to compensate for the interference with the enjoyment of fishing rights. A typical example of this type of claim is provided by *Roy Brodrick and Others v. Gale and Ainslie Limited* 21 December 1992, Swindon County Court (unreported). In that case Rainbow Trout escaped from a fish farm into the river Kennett. HHJ Dyer found that the Defendant fish farm was liable in nuisance and negligence. In considering damages for loss of amenity the Judge observed:

"Among fly fishermen the brown trout is considered to be the aristocrat. Such fish are considered to be cunning and yet to be excellent fighters when hooked... Fly fishing in trout streams where the brown is the only quarry carries a high premium. Flyfishing clubs, such as the plaintiff club go to great lengths to keep there water free of rainbows and grayling."

The flyfishing club had fishing rights over about 4 miles of the river Kennett. The Judge awarded damages to the plaintiff club for the diminution in the value of its property, plus loss of enjoyment based upon the rental per rod, following *Burgess v Gwynedd River Authority* (1972) 24 P & CR 150 (Lands Tribunal). In that case C.'s fishing rights had been substantially damaged by works carried out by the river authority to prevent further flooding; the works, though necessary, were too drastic and thus unreasonable as they paid no heed to the fishing interests, floods, even very big ones, being unlikely to affect the river permanently; the authority had committed an actionable wrong and an injury within the meaning of the Land Drainage Act 1930 s34(3) for which they must pay full compensation, which was determined at £7,000, arrived at on a rental per rod basis.

Loss of profit

Any claim made by a business arising from toxic damage to water will involve a claim for loss of profit as well as any claim that may exist for the reinstatement of the fishery. Such a claim will be based on the estimated loss of income less saved expenditure. Claims for loss of profit are much more readily established on the basis of accurate historical data rather than speculation of what may have happened in the future. It is submitted that a claim for loss of amenity or loss of profit following a pollution incident is made in response to direct damage and cannot be construed as pure economic loss. This will only be important in the context of a negligence/private nuisance action.

It should be noted that s.21 of the Capital Gains Taxes Act 1979 provides that a charge to CGT arises where a capital sum is derived from an asset notwithstanding that the asset has been disposed of. The section specifically refers to compensation as being such a capital sum. There is an exemption form tax where the compensation is used to restore the asset. Tax will not therefore be payable in respect of the reinstatement part of a claim. A charge to tax is however likely in the case of a loss of amenity payment.

Where possible the taxable element of a claim should be grossed up to reflect the tax liability. Alternatively the paying party should give an indemnity against any liability that may arise in the future. This paragraph cannot do justice to a complex issue. The possible liability to tax and the availability of exemptions has to be considered on the facts of each case.

Other consequential loss

In addition to restocking costs a claimant can, of course, recover any expense to which he has been put as a result of the wrongful act. This may include clean-up costs but only where actual expense has been incurred as opposed to voluntary labour. In the case of a fishing club a claim can be made for loss of ticket income.

12.A typical water pollution case

This freshwater river pollution case has been adapted from a recent pollution incident. It illustrates several of the issues discussed above.

Toxi-Chem Ltd discharge of a quantity of ammonia into the river Murky. The pollution persists for about 2 weeks and as killing fish and plant life. The expert evidence indicates total fish kill along a 4 mile stretch and partial fish along a 3 mile stretch. The land abutting the affected stretch of river is owned by an angling association.

As the riparian owner the angling association has a right of action against anyone who unlawfully does any act which disturbs the enjoyment of the fishery. Interference with the Angling Association's rights gives rise to an action in nuisance for damages. Similarly the Angling Association may bring a claim for trespass (see *Nicholls v Ely Beet Sugar Factory Ltd* [1936] Ch. 343.). It is likely that a court would take the view that this was a non-natural user of land and that the escape of the ammonia gives rise to damages under the rule *Rylands v Fletcher*. Since the Toxi-Chem owe the Angling Association a duty to take reasonable care the fourth cause of action available is negligence. Ordinarily expert evidence would be required on this issue although in certain circumstances it may be possible to plead a case on the basis of res ipsa loquitur, if, for example, Toxi Chem are successfully prosecuted by the NRA. Any conviction should be pleaded and in such circumstances it may in a serious case it may be possible to put pressure on a defendant with an application for summary judgement.

Heads of Damage

These may include the following:

(1) Clean up site;

(2) water to waste;

(3) value of fish;

(4) loss of income;

The principle that the Angling Association should be put back in the position that they were in before the pollution means that the measure of damages is arguably the cost of restocking the stretch of river. This is subject to it being reasonable to do so and a court being satisfied that it would do so. It is submitted that the correct approach for the court to take would be to allow recovery if it was reasonable for the Angling Association to replace the fish and if the expert evidence showed that the fish population had not and would not recover naturally and within a reasonable period of time. Replacement calculations are not simply "pound for pound". The replacement fish will probably be younger and smaller and since they are unlikely to be wild fish some increment in the damages may be allowed for the fact that they will not, for a period, offer such good sport as those killed.

CHAPTER TWENTY ONE

AIR POLLUTION

Introduction

In 1952 an estimated 4,000 Londoners died from a smog that persisted for 5 days and, whilst the sulphurous smogs of the fifties have receded, air pollution remains a serious health problem today. The increase in the volume of traffic on our roads, for example, has led to different forms of air pollution caused by nitrogen dioxide and other exhaust emissions.

In January 1995 the Department of Environment published *Air Quality: Meeting the Challenge* which concluded that there was a need to develop a general strategy for air quality. Air quality is subject to extensive statutory controls and a number of European Directives dealing with gases from engines, sulphur in the atmosphere, lead in the air and chloroflurocarbons. Those controls are not considered in detail in this chapter which concentrates on the practical aspects of running an air pollution action and in particular the evidential hurdles faced by potential plaintiffs.

Air pollution impacts upon individuals at every level, from highly localised nuisances to depletion of the ozone layer and acid rain. It can have a detrimental effect on property through particulate deposition causing depreciation of property value ("property blight") and substantial clean-up costs. Actions based upon air pollution range from the nuisance complaints brought by local residents to restrain the odour caused by pigfarms, to actions brought by farmers for compensation for damage to cattle and property blight caused by toxins emitted from incinerators.

Polluters and Pollutants

In many air pollution cases the primary difficulty faced by the plaintiff will be in identifying the source of the pollution. Often the key to identifying the source of the pollution will lie with the analysis of samples of the pollutant. The chemical composition of the pollutant will often reveal the fingerprints of the polluter or at least narrow down the possible sources. Deposits containing PCBs, for example, are more likely to originate from an incinerator burning industrial waste which contains halogenated oils than from a municipal waste incinerator burning paper. Analyzing the pollutant is therefore the first step in identifying the source of the pollution and the potential defendant. The table below sets out some of the sources of common pollutants.

SOURCE	POTENTIAL WASTE PRODUCT
Power generation processes i.e. coal, oil, gas and nuclear generators	carbon monoxide (CO), sulphur dioxide (SO2), particulate material, radio-active waste
Industrial processes (mineral, chemical, metal and extractive industries)	heavy metals, polycyclic hydrocartbons, gases and dust
Incinerators	waste products depend on the type and size of material incinerated; the temperature of incineration; the residence time; and the amount of excess oxygen
Road traffic	nitrogen dioxide (NO2), CO, very fine particles
Industrial processes such as animal by-product rendering or knacker's yards	highly odorous compounds
Dust	smuts from chimneys, industrial sites, construction sites

Airborne pollutants may be divided into two broad categories, gases (eg NO_2) and particulate matter, such as dust. Dust is the particulate matter most commonly encountered and warrants more detailed consideration. There are three main types of dust (see table below). The type of dust will reflect its source, the mechanism of its travel and its effects on members of the public.

Pollutant	Size (mm)	Description	Source	Distance travelled
Dust: Macro deposits	0.5-10	large individual obtrusive deposits visible to the human eye	smut from chimneys; commonly caused by incomplete combustion of fuel oil	up to 300m (short chimneys) or 1000m (tall chimneys)
Dust: Gritty deposits	0.2-1.0	feels gritty to touch	unpaved roads/heavy materials handling /piling	200m if not from elevated source i.e. chimney
Dust film	0.5-0.01	most frequently occurring dust nuisance. Too small to be seen with naked eye	cement dust from building sites	maximum deposition within about 10 chimney heights of source
Fume	.001	any airborne solid matter smaller than dust (CAA 1993 s64 (1))	industrial processes	depends upon height of chimney

Of the differing forms of dust nuisance the most frequently encountered is a dust film causing soiling ("dinginess"). A dust deposit can cause a clean surface to become soiled in this way within a few hours. The degree of nuisance caused will depend upon the following factors:

(i) the rate of obscuration of the surface by dust particles;

(ii) the optical properties of the surface exposed to the dust film;

(iii) the optical properties of the dust film;

(iv) the nature of the illumination of the surface;

(v) the frequency of dust deposition incidents; and

(vi) the size of the area affected.

1. The mechanism of pollution

In seeking to establish a link between an alleged polluter and the person or property injured the practitioner will often need to have recourse to meteorological evidence. In relatively straight forward cases where there is no dispute as to the source of the pollution, for example where the plaintiff suffers an intolerable odour from an adjacent pigfarm, meteorological evidence can sometimes be dispensed with. However, where, for example, it is alleged that toxic matter has been deposited on the plaintiff's land from one of a cluster of nearby factories it will be important to establish the source of the matter, how it came to be deposited on the plaintiff's land and in what concentration it has been deposited.

In cases where the source of the pollutant is in dispute expert meteorological evidence will be required before the claim can be pleaded. Particular consideration will need to be given to explaining any concentrations of pollution (one of the notable features of the Chernobyl pollution incident was that it resulted in localised concentrations of pollution thousands of miles from the source).

Methods of Toxin Deposition

Pollutants carried in the air may be deposited on land in a number of ways.

(i) *Dry Deposition* (i.e. particle fall out): This is one mechanism whereby pollutants may be carried from a chimney stack. Where wind is multi-directional the concentration of deposits is likely to be uniform in all directions around the stack.

(ii) *Wet Deposition*: Wet Deposition is a very effective means of deposition from a chimney stack. Consideration needs to be given to whether the pollutant is hydrophobic e.g. dioxins. Most rain bearing winds in Britain are Westerlies or South Westerlies which will tend to shed their water vapour on the Western side of any mountains which may lead to concentrated deposits of a pollutant some distance from the source.

(iii) *Occult deposition*: This type of deposition takes place where cloud is driven against the hillside. In some areas this accounts for a significant amount of the precipitation and may therefore contribute to the transport of pollutants.

Dust deposition

(i) Macro deposits: the most common form of macro deposits are caused by incomplete combustion of oil in chimneys ("acid smuts"). The distance travelled by is dependant on the height of the chimney. With chimneys up to 50m the acid smuts will travel up to 300m. If the height of the chimney is 70m or more the distance may exceed 1000m.

(ii) Gritty deposits: these do not travel far except where emitted from large chimneys. Grit problems caused by dirty surfaces or stock piles are often associated with strong winds. The mechanism of transport is "saltation" where the particles bounce across the surfaces and off of each other assisted by the wind.

(iii) Films of Dust: These are particles which are small enough to be dispersed on the wind rather than moving in salatating motion. Nuisance conditions from a ground level source are usually limited to 200m.

2. Statutory Outline

The Clean Air Act 1993 (the CAA 1993)

The CAA 1993 consolidates the Clean Air Acts of 1956 and 1968. Section 1 of the CAA 1993 prohibits the emission of dark smoke from chimneys; Section 2 prohibits the emission of dark smoke from any industrial or trade premises; and Section 4 provides that new furnaces must be constructed so that they are so far as practicable, smokeless. Domestic chimneys are controlled by way of the smoke control area order (ss18-20) whereby a local authority may by order declare the whole or any part of the district of the authority to be a smoke control area and thereby make it an offence to burn other than authorised fuel. Section 33 provides that a person who burns insulation for a cable with a view to recovering metal from the cable shall be guilty of an offence unless the burning is part of a process subject to Part I of the EPA 1990.

Environmental Protection (Prescribed Processes and Substance) Regulations 1991.

The regulations provide that certain processes are controlled under Part 1 of the EPA 1990. Those processes in Part A of the Regulations are subject to control by HMIP and those in Part B are subject to control by Local Authorities. Detailed consideration of this area falls outside the scope of this book but the practitioner should always consider whether drawing a pollution problem to the attention of the appropriate authority will provide a practical alternative to litigation.

3. Remedies in the Magistrates' Court

The statutory nuisance provisions under Part III of the EPA largely mirror those which have been considered in detail in relation to noise nuisance. The relevant statutory nuisances are set out in section 79 of the EPA: Section 79(1)(b) covers any smoke emitted from premises so as to be prejudicial to health or a nuisance; Section 79(1)(c) covers fumes or gases emitted from premises so as to be prejudicial to health or a nuisance; and Section 79(1)(d) covers any dust, steam, smell or other effluvia arising on industrial, trade or business premises and being prejudicial to health or a nuisance.

It should be noted that by Section 79(7) "dust" does not include dust emitted from a chimney as an ingredient of smoke; "fumes" means any airborne solid matter smaller than dust; and "gas" includes vapour and moisture precipitated from vapour. As with noise nuisance an individual may make a complaint to a Magistrates Court under section 82 of the EPA 1990 and a local authority may serve an abatement notice under section 80. This procedure is set out in detail in Chapter 19 in relation to noise nuisance.

Whether a complainant brings proceedings in the Magistrates Court or in the Civil Courts will depend upon the nature of the nuisance and on the means of the plaintiff. Broadly speaking where the primary remedy sought is the cessation of the nuisance (rather than compensation) and where dispute is relatively simple, where for example neighbours are in dispute, the informality of the Magistrates Court may be preferred (particularly where the complainant does not qualify for legal aid). Conversely, where the nuisance arises on industrial or trade premises the availability in the Magistrate's Court of the defence of BPM means that civil proceedings may be preferred although they are generally more expensive. It should be noted that by s79(10) the defence of BPM does not apply in the case of a nuisance falling within para 79(1)(b) except where the smoke is emitted from a chimney or in the case of 79(1)(c).

4. Remedies in the Civil Courts

The primary causes of action in the field of atmospheric pollution are: (i) nuisance (and the rule in *Rylands v. Fletcher*); and (ii) negligence. The general principles in relation to each of these causes of action are discussed in Chapter 13. However the cases set out below illustrate how the courts have applied of those principles in air pollution actions.

As with all nuisance whether or not smoke or dust amounts to a nuisance will depend upon the character of the neighbourhood and the background air quality. As we have previously noted what is a nuisance in Belgravia Square may not be a nuisance in Bermondsey. As Mellor J observed in *Tipping v St Helen's Smelting Co* (1863) 4 B & S 608 at 610:

"The law does not regard trifling inconveniences; everything must be looked at from a reasonable point of view, and therefore in an action for nuisance to property by noxious vapours arising on the land of another, the injury to be actionable must be such as visibly to diminish the value of the property and the comfort and enjoyment of it.... In determining that question time, locality, and all the circumstances should be taken into consideration."

In *West v Bristol Tramways Company* [1908] 2 KB 14, the defendants were a tramway company who paved parts of a road on which their tramway was laid. The wood paving was coated with creosote which gave off fumes and injured plants and shrubs belonging to the plaintiff, a market gardener. It was open to the defendants to use a different form of wood paving which would not have caused the damage. A jury found for the plaintiff. The Court of Appeal held that although the defendants did not know that the use of creosoted wood might cause damage and were not guilty of negligence they were liable under the rule in *Rylands v Fletcher* for the damage caused by the fumes.

In *Tutton v A.D. Walter Ltd* [1981] QB 61 the plaintiffs kept bees near land farmed by the defendant company and on which it grew a crop of oil seed rape. The flowers of rape were particulary attractive to bees. The crop was affected by pests to the extend that it required control by spraying with an insecticide. The insecticide was known to be dangerous to bees and the advice to farmers from both government agencies and the manufacturers warned against spraying during the flowering period because of the risk to bees. The defendant, having given a warning only 24 hours earlier to only 2 of the 5 plaintiffs, sprayed the field with insecticide killing the bees. It was held (Denis Henry QC sitting as a deputy High Court judge): (i) that the defendant owed a common law duty of care to neighbouring bee keepers since it knew of their presence in the neighbourhood, had knowledge of the danger to bees of spraying during the flowing period and had the bee keepers in contemplation before spraying. The defendant was in breach of the duty owed to the plaintiffs; (ii) that the warning given by the defendant to some of the plaintiffs was inadequate.

In *Wheeler v JJ Saunders Limited and Others* (1995) Times 3 January the Court of Appeal dismissed an appeal by the defendants from an order that they were liable in nuisance to neighbouring landowners as a result of smells emanating from their pig weaning houses. The decision is of particular note because the Court of Appeal held that the grant of planning permission enabling further pig farming on a site already used for that purpose did not exempt the defendants from liability in nuisance for smells which were the inevitable result of the implementation of the planning permission.

Where nuisance is caused one of the plaintiff's most important remedies will be injunctive relief. In the case of *Bone v Seale* [1975] 1 WLR 797 the plaintiffs owned and occupied properties adjacent to the defendant's pig farm. They brought an action for an injunction restraining the defendant from causing nuisance by smell from the farm and for damages. The nuisance had existed for 12½ years and caused no diminution in value. The trial judge granted the injunction and awarded damages of £6,324.66 on the basis of £500 per anum. The defendant appealed and the Court of Appeal varied the order to the extent that it held that applying general principles the correct figure for damages for loss of amenity was £1,000 to each plaintiff. See also Chap.13 p.147.

5. Evidence

Where the primary cause of action is nuisance the starting point is the collation of good anecdotal evidence. A potential plaintiff should obtain the following by way of primary evidence:

(i) Anecdotal evidence of the plaintiff.

(ii) Anecdotal evidence of others eg. neighbours.

(iii) A notebook/diary should be kept by the plaintiff and by neighbours. It should detail the dates, times, duration and source of any smoke, odour or other airborne pollution and indicate the prevailing weather patterns (eg. wind direction and whether raining).

(iv) Where dust or other matter is deposited samples must be obtained.

(v) If the pollution complained of is dust the plaintiff would be wise to have recourse to some objective measure of the dust level. This can be done by means of a dust gauge. There are two types of British Standard dust Gauge: (a) Bowl Gauge BS 1747 Part 1; and (b) Directional Gauge BS 1747 Part 5. The differing designs of these gauges mean that the results, although often of the same general magnitude, are not strictly comparable. Both types of gauge have specific uses in the assessment of dust deposition. Deposit figures are only valid for a small area around a gauge, and do not necessarily give much indication of average pollution in the rest of the town or region. This is exactly what would be expected from the variable nature and relatively short range of dust travel in nuisance situations.

(vi) In a case which involves smoke from a chimney photographic and video evidence should be obtained where possible.

CHAPTER TWENTY TWO

CONTAMINATED LAND

The Environment Committee of the House of Commons (the Rossi Committee) estimated, a few years ago, that the number of potentially contaminated sites in the United Kingdom were in the range of 50,000 to 100,000 as a result of a history of waste disposal by landfill, and of operational use for such things as gas works, power stations, textile plants, sewage works, chemical works and the like.

Up until very recently 90% of the nation's municipal waste went to landfill. It is probably no exaggeration to say that there were thousands of such sites which are now methane active and/or leaking polluted water. Residential development has since taken place on or near many such sites. Controlled waters are near such sites, and the underground plume is heading towards such controlled waters or already polluting them. Some of these sites are still owned by local authorities who filled and operated them. Others have long since been sold on to unwitting purchasers and may, for example, now be owned by tens or hundreds of domestic owner occupiers.

No area of pollution law has given rise to more controversy or anxious concern about rights and remedies as the question of who should foot the bill for contaminated land. In the 1990 EPA two sections, Section 143 which would have required a national register of land which had been the subject of contaminative uses, and Section 61 which would, in some circumstances, have required waste regulation authorities to clean contaminated land and pass the clean up charges onto the owner for the time being of the land, are both to be repealed. In other words the government has been forced to retreat in the face of a coalition involving property, industry and commerce which argued that property values would be blighted, asset backing undermined, and that the provisions would lead to a crisis of unmanageable proportions.

1. Environmental Liability

Broadly, environmental liabilities may be divided into three areas:

(i) criminal liability for regulatory non-compliance (subject to fines and/ or custodial sentences);

(ii) tort liability for damage caused to persons and their property eg. employers, neighbours, to be compensated in the form of damages or an injunction to prevent further damage;

(iii) "clean up" liability as imposed by the regulatory authorities pursuant to their statutory authority and their powers under the waste management regime which is Part II/IIA of the EPA.

"Owners", "Occupiers", "Persons Responsible", "Persons in Control", "Appropriate Persons" may all be held liable. Taking a landfilling operation as an example, the principal heads of liabilty are as follows:

Environmental Protection Act 1990

S33 - the offence of unlicenced disposal of waste or managing waste in a manner likely to cause environmental pollution or harm to health (s33 (1) (c)).

s34 - breach of the duty of care in relation to waste.

s59 - providing for the remediation of unlicenced deposit of waste.

s73 - providing for civil liability.

Part III - which regulates statutory nuisances.

The new legal framework involving local authorities, the environment agency and central government to be inserted as Pt.IIA in the EPA, building on nuisance law, and providing for "remediation notices" to be served on "appropriate persons" requiring specific remediation, failure to comply with which will result in heavy financial penalties plus chargeback of the reasonable cost of any remediation work which the enforcing authority has had to carry out itself.

Water Resources Act 1991

s85 - the offence of pollution/unconsented discharge of controlled waters.

s161 - providing for carrying out of remedial works by the NRA.

Common Law

Civil liability (principally nuisance, negligence, and *Rylands v Fletcher*)

Liabilities under the lease or contract for both the seller and the purchaser; liabilities under the lease for both the landlord and the tenant.

2. Recent Developments

It is beyond the scope of this work to give a detailed review of liability for contaminated land. That said, in the three years since the last edition of this work developments in case law and statute law have taken place which makes it more possible to discern where liability is likely to lie in given types of case, and also to identify areas of overlapping liability as between civil, regulatory and criminal schemes. It is necessary to review these to the extent that they bear on liability for contaminated land in tort.

The principal developments have been:

a) the decision by the House of Lords in *Cambridge Water Co Ltd v Eastern Counties Leather Plc* [1994] 1 All ER 53 which considerably clarified the common law relating to liability for long term contamination;

b) the proposed "remediation" regime now to be introduced into the 1990 EPA which now leans heavily on the statutory regime applicable to water pollution;

c) decisions of the courts on the proper interpretation of the words "causing and permitting" in the context of water pollution, which will probably now have direct application to the new land remediation regime just referred to;

d) the policy of the NRA both in relation to water pollution prosecution, and in relation to its "clean up" powers under s161 of the WRA 1991, which may well provide insight into the likely approach to prosecutions and clean up in respect of contaminated land.

These matters, are considered in turn.

3. Cambridge Water

The facts are well known and may be stated briefly. *Eastern Counties Leather Plc* (ECL) was an old established leather manufacturer which used chemical solvent in its tanning process; (in more innocent days, incidentally, this used to be sold directly to the public as "Dab-it-off" for getting stains out of their clothes). In the course of the process there were regular spillages of relatively small amounts of solvent onto the concrete floor of the tannery prior to but not after a change of operational methods in 1976. The total spillage over the period of years up to 1976 was assessed at being at least 1,000 gallons.

The spilled solvent, which was not readily soluble in water, seeped through the tannery wall into the soil below until it reached an impermeable strata 50 metres below the surface from where it percolated along a plume at the rate of about 8 metres a day until it reached the strata from which the Cambridge Water Co. Ltd. (CWC) extracted water for domestic use via a borehole. The distance between the borehole and the tannery was 1.3 miles and the time taken for the solvent to seep from tannery to borehole was about 9 months. In 1983 following the introduction of EEC driven maximum admissible concentrations for this solvent, tests at the borehole established that the concentrations exceeded the permissible level, the CWC had to cease use of the borehole, and in broad terms, inclusive of interest, CWC had to pay roughly £1 million to replace this source of supply. CWC sought to recover this sum against ECL in nuisance, negligence and *Rylands v Fletcher*.

The judge at first instance, Kennedy J, held that it was not reasonably foreseeable by ECL in 1976 that the spillages might cause any pollution. That, in his view, lead to the claims in negligence and nuisance failing. The claim in Rylands v Fletcher failed because the judge held that the tannery was not a "non-natural" user of land.

CWC appealed and the Court of Appeal allowed the appeal saying that where a nuisance was "an interference with a natural right incident to ownership then the liability is a strict one". The Court of Appeal sought to extract this proposition from *Ballard v Tomlinson* [1885] 29 Ch. D115, a case that was probably surprised to find itself forced into the judicial spotlight after 100 years of peaceful non-citation.

The House of Lords allowed ECL's appeal on the grounds that, irrespective of when the claim was put in negligence, nuisance, all *Rylands v Fletcher*, it was a necessary precondition that "damage of the relevant type" was reasonably foreseeable at the time of the leakage.

This disposed of CWS's claim (and left CWC, on any view, a wholly innocent party, with a bill for £1 million), but Lord Goff, with whose speech the other members of the House all agreed, went on to deal with the argument, raised by CWC, that whilst ECL may not have foreseen the type of damage <u>at the time of the spillage</u>, given that the pollutant remained in the pools beneath (and therefore part of,) their land, ECL can be liable for all the damage caused by the pollution leaving their land after they were told about the problem. Lord Goff's speech, in disposing of this argument, is of such importance that it ought not to be summarised. He said at 77 c-h as follows:

"Turning to the facts of the present case, it is plain that, at the time when the PCE was brought on to ECL's land, and indeed when it was used in the tanning process there, nobody at ECL could reasonably have foreseen the resultant damage which occurred at CWC's borehole at Sowston.

However there remains for consideration a point taken in the course of argument, which is relevant to liability in nuisance as well as under the rule in *Rylands v Fletcher*. It is appears that, in the present case, pools of neat PCE are still in existence at the base of the chalk aquifer beneath ECL's premises, and the escape of dissolved phase PCE from ECL's land is continuing to the present day. On this basis it can be argued that, since it has become known that PCE, if it escapes, is capable of causing damage by rendering water available at boreholes unsaleable for domestic purposes, ECL could be held liable, in nuisance, or under the rule in *Rylands v Fletcher*, in respect of damage caused by the <u>continuing</u> escape of PCE from its land occurring at any time after such damage had become foreseeable by ECL.

For my part, I do not consider that such an argument is well founded. Here we are faced with a situation where the substance in question, PCE, has so travelled down through the drift and the chalk aquifer beneath ECL's premises that it has passed <u>beyond the control of ECL</u>. To impose strict liability on ECL in these circumstances, either as the creator of a nuisance or under the rule in *Rylands v*

Fletcher, on the ground that it has subsequently become reasonably foreseeable that PCE may, if it escapes, cause damage, appears to me to go beyond the scope of the regimes imposed under either of these two related heads of liability. This is because when ECL created the conditions which have ultimately lead to the present state of affairs - whether by bringing the PCE in question on to its land, or by retaining it there, or by using it in its tanning process - it could not possibly have foreseen that damage of the type now complained of might be caused thereby. Indeed, long before the relevant legislation came into force, the PCE had become <u>irretrievably lost in the ground below</u>. In such circumstances I do not consider that ECL should be under greater liability than that imposed for negligence. At best, if the case is regarded as one of nuisance, it should be treated no differently from, for example, that case of the landslip in *Leakey v National Trust* [1980] 1 All ER 17, [1980] QB 485." (our underlining)

This, so far as we are aware, is the first judicial pronouncement on liability for continuing pollution where the creator did not foresee the damage at the time of the acts/omissions complained of, but has been made aware of it subsequently. To this extent the speech made important new law, but, in addition, Lord Goff clarified old law in holding that *Rylands v Fletcher* was an extension of the law of nuisance, which normally applies to a state of affairs, to an isolated escape; but that foreseeability of the type of damages is required in nuisance as in *Rylands v Fletcher*; and that the liability of the <u>creator</u> of a nuisance is different and more strict to that of a person who merely <u>continues</u> a nuisance, not having created it.

This last point is of considerable importance, and enables us to suggest that the liability in nuisance for contaminated land may currrently be summarised as follows:

a) Providing the user is held unreasonable, then, if, but only if, the type of damage was reasonably foreseeable at the time of the leakage, liability is strict in the sense that the defendant will still be held liable notwithstanding that he can show that he took all reasonable steps to prevent the nuisance occurring.

b) Further, a person is liable for the continuance of a nuisance when he has originally created a nuisance which in the nature of things is likely to be continued and is continued, even though he has ceased to be in possession of or interested in the land on which the nuisance exists, and has no power to remove it without being guilty of a trespass, see Halsbury's Laws, 4th Ed. Vol. 34 para 365; *Roswell v Prior* [1701] 12 MoD Rep 635; *Thompson v Gibson* [1841] 7 M & W 456; followed in Australia in *Fennel v Robson Excavations* [1977] 2 NSW LR 486, and in the American case of *Tadjer v Montgomery County* [1985] 487 A(2d) 658.

c) The liability of the creator is strict in the sense that the court will not give weight to the defendant's means and/or the proportionate benefit to be conferred on the plaintiff: if the nuisance can be abated, the defendant will be required to abate it and/or pay damages.

4. Liability of the Mere Continuer of a Nuisance

An occupier of land is liable for a nuisance, even though he has not created it, if he has continued it while he is in occupation and an occupier of land continues a nuisance if, with knowledge (actual or constructive) of its existence, he fails to take reasonable steps to bring it to an end, (see Halsbury's Laws 4th Ed. Vol. 34 para 365.) But, the plaintiff has the burden, as against a mere continuer, of proving:

a) that the defendant was negligent in failing to take reasonable steps to bring the nuisance to an end;

b) that the person so failing was in a position to take effective steps to that end, for example that the person had access to the site;

c) that, in demonstrating a failure to take reasonable steps, it is reasonable taking into account the defendant's financial circumstances, the cost of works, and the likely benefit to the plaintiff, see *Goldman v Hargrave* [1967] 1 AC   645 [1966] 2 All ER 989 PC; *Leakey v National Trust* [1981] All ER 17 [1982] WLR 65.

Applying the foregoing principles to the case where a municipal waste tip is built on and sold on to householders and then becomes methane active, if, but only if, the local authority filled the tip after the date on which it ought to have known of the methane producing propensities of such waste it will be held liable in nuisance because, firstly, methane type damage was reasonably foreseeable at the time it did the acts complained of, and, secondly, failing to take any precautions, in the light of the knowledge actual or constructive, would be deemed to be an unreasonable user; and, notwithstanding the local authority's sale and disposal of the land, its liability, *qua* creator of the nuisance, would continue, subject to limitation.

By contrast, an action in nuisance by an adjacent landowner against one or more of the homeowners that had purchased their homes on the active landfill would fail because, even though the homeowners were now the occupiers of the land with knowledge of the existence of the nuisance, there are no steps which the homeowners could reasonably take, particularly given their financial means, to bring the nuisance to an end.

Thus, in general terms, the Cambridge Water decision will be of comfort to those who purchase contaminated land, for it must follow that, as long as the purchaser can show that the pollutant is "irretrievably lost", and/or given the person's means it is not possible to demonstrate, in all the circumstances of the case, that there are reasonable steps the person could take to bring the nuisance to an end, he cannot be sued successfully in the torts of nuisance, negligence or *Rylands v Fletcher*.

The problem, as we shall see, is that, whilst the civil law treats him kindly, the regulatory scheme, and the criminal law, may not be so reassuring.

5. The Proposed Remediation Scheme

Although the proposed statutory scheme for contaminated land is not even on the statute book, we consider that it is sufficiently probable that the Bill will be introduced into law with its broad outline unamended to deal with it in this chapter. The guiding theme will be the "suitable for use" approach, under which contamination is generally dealt with as land comes up for redevelopment and the clean up standard is dictated by the proposed end use.

The new legal framework will involve local authorities, the environment agency, and central government. Their roles are spelled out in an exceedingly long (15 page) clause in the Bill which will be inserted into the 1990 Act following the committee stage in the Commons which threatens to give rise to changes but not to emasculate the present Clause 54 which will become Part IIA of the EPA.

The clause is based on old established statutory nuisance legislation which was amended by the EPA and is Part III of the EPA. Under Part III, local authorities have a duty to inspect their areas "from time to time" with a view to detecting various prescribed nuisances - eg air pollutants, waste deposits and noise - which are "prejudicial to health or a nuisance".

Where a nuisance is detected an abatement notice must be served on the person responsible or, in some cases, on the owner or occupier of the premises concerned. There is an appeal procedure and then an enforcement procedure under which non-compliance with the notice is an offence unless the defendant proves that he was using "the best practicable means" to prevent or mitigate the nuisance. Further, where a notice is not complied with, the local authority may abate the nuisance itself and seek to recover the costs "reasonably incurred" from the person responsible. The proposal, in relation to contaminated land, is to use a similar procedure.

Contaminated land is defined as any land appearing to a local authority "to be in such a condition, by reason of substances in, on or under the land," that "harm" or water pollution "is being, or is likely to be, caused". In turn, harm is defined as "harm to the health of living organisms or other interference with the ecological systems of which they form part and, in the case of man, includes harm to his property" - a definition which appears in similar terms elsewhere in the EPA.

These definitions amount to a considerable extension of current nuisance law and also underline why it has so rarely been invoked to deal with land contamination problems. Nuisance law is concerned primarily with human health and well being. In contrast, the new definition also embraces other organisms and their habitats and water pollution, and makes it clear that damage to property is encompassed as well.

Under the statutory scheme once a contaminated site is identified by a local authority procedures are put in place according to the status of the contaminated land.

The principal vehicle for securing the assessment and clean up of contaminated sites is the "remediation notice". The enforcing authority, which may be the local authority or the environment agency according to the status of the site, will be placed under a duty to serve a remediation notice on the "appropriate person" specifying what remediation must be carried out and a deadline for compliance.

The remediation notice will be required to specify "only things which it considers reasonable, having regard to <u>the likely costs and the seriousness of the harm or water pollution involved</u>", and to any guidance issued by the Secretary of State.

As with the current Part III statutory nuisance regime appeals against remediation notices would go to a Magistrates Court or to the Secretary of State in certain cases giving the appropriate person an opportunity to have revoked or varied the remediation notice.

There is however a very significant new feature in relation to the "appropriate person". Under Part III statutory nuisance an abatement notice must be served on the "person responsible" for the nuisance, or if he cannot be found, on the owner or occupier of the premises concerned. The Bill by contrast establishes a clearer hierarchy and uses different terminology on this vital point.

In the first instance, the "appropriate person" upon whom a remediation notice may be served must be "the person, or any of the persons, who caused or knowingly permitted" the substances which has resulted in land being identified as contaminated to be present in, or on or under the land.

The expression "caused or knowingly permitted" has been borrowed from water pollution law, and the courts will thus be able to refer to a considerable body of case law in interpreting it, (see Chapter 17).

The Bill then goes on to provide for cases where the person who caused or knowingly permitted the contamination. In such cases the "appropriate person" will then be the owner or occupier.

Where a remediation notice is not complied with, the enforcing authority will be entitled, but not obliged, to carry out the specified work itself and recover the "reasonable costs" it incurs from the person upon whom the notice had been served. In charging back the authorities will be required to "have regard to any hardship" caused to a landowner and the authorities will be able to allow payment in instalments spread over up to thirty years. Appeals against charging notices will go to County Court.

Further, it will be a criminal offence not to comply with any requirement of a remediation notice "without reasonable excuse" in the case of industrial, trade or business premises the maximum fine would be £20,000 and £2,000 per day.

6. "Causes or Knowingly Permits"

The recent cases in water pollution law were dealt with in Chapter 17 and we do not repeat them here. The point to emphasise in this context is that there is no pre-condition of "unreasonable user" or "foreseeability of damage of the relevant type" for criminal liability.

Suppose, therefore, that in the *Cambridge Water* case, instead of a borehole it had been controlled water or land which was contaminated by the solvent, ECL could have been successfully prosecuted under s85 of the WRA 1991 and as an "appropriate person" under the proposed contaminated land framework, notwithstanding that the victim of the pollution would not, on Cambridge Water principles, have had any civil remedy at common law against ECL.

Thus there is a tension between the criminal liability and the civil liability of the creator of the contamination. The tension is even more pronounced in the case of the subsequent owner of land who is a "continuer". As we have seen, to achieve a common law remedy the victim of the pollution has to surmount a series of hurdles which make the action more difficult to maintain against a "continuer" than against a "creator". By contrast, the NRA in water pollution, and the prosecuting authority for land contamination would seem, for the purposes of "knowingly permitting", to be required to show no more than that the "continuer" has knowledge, actual or constructive, of the pollution, and that there are steps that the "continuer" can take to prevent its continuance.

Suppose the facts of the Cambridge Water case, as adapted above, but with one additional amendment; suppose that we are dealing, not with ECL, but with a subsequent owner who has not himself contributed in any way to the solvent spillage. Then, on the basis of Lord Goff's findings that the pools of neat solvent at the base of the chalk aquifer beneath the premises were "beyond the control of" the owner and/or "irretrievably lost in the ground below", there would probably be no criminal liability because, although not tested as yet by the courts, the words "knowingly permit" would seem to connote a finding that there are actions that could be taken to prevent/abate/remove the pollution, but which the defendant has not taken.

Given modern clean up technology, we consider that the Cambridge Water scenario of "beyond the control" of the occupier will be the exception rather than the rule. In the great majority of cases there will in fact be steps that <u>can</u> be taken to remediate and prevent continuing pollution. For example, in the case of a closed landfill from which a polluting leachate is escaping, there can be sunk, around and under the landfill, an impermeable layer of bunding, but the costs of such an exercise are immense. If the owner is faced with a civil action he can pray in aid these costs, his own limited resources, and, arguably, will be excused liability on this footing. There is no such saving in the express words governing criminal liability but it would seem, that if criminal proceedings are brought, the owner is liable to be successfully prosecuted providing there are some steps that he could take to control the pollution however expensive they may be.

In short the "mere continuer" seems to be under the shadow of criminal sanctions rather than civil liability, which is an odd state of affairs, and, as we shall see, so far as the cost of remediation is concerned, whilst the victim of the pollution appears to have no civil redress, the regulatory authority appears to be in a stronger position.

7. The Use by the NRA of the Clean Up Provision; S161 WRA

The NRA has extensive powers under s161 of the Water Resources 1991 to remedy pollution.

In summary:

Where it considers that any poisonous obnoxious or polluting matter or solid waste matter

... is likely to enter or be present in or have been present in controlled waters

... then it can carry out works to prevent such entry, remove or dispose of such matter, remedy or mitigate any pollution which has occurred and restore flora and fauna

... once works have been completed the NRA can recover its costs from the person who caused or knowingly permitted the matter in question to be at the place from which it was likely to enter controlled waters or to be present in them.

This is a further imposition of strict liability for expenses incurred as a result of a pollution incident or environmental danger by statute.

There is no requirement for a separate cause of action or successful prosecution.

There is no apparent limitation period beyond which a party is saved from the risk of being required to reimburse clean up costs.

It may be that the existence of the section and threat of an extensive NRA clean up operation may force responsible parties into voluntarily cleaning up areas of contamination and, in practice, the clean up bill from the NRA is usually paid either in the hope that it will encourage the NRA not to bring a prosecution under s85, or, if one is brought, so that the defendant may pray in aid in mitigation of punishment the fact that he has paid in full the NRA's cost of clean up.

Where the party refuses to pay a clean up demand under s161, the NRA will take proceedings in the County Court. So for example in *Clarke v NRA*, July 1993, Cambridge County Court, the NRA recovered £90,000 for expenses arising out of water pollution by a pig farm. In that case, incidentally, the prosecution had failed, in that the pig farmer, having been convicted, had successfully appealed against the conviction and had it set aside, see ENDS, May 1994, page 45.

The proposed statutory framework for dealing with contaminated land broadly follows the scheme under s161, save only for the very important hierarchy for identifying "appropriate persons" upon whom to impose liability.

The aim plainly is to impose a duty on the enforcement authority to pursue the creator of the land contamination rather than the subsequent "innocent" owner/continuer. Where, but only where, the creator of the contamination cannot be found the authority will be allowed to impose liability on the owner/occupier. Plainly, the legislature is trying to avoid a situation where the enforcement agency can apparently cherry pick for the deepest pocket without regard for culpability or responsibility for the contamination.

It is not proposed that there is anything in the new provision that will limit private rights, and, in a case where the "appropriate person" considers that the enforcement authority have sought to impose liability on the wrong person, it will presumably be open to him to allow the enforcement authority to commence its proceedings against him in the County Court, and there to third party the person who he alleges is actually responsible as a "causer" of the pollution.

8. Conclusion

Given the developments set out above, the imposition of liability for contaminated land is becoming clearer. That said, given the sums involved, this field is likely to be a fertile area for litigation in the coming years. In particular, we shall watch closely the case where, unlike *Cambridge Water*, the contaminant is not irretrievably beyond the control of the owner when he learns about it. This is likely to be a common case. Take toxic waste buried to a moderate depth, which could be removed and neutralized, albeit at great expense. The indications are that the owner is not liable to an adjacent landowner affected by the contamination in a civil claim since, having regard to his means, he cannot reasonably be expected to make the expenditure, yet he will be liable to substantial financial penalties under criminal process, and, in an instance where the creator of the pollution cannot be found, will be liable to repay the costs of clean up to the enforcement agency.

Whilst at first sight it may seem an odd result that the owner can escape civil liability to an adjacent landowner affected by the pollution on the one hand, and yet cannot escape liability for clean up costs imposed by the enforcement agency on the other, there is some justification for this result because whereas the adjacent landowner could simply pocket the damages and not spend them on remediation, a liability to the enforcement agency means, by definition, that the land will in fact have been remediated.

9. Qualitative Standards: land contamination

In the fields of air, water and noise pollution there are qualitative standards with statutory force as we have seen in the last three chapters. The *Cambridge Water* case is itself an example of tort liability turning on such standards.

There are no standards with statutory force in land contamination primarily because the EC member states have remained unable to agree a Directive on contaminated land notwithstanding that drafts have been circulating for five years.

The ICRCL Guidelines

The only guidance published within the UK are the guidelines published in 1987 by the Inter-departmental Committee on the

Redevelopment of Contaminated Land, known as the ICRCL guidelines. There are two levels in the scheme: threshold and action. Below threshold means uncontaminated. Where concentrations exceed "action" levels, remedial action or a change of end use is required. Levels vary according to end use, eg the levels are higher for industrial than for residential end use.

Any practitioner with a contaminated land action should certainly consult, and if possible rely on exceedences in relation to these guidelines. That said he should have in mind the following limitations:

a) guidance only; therefore no statutory force;

b) the guidelines are in any event limited; they tend to be restricted to compounds associated with former coal carbonisation sites. So, for example, there is little to assist when dealing with a petrol/oil spill ie a   hydrocarbon-contaminated site;

c) the guidelines explicitly state that they must not be used for any other purpose.Whether litigation falls under the shadow of this exclusion has yet to be determined.

The Dutch VPR Levels

In the absence of national standards applicable to soil contamination particularly for such compounds as petroleum hydrocarbons contamination investigations by the most prestigious consulting engineers in the UK, Germany and Belgium have for some time used the Dutch VPR (Voorlopige Praktijkrichtlijnen) levels as a benchmark for assessing soil contamination (and groundwater). The VPR criteria provide guidelines to assess contamination and appropriate remedial action. There are three levels of concern as follows:

Concentrations exceeding level A: Background levels have been exceeded.

Concentrations exceeding level B: Significant contamination; further investigation to identify source required.

Concentrations   exceeding level C: Severe contamination. Risk analysis based on site-specific factors leading to appropriate clean-up criteria.

Plainly, the VPR levels are not mandatory in the UK and it remains to be seen how the courts will treat them. It is submitted that they have been applied sufficiently in Europe to constitute an arguable negligence/nuisance benchmark, certainly for a multi-national company.

CHAPTER 23

GRAHAM V. RECHEM:

Cattle disease and alleged dioxin poisoning

1. Background

In a judgment given on 16th June 1995 the Court ruled that the Graham claim against Re-Chem failed on the facts. The case nonetheless raises a number of important points, notably in relation to the Judge's rulings on the law, and also on the organisation and management of a trial of this magnitude. Accordingly, we have added a chapter on this case as the book goes to press. For this reason it has not been possible to index this chapter in the usual way.

It is perhaps not surprising that the longest trial of a civil action on record is in the USA, and still less surprising that it concerned an alleged toxic chemical poisoning incident. The case is *Kemner v. Monsanto*. The trial began in February 1984 and ended in October 1987. The Judge, who sat with a jury, heard the case for a total of 667 court days.

The longest single party civil action in the UK is also an alleged toxic poisoning claim. *Graham v. Re-Chem* lasted 198 court days at the end of which, as he put it, the Judge dismissed the claim "with a heavy heart" realising only too well that it represented a devastating blow to the hopes and beliefs which had been cherished by the Grahams for the last 12 years or so. In so doing the Judge found against the Grahams on certain important issues of fact, and also, in general terms, preferred the scientific expert evidence adduced by Re-Chem to that adduced by the Grahams.

The central dispute in the trial was the alleged contamination of the Grahams' farm land by aerial transmission and deposition of toxic chemicals said to have been emitted from a nearby incinerator owned and operated by Re-Chem for the commercial destruction of hazardous wastes. It was the Grahams' case that between 1980 and 1983 their dairy cattle had been poisoned as a result of ingesting the toxic chemicals whilst grazing on the contaminated pasture and had died or had to be disposed of as a result. Although the basic subject matter of the action can thus be summarised shortly, it did give rise to a large number of factual and technical issues, the latter of being great scientific complexity. Roughly 100 witnesses gave evidence in all.

2. Rulings in Law

The Grahams' case in nuisance was that Re-Chem created a nuisance in the operation of their incinerator by the emission of toxic substances, namely dioxins, furans and PCBs together with, on occasion, molybdenum which caused harm to the Grahams' use and enjoyment of their pasture.

It was submitted on behalf of the Grahams that unless Re-Chem could bring itself within the principle of "reasonable user", i.e. that Re-Chem's use of the plant as a toxic waste incinerator had been part of the normal give and take between neighbouring occupiers of land, Re-Chem would be liable for all the foreseeable damage caused by emissions from the incinerator, even if all due care had been used in the conduct of its incineration business.

They relied·on the speech of Lord Goff in *Cambridge Water Co v. Eastern Leather plc* (1994) 2 WLR 53 at page 74, where he stated:

"Of course, although liability for nuisance has generally been regarded as strict, at least in the case of a defendant who has been responsible for the creation of a nuisance, even so that liability has been kept under control by the principle of reasonable user - the principle of give and take as between neighbouring occupiers of land, under which "those acts necessary for the common and ordinary use and occupation of land and houses may be done, if conveniently done, without subjecting those who do them to an action:" see *Bamford v. Turnley* (1862) 3 B&S 62, 83, per Bramwell B. The effect is that, if the user is reasonable, the defendant will not be liable for consequent harm to his neighbour's enjoyment of his land; but if the user is not reasonable, the defendant will be liable, even though he may have exercised reasonable skill and care to avoid it".

In upholding this submission the Court held that incineration of chemical waste is not "reasonable use" of land in the law of nuisance, (i.e. it is not necessary "for the common and ordinary use and occupation of the land"). Accordingly, the creator of a nuisance cannot avoid liability on the basis that he took all reasonable care. In this sense the liability of an incinerator of chemical waste in nuisance is strict, applying *Cambridge Water*.

A second ruling concerned the question of "foreseeability". Following *Cambridge Water,* it was plain that Re-Chem's liability in damages was confined to damage of a type which Re-Chem could reasonably foresee.

It will be recalled from Chapter 12 (p.123) that the degree of specificity of what needs to be foreseen in order to attract liability remains an open question.

In *Graham v. Re-Chem*, the evidence demonstrated that the mechanism within the incineration process (known as "de novo synthesis") by which the dioxins were formed did not become known in the scientific community until 1985, i.e. after the material period. Accordingly, Re-Chem argued, basing their argument on <u>Cambridge Water</u>, that the type of harm was not foreseeable because, at all material times, the mechanism by which the dioxins were formulated was unknown to Re-Chem.

The Court rejected this argument and held that for the purposes of liability in nuisance in incineration cases actual knowledge of the precise chemical processes whereby the toxic compounds in question were created was <u>not</u> a necessary ingredient. It was sufficient that at all material times it was known that dioxins were toxic and could cause ill-health and death in animals and that the operation of a waste incinerator could and did result in the emission of substances known to be toxic to the environment.

In dealing with the law on "causation", the Court made a further important ruling.

On behalf of the Grahams it was submitted that to succeed in their claim it was not necessary to prove that the emissions were the sole cause of the physical injury alleged to have been suffered by their cattle. It was argued that once it was proved that the toxic emissions were the result of a lack of care on the part of Re-Chem, the damage necessary for negligence would be established by proof that those emissions "materially contributed" to the ill-health and injury suffered by the Grahams' cattle. Reliance was placed upon the decision of the House of Lords in *Bonnington Castings Limited v. Wardlaw* (1956) AC 613, recently re-affirmed by the House in *Wilsher v. Essex Area Health Authority* (1988) AC 1074. In *Wardlaw's* case Lord Reid gave the leading speech and said:

".... He (i.e. the Plaintiff) must make it appear at least that on a balance of probabilities the breach of duty caused or materially contributed to his injury" (p.620)

... "What is a material contribution is a question of degree. The contribution which comes within the exception de minimus non curat lex is not material, but I think any contribution which does not fall within that exception must be material" (p.621).

Accordingly, it was contended that it was not even necessary to show that the emissions from Re-Chem were the dominant cause of the injuries suffered, although it was their submission that the emissions were in fact the dominant cause. It was claimed that the Grahams would be entitled to succeed and to recover damages in full if the emissions from Re-Chem materially contributed to the ill-health suffered by the Grahams' cattle. Thus, for example, causation of damage by Re-Chem would be sufficiently established if the finding of fact was that negligent emissions from Re-Chem alone would not have caused all the problems, but that they did so when added to the "background" levels of PCBs and dioxins or to those contributed in some degree by another industrial source.

The Court accepted these submissions of law on behalf of the Grahams and held that in order for the Grahams to recover damages in respect of the injuries suffered by their cattle, *whether in nuisance or in negligence*, it would be sufficient to establish that the alleged emissions from Re-Chem's plant caused or materially contributed to the ill-health of their cattle.

Although the principle of "material contribution" is a settled principle in the tort of negligence, and although some of the older "injunction" cases in nuisance show that the averment that the defendant is one of many polluters is no defence, this is the first instance, to the best of our knowledge, where the Court has ruled in a nuisance damages action that the principle of "material contribution" applies.

Finally, in relation to matters of law, the Judge in *Graham v. Re-Chem* accepted the proposition that theoretical or inductive evidence should not be allowed to displace proven facts, a proposition which was based squarely on the judgment of Henchy J. given on behalf of the Supreme Court in *Hanrahan v. Merck Sharpe and Dohme (Ireland) Limited* (1988) ILRM 629 at pages 644-645.

This is an important finding. In the *Hanrahan* case the eye witness evidence of the farmers established cattle problems which were only consistent with having been caused by the defendant chemical company's emissions. The Judge at first instance, however, was greatly impressed by the extent and volume of environmental monitoring data, much of which had been carried out by the local authority, which failed to disclose any positive findings upon which the plaintiffs could rely. Accordingly, the Court dismissed Farmer Hanrahan's claim. The Supreme Court, allowing the appeal and entering judgment for the farmer, said that where the primary evidence established that the problems were only consistent with having been caused by the defendant's emissions, then that finding of fact should follow. Theoretical or inductive evidence, i.e. inferences to be drawn to the contrary from the environmental monitoring data, must take second place and must not be allowed to prevail over the primary evidence.

Having dealt with the main findings and matters of law, which will be of importance for practitioners in cases in the future, we now go on to deal with matters concerning the development and management of such a substantial trial which, again, may be of assistance in the future.

3. The Proceedings

The writ was issued in March 1988. The plaintiffs were granted legal aid in England. The proceedings were issued in England and not Scotland for two reasons, first the plaintiffs were partners in the farming business and legal aid was not available for partnerships in Scotland and second the defendants were a company domiciled in England. The total claim as finally presented was for £1.5 million.

The investigation and trial of the case involved experts in the following areas of expertise:

Incineration, both the engineering and chemical aspects;

> The sampling, monitoring and analysis of emissions and depositions, particularly in connection with dioxins, furans and PCBs and metals;

> Meteorology, including meteorological modelling;

> Veterinary, both with regard to what may be called normal cattle diseases and problems and specifically with regard to the effects of dioxins and related chemicals, including PCBs on livestock and cattle in particular.

Accountancy and valuation evidence.

The evidence on sampling and analysis and the toxic effects of dioxins was particularly complex and difficult and called for special expertise.

4. The Trial

The trial started on 18th October 1993. The plaintiffs' opening speech, which was submitted in written form, took about $3^{1}/_{2}$ days to deliver. There was then a short break followed by an opening from the defendants, also written and also lasting about $3^{1}/_{2}$ days. The judge then went on a site visit.

The evidence of the lay witnesses was in the form of written statements which stood as the evidence in chief but which could be supplemented by oral examination in chief to explain or elucidate points or deal with matters which had arisen after the statement had been prepared.

The order of evidence agreed was that all the plaintiffs' lay witnesses were called first followed by the defendants' lay witnesses. After all the lay evidence the experts were called, their evidence in chief being in the form of their expert reports. The order of experts was first the incinerator experts plaintiffs' and then defendants, followed by meteorological experts, plaintiffs' and defendants, veterinary first "ordinary" then "dioxin" again plaintiffs' followed by defendants'. The defendants then called their sampling experts, the plaintiffs' sampling expert having been called with the incinerator experts, and finally the quantum experts were called plaintiffs and then defendants.

There were some 25 ring binders of scientific articles and expert literature and a very substantial number of documents which had been disclosed on discovery by both the plaintiffs and the defendants.

The plaintiffs called about 60 lay witnesses, some 30 of which whose evidence was short were heard by video link from Scotland.

The defendants called 22 lay witnesses about 5 of whom were so called "hybrid" witnesses, that is witnesses who had expertise but were called to give factual evidence.

The trial lasted 198 court days and finished on the 16th December 1994. Judgment was reserved and was given on 16th June 1995.

Andrew Graham gave evidence for 32 days, about 30 of which were in cross examination,(thought to be a record). Irene Graham gave evidence for 15 days also mostly cross examination. Although the plaintiffs counsel heavily criticised these cross-examinations, the court held that they were reasonable in all the circumstances and, indeed, made adverse findings on credibility which may be said to have vindicated the protracted cross examinations.

The lay evidence, including hybrid witnesses, was completed on day 119 of the trial. The expert evidence took 67 days.

At the conclusion of the evidence there was break for the preparation of final submissions. These were presented in written form. The judge adjourned to read the written submissions. Oral submissions were accordingly allowed 3-4 days for each party.

For the lay witnesses their statements, subject to elucidation where needed, stood as the evidence in chief but there was no agreement on the limitation of the time for cross-examination or re-examination. Efforts were of course made to estimate the likely length of a witness's evidence for the purpose of scheduling the subsequent witnesses many of whom had to come from Scotland.

For the experts the parties agreed, with the encouragement of the judge, a strict time table for elucidatory examination in chief and for cross examination and re-examination. This was adhered to on the whole successfully although sometimes it meant extra long sittings.

During the course of the case a number of additional expert reports were introduced, usually by the defendants. This caused problems for the plaintiffs who needed specific legal aid authority to respond.

The evidence in the case, except for the video link evidence, was recorded by the "Livenote" transcript system. By this system the court reporters type the evidence straight into personal computers used by the judge, counsel and solicitors. There is a facility to annotate the transcript as it is being entered into the computer which is very helpful for the preparation of cross- or re-examination or for reference for future submissions. A daily correction both in hard copy and on disc is delivered each evening. This system saved a lot of time for the advocates, and increased efficiency generally.

Although the claim was a considerable one for private individuals the costs on both sides will exceed it substantially. However for both parties the importance of the case was not to be measured in money terms alone. For the plaintiffs their whole way of life as farmers, a way of life which had been followed for generations in both their families, was at stake. Presumably the defendants' reason for investing such large sums in costs which will probably be irrecoverable was that an adverse result, even by way of settlement, could be severely detrimental to the future of their business. This is an extreme case but it does illustrate something which is not uncommon in litigation, namely that there can be wider issues and interests than the economics of a case would seem to suggest.

Although this was a very long trial on a matter which the judge recognised as having an interest much wider than the interests of the parties, the use of written statements and written submissions together with the Livenote transcript kept it within manageable proportions.

APPENDIX 1

Useful addresses

Organisations:

CALIP

(Campaign Against Lead in Petrol), 1, Moat Court, Ashstead, Surrey, KT21 2LP.

NSCA

(National Society for Clean Air), 136, North Street, Brighton, East Sussex, BN1 1RG.

Greenpeace

Canonbury Villas, London N1 2HB.

Marine Conservation Society

9,Gloucester Road, Ross-on-Wye, Herefordshire.

ACOPS

(Advisory Committee for the Protection of the Sea), 11, Dartmouth Street, SW1H 9BN.

The Council for the Protection of Rural England

Warwick House, 25, Buckingham Palace Road, SW1 WOPP. Also Council for the Protection of Rural Wales (Ty Gwyn,31, High Street, Welshpool, Powys.

Friends of the Earth

26, Underwood Street, N1 7JQ.

The Ramblers Association

1-5 Wandsworth Road,London, SW8 2LX.

Legal

Environmental Law Foundation,

Lincoln's Inn House, 42, Kingsway, London, WC2B 6EX; Tel: 0171 404 1030; Fax: 0171 404 1032.

Association of Personal Injury Lawyers (APIL)

10A Byard Lane, Nottingham, NG1 2GJ; Tel: 0115 958 0585; Fax: 0115 958 0885.

United Kingdom Environmental Law Association

61, Charterhouse Street, London EC1M 6HA

APPENDIX 2

NRA Offices

HEAD OFFICE: BRISTOL
Rivers House, Waterside Drive, Aztec West, Almondsbury, Bristol
BS12 4UD
Tel:01454 624400 Fax: 01454 624409

HEAD OFFICE: LONDON
Eastbury House, 30-34 Albert Embankment, London SEl 7TL
Tel; 0171 820 0101 Fax: 0171 820 1603

ANGLIAN;
Anglian NRA, Kingfisher House, Goldhay Way, Orton Goldhay;
PETERBOROUGH PE2 5ZR
Tel:01733 371811 Fax: 01733 23f840

NORTH WEST:
North West NRA, Richard Fairciough House, Knutsford Road,
WARRINGTON WA4 1HG
Tel:01925 53999 Fax: 01925 415961

SEVERN TRENT:
Severn Trent NRA, Sapphire East, 550 Streetsbrook Road, SOLI-
HULL
B91 lQT
Tel:0121 711 2324 Fax: 0121 711 5824

SOUTHERN:
Southern NRA, Guildbourne House, Chatsworth Road, WORTHING,
West Sussex BN11 1LD
Tel:01903 820692 Fax: 01903 821832

SOUTH WEST
South West NRA, Manley House, Kestrel Way, EXETER EX2 7LQ
Tel:01392 444000 Fax: 01392 444238

THAMES;
Thames NRA, Kings Meadow House, Kings Meadow Road, READ-
ING Berks RG1 8DQ
Tel:01734 535000 Fax: 01734 500388

WELSH;
Welsh NRA, Rivers House/Plas-yr-Afon, St Mellons Business Park,
St Mellons, CARDIFF CF3 0LT
Tel:01222 770088 Fax: 01222 798555

NORTHUMBRIA & YORKSHIRE:
Yorkshire NRA, Rivers House, 21 Park Square South, LEEDS LS1
2QG
Tel:0113 2440191 Fax: 0113 2461889

Table of Cases

Ballard -v- Tomkinson [1885] 29 Ch D 115, 216, 243

Barnes -v- Irwell Valley Water Board [1939] 1 KB 21, 118

Billings -v- Riden (1957) 3 All ER 1 HL, 135

Blair -v- Deakin [1887] 57 LT 522, 145

Bliss -v- Hall [1838] 4 Bing NC 183, 145

Blythe -v- Birmingham Waterworks Co [1856] 11 Exch 781, 120

Bolton -v- Stone [1951] AC 850, 124, 136

Bone -v- Seale [1975] 1 WLR 9, 148, 238

Bourgoin SA -v- Minister of Agriculture [1986] 1 QB 716, 177

Boyce -v- Paddington Corporation [1903] 1 Ch 109, 190

Bradford Corporation -v- Pickles [1895] AC 587, 216

Bristol City Council -v- Higgins The Times 9 September 1994, 214

Broder -v- Saillard (1896) 2 Ch D 692, 209

Budden -v- BP & Shell (unreported, 21 May 1980 CA), 119, 120

Burgess -v- Gwynedd River Authority (1972) 24 P & CR 150, 227

Byron Shire Business -v- Byron Council (Environmental Law and Management December 1994 201), 193

Cambridge Water Co -v- Eastern Countries Leather plc [1994] 1 All ER 53 (HL), 122, 123, 125-127, 130, 136, 141, 144, 147, 161, 164-166, 168, 216, 220, 243-245, 250, 253

Caparo Industries plc -v- Dickman [1990] 2 AC 605, 149, 150

Cargill -v- Gotts [1981] WLR 441, 222

Castle -v- St Augustine's Links Ltd [1922] 38 TLR 615, 161

Cattle -v- Stockton Waterworks [1875] LR 10 QB 453, 169

Charing Cross Electricity Supply Co -v- Hydraulic Power [1914] 3 KB 772, 167

Clarke -v- National Rivers Authority July 1993 (no reference), 252

Colls -v- Home and Colonial Stores Ltd [1904] AC 179, 138

Colwell -v- St Pancras Borough Council [1904] 1 Ch 707, 209

Cook -v- South West Water (unreported, 15 April 1992), 223

Council of Civil Service Unions -v- Minister for the Civil

Service [1985] AC 374, 37

Courtney -v- Collett (1697) 12 MoD Rep 164, 220

Crump -v- Lambert [1867] LR 3 Eq 409, 145

Cutler -v- Wandsworth Stadium [1949] AC 398, 175

D & F Estates Ltd -v- Church Commisioners [1998] 3 WLR 368, 131

Dear -v- Thames Water [1993] 4 Water Law 116, 145

Department of Transport -v- North West Water Authority [1984] AC 336, 142

Devon Lumber Co Ltd -v- MacNeill and Others [1988] 45 DLR (4th) 300, 138

Donoghue -v- Stevenson [1932] AC 562, 118

Dunn -v- North Western Gas Board [1964] 2 QB 806 [1963] 3 All ER 916 CA, 168

Dunton -v- Dover District Council (1977) 76 LGR 87, 209

East Lothian Angling Association -v- Haddington Town Council 1980 SLT 213, 219

East Suffolk Rivers Catchment Board -v- Kent [1941] AC 74 [1944] All ER 527, 133

Eckersley -v- Binnie [1988] 18 Con LR 1, 124, 125

Embury -v- Owen (1851) 6 Ex 353, 217

Emms -v- Poly [1973] 227 EG 1659, 148

Factortame Ltd -v- Secretary of State for Transport (No 2) [1991] AC 603, 177

Fennel -v- Robson Excavations [1977] 2 NSW LR 486, 246

Fletcher -v- Bealey [1885] 28 Ch 688, 193

Francovich -v- Italian Republic (joined cases C-6/90 and C-9/90), 177

Gaskill -v- Rentokil (1994, unreported), 69

Geddis -v- Proprietors of Bann Reservoir [1878] 3 APP CAS 430 (HL), 133, 167

Gillingham -v- C.V. Medway (Chatham) Dock Co [1992] 3 WLR [1992] 3 All ER 923, 139, 140

Goldman -v- Hargrave [1967] 1 AC 645 [1966] 2 All ER 989, 144, 246

Gorries -v- Scott (1874) LR 9 Ex 125, 175

Gouriet -v- Union of Post Office Workers [1978] AC 435, 159

Graham -v- Rechem International Ltd (no reference), 54, 72, 107-109, 145

Hale -v- Jennings Brothers [1938] 1 All ER 579 CA, 168

Halsey -v- Esso Petroleum Co Ltd [1961] 1 WLR 683, 137, 146, 148, 158, 190, 203, 204

Hammersmith LBC -v- Magnum Automated Forecourts Ltd [1978] 1 WLR 50, 192

Hanrahan -v- Merck Sharp & Dhome (Ireland) Ltd (1988) ILRM 629, 61, 76

Harper -v- Haden [1933] 1 Ch D 298, 161

Loveday -v- Renton (1988, unreported), 61

Malone -v- Laskey [1907] KB 141, 135, 147

Manchester Corporation -v- Farnworth [1930] AC 171, 195

Marquis of Granby -v- Bakewell Urban District Council (1921) 87 JP 105, 226

Mason -v- Clarke [1955] AC 778, 219

Martell -v- Consett Iron Co [1955] Ch 363, 189

Mc Cartney -v- Londonderry Lough Swilly Railway Co [1904] AC 301, 217

McGhee -v- National Coal Board [1973] 1 WLR 1, 59-61

McGillivray -v- Stephenson [1950] All ER 942, 212

Merlin -v- British Nuclear Fuels plc [1990] 3 WLR 383, 95, 100, 128, 165, 171

Metropolitan Asylum District -v- Hill [1881] 6 App Cas 193 (HL), 133, 194

Metropolitan Board of Works -v- McCarthy (1874) LR 7 HL 243, 224

Metropolitan Properties -v- Jones [1939] 2 All ER 202, 207

Midland Bank plc -v- Bardgrove Property Services Ltd [1992] 37 EG 126, 128, 194

Miles -v- Forest Rock Granite Co (Leicestershire) Ltd [1918] 34 TLR 500 CA, 168

Miller -v- Jackson [1977] QB 966, 130, 190, 195

Monk -v- Warbey [1935] KB 75, 175

Murphy -v- Brentwood DC [1991] AC 398, 131, 149

Myatt -v- Teignbridge District Council 20 June 1994 (Garner), 213

National Rivers Authority -v- Welsh Development Agency [1993] ENVLR 407, 186

National Rivers Authority -v- Yorkshire Water Services [1995] 1 All ER 225 (HL), 186-188

Network Housing Association Ltd -v- Westminster City Council, The Times 8 November 1994, 213

Newman -v- Real Estate Debenture Corporation [1940] 1 All ER 131, 209

Nicholls -v- Ely Beet Sugar Factory Ltd [1936] Ch 343, 229

North Western Utilities Ltd -v- London Guarantee and Accident Co Ltd [1936] AC 108, 167

O'Reilly -v- Mackman [1983] 2 AC 237, 177

Patricia Hunter and Others -v- London Docklands Development Corporation, unreported 4 November 1994, 127

Peabody Donation Fund (Governors) -v- Sir Lindsay Parkinson [1985] AC 210, 174

Perry -v- Kendricks Transport [1956] 1 All ER 154 [1956] 1 WLR 85 CA, 166, 168

Pride of Derby and Derbyshire Angling Association -v- British Celanese Ltd [1953] Ch 149, 194, 220

Pwllbach Colliery Co Ltd -v- Woodman [1915] AC 634 HL, 137

R -v- Battsby [1850] 16 QB 1022, 137

R -v- City Equitable Fire Insurance Co Ltd [1925] Ch 40, 182

R -v- Clerk to Birmingham City Justices ex parte Guppy JP Vol 152 159, 212

R -v- Deputy Governor of Parkhurst Prison ex parte Hague [1991] 3 WLR 340, 174

R -v- Exeter City Council ex parte Thomas [1989] The Times 11 May, 132

R -v- Fenny Stratford Justices ex parte Watney Mann (Midlands) Ltd [1976] 2 All ER 888, 213

R -v- Henderson and Battley (no reference), 126

R -v- Hunt [1992] 1 CL 57, 130

R -v- Legal Aid Area No 8 (Northern) Appeal Committee ex parte Parkinson, The Times 13 March 1990, 37

R -v- Legal Aid Committee No 10 (East Midlands) ex parte McKenna, The Times 20 December 1989, 37

R -v- Secretary of State for Social Services ex parte Hincks (1973) 123 SJ 436, 176

Rameshur Pershad Narain Sing -v- Koonj Behari Pattuk (1874) 4 App Cas 121, 216

Ratttray -v- Daniels (1959) 17 DLR (2d) 134, 208

Re -v- Saxton [1962] 1 WLR 968, 104

Read -v- Croydon Corporation [1938] 4 All ER 631, 177

Read -v- Lyons [1947] AC 156, 144, 147, 165, 168

Redland Bricks Ltd -v- Morris [1970] AC 652, 189

Richards -v- Lothian [1913] AC 263, 167

Ricket -v- Metropolitan Railway Co [1867] LR 2 HL 175, 159

Robinson -v- Kilvert [1889] 41 Ch D 88

Rooks -v- Barnard [1964] 1 All ER 367, 169

Rose Theatre Trust Co, ex parte [1990] 1 QB 504, 191

Roswell -v- Prior [1701] 12 MoD Rep 635, 246

Roy Brodrick and Others -v- Gale and Ainslie Limited 21 December 1992 (unreported), 227

Rushmer -v- Polsne & Alfieri Ltd [1907] AC 121 (HL(E)), 208

Ryeford Homes Ltd -v- Sevenoaks DC [1989] NLJ 255, 131

Rylands -v- Fletcher [1861-73] All ER REP 1, 122, 136, 147, 164-169, 219-221, 229, 237, 242-245, 247

St Helen's Smelting Co -v- Tipping [1865] 11 HL Cas 642, 137, 146

Salvin -v- North Brancepeth Coal Co [1874] 9 Ch App 705, 137

Scott -v- London & St Katherine Docks Co [1865] 3 H & C 596, 121

Scott Whitehead -v- National Coal Board [1987] P & CR 263, 119

Shelfer -v- City of London Electric Lighting Co [1895] 1 CH 287, 141

Shiffman -v- Venerable Order of The Hospital of St John of Jerusalem [1936] 1 All ER 557, 168

Shoreham by Sea Urban District Council -v- Dolphin Canadian Proteins Ltd [1972] LGR 261, 156, 190

Smeaton -v- Ilford Corporation [1954] Ch 450 [1945] 1 All ER 923, 168

Snell -v- Farrell [1990] 72 DLR 289, 61

Soltau -v- De Held (1851) 2 Sim (NS) 133, 210

Stapley -v- Gypsum Mines [1953] AC 663, 60

Sturges -v- Bridgman (1970) 11 Ch D 852, 207

Tadjer -v- Montgomery County [1985] 487 A (2d) 658, 246

Tate & Lyle Industries Ltd -v- Greater London Council [1983] 2 AC 509, 142

Tetley -v- Chitty [1986] 1 All ER 663, 205, 208, 209

Thompson -v- Smiths Shiprepairers (North Shields) Ltd [1984] 1 QB 405, 118

Thornton -v- Kirklees MBC [1979] QB 626, 177

Tipping -v- St Helen's Smelting Co (1863) 4 B & S 608, 237

Tutton -v- A.D. Walter Ltd [1981] Qb 61, 237

Vanderpant -v- Mayfair Hotel Co [1930] 1 Ch 138, 210

Wagon Mound (No 2) [1967] 1 AC 617, 122, 124, 150, 165

Walter -v- Selfe [1851] 4 De G & Sm 315, 137

Ward -v- Hobbs (8178) 4 App Cas 13, 175

Watt -v- Kesteven CC [1955] 1 QB 408, 176

Watts -v- Morrow [1991] 1 WLR 421, 149

Weller & Co -v- Foot and Mouth Disease Research Institute [1966] 1 QB 569 [1965] 3 All ER 560, 131, 169

Wellingborough District Council -v- Gordon [1991] JPL 874, 214

West -v- Bristol Tramways [1908] 2 KB 14, 167, 237

Wheeler and Another -v- J.J. Saunders Ltd and Others CA The Times 4th January 1995, 140, 143, 238

Whitehouse -v- Jordan (no reference), 99

Wilsher -v- Essex Area Health Authority [1988] AC 107, 60

Wilson -v- Ministry of Defence [1991] 1 All ER 638, 131

Wood -v- Conway Corporation [1914] 2 Ch 47, 137

Wrothewell -v- Yorkshire Water Authority (unrepoerted, 1987), 183

Wychavon District Council -v- National Rivers Authority [1993] 2 All ER 440 (DC), 186, 188

Young John & Co -v- Bankier Distillerry Co (1893) All ER Rep [1891-4] 439 HL, 218

Table of Statutes

Table of Statutory Imstruments

INDEX

pleadings 51

CABLE BURNING 235

CAUSATION
Evidence
primary 61
biological 63
Legal principles 59
Material contribution 59,60

CLIENT
Advertising for 22-23
Duty to 22
Groups 23

CONTAMINATED LAND
Environmental Agency 181
ICRCL Guidelines 253,254
liability for
criminal 240,241
tort 240,241
clean up 240,242
Nuisance 245-247
NRA 251-253
Qualitative standards 253
Register 240
Rylands v Fletcher 243,244
Statutory remediation 247-249
VPR levels 254,255

COSTS
Legal aid from 39,40

COUNTY COURT
Air pollution actions
Jurisdiction 49
Noise pollution actions

CRIMINAL LIABILITY
Causing or knowingly permitting 185-188Companies 182